This publication has been provided by the

GULF LIBRARY ACQUISITION ENDOWMENT

Established through a generous gift from

The Gulf Oil Foundation

to promote

scholarly research and academic excellence

among the faculty and students

of Duquesne University

A Plague of Insurrection

University of Pennsylvania Press
MIDDLE AGES SERIES
Edited by
Edward Peters
Henry Charles Lea Professor
of Medieval History
University of Pennsylvania

A listing of the available books
in the series appears at the
back of this volume

A Plague of Insurrection

Popular Politics and Peasant Revolt in Flanders, 1323–1328

William H. TeBrake

University of Pennsylvania Press

Philadelphia

Copyright © 1993 by the University of Pennsylvania Press
All rights reserved
Printed in the United States of America

Library of Congress Cataloging-in-Publication Data
TeBrake, William H. (William Henry), 1942–
    A plague of insurrection : popular politics and peasant revolt in Flanders, 1323–1328 /
William H. TeBrake.
        p.   cm. — (Middle Ages series)
    Includes bibliographical references and index.
    ISBN 0-8122-3241-0. — ISBN 0-8122-1526-5 (pbk.)
    1. Flanders—History.   2. Peasant uprisings—Flanders.   3. Flanders—Politics and
government.   4. Flanders—Rural conditions.   5. Peasantry—Flanders—History.
6. Flanders—Social conditions.   I. Title.   II. Series.
DH801.F46T43   1993
949.3′1—dc20   93-8222
                                                                                          CIP

D H 8 0 1
. F 4 6
T 4 3
1 9 9 3

Contents

List of Maps   vii

Preface   ix

Introduction: Peasant Unrest in Flanders and Europe   1

1. Flanders and Its People on the Eve of Revolt   15

2. For a World Without Corruption   45

3. For a World Without Privilege   67

4. Stalemate, Invasion, and Victors' Vengeance   108

5. Ordinary People in a Changing World   132

Appendix A: Economic and Social Conditions of the Rebels   139

Appendix B: Peasant Captains, 1323–1328   145

Bibliography   157

Index   165

JUL 1 2 2001

List of Maps

Figure 1: Location of Flanders   18

Figure 2: Rural Districts of Flanders   24

Figure 3: Cities and Towns of Flanders   27

Figure 4: Campaign in the Southwest   79

Figure 5: Greatest Extent of Peasant Revolt   87

Figure 6: Campaign in the Northeast   92

Figure 7: Battle of Cassel   122

Preface

This work is the result of nearly two decades of frequently interrupted effort. I first became interested in the fourteenth-century peasant revolt of Flanders during the spring semester of 1974, while auditing Professor Michael Baylor's seminar on Medieval Peasant Revolts at the University of Texas at Austin. Because my dissertation demanded most of my attention, however, I conducted only a preliminary investigation at that time, enough for a short oral presentation to the seminar. Since then, other research projects and the demands of teaching, including three years in temporary positions with an almost constant need to develop new courses, prevented full-time attention to the topic. Though I continued to maintain an interest by collecting relevant sources and developing a working bibliography, I was unable to give the topic the attention it deserved until the late 1980s.

The eventual completion of this study illustrates how teaching and research can influence each other. While it is fairly commonplace for the results of research to inform and improve teaching, in this case it was my experience in teaching that induced me to make the Flemish project a higher research and writing priority. I have tried to teach about the Flemish peasant revolt in every medieval history course I have offered at the University of Maine. Such efforts were considerably reinforced, however, when I joined a former colleague in offering a seminar on Peasants in History at the University of Maine in 1981 and 1983. While I was responsible for the medieval sections, Professor Allan Greer, a Canadianist with a strong competence in early modern European history as well, covered later Europe and especially a comparative section involving early modern Quebec. In order to give the seminar greater cohesion in its second rendition, we focused specifically on peasant revolts, and this time I expended considerable effort reconstructing the events in Flanders during the 1320s—I offered a shortened version of this material at the annual medieval conference at Western Michigan University, Kalamazoo, in May 1983. But it was my solo attempt to offer a seminar on Peasants in European History during the spring term of 1986 that finally convinced me of the need to give the revolt more attention, particularly because of the continuing impossibility of assigning relevant reading material.

Though most of my research and writing over the past two decades has focused on the northern Low Countries, especially medieval Holland, shifting my attention to medieval Flanders was not as big a change as it might appear to be at first glance. In fact, it is virtually impossible to study medieval Holland without learning a great deal about Flanders in the process. First of all, because of its early economic development and urbanization, Flanders often serves as the standard against which historians measure other parts of the Low Countries. In addition, even though they often quarreled, especially over control of portions of Zeeland that lay between them, a whole range of similarities produced common experiences for the principalities of Holland and Flanders. For example, both first appeared as outposts of resistance to Viking attacks during the ninth century. Further, there was a great deal of similarity in the physical environments of Holland and maritime Flanders, and the ways in which the residents of these coastal lowlands used their surroundings often were virtually identical. Finally, there were always very intense economic and cultural relations between the two, so much so that the language spoken in the Flemish towns, derived from old Frankish dialects, replaced the Frisian dialects of Holland during the high Middle Ages. Though traveling from Holland to Flanders today represents movement from one nation-state to another, the differences are not and never were as great as this fact might otherwise indicate. The biggest disparities were always in the more precocious development of Flanders compared to the northern principalities.

I wish to thank all those who gave me encouragement or assistance along the way: Michael Baylor for introducing me to the topic; my brother Wayne TeBrake, historian of early modern revolution, for reading and commenting upon every aspect of this project; Allan Greer for the dialogue we engaged in concerning the study of peasant revolts; my wife Janet K. TeBrake, who never typed a page of the manuscript but offered instead her expertise as an historian of nineteenth-century Irish peasants in revolt; David Nicholas who gave my 1983 presentation in Kalamazoo the rigorous criticism that it deserved. A small research grant from the University of Maine Faculty Research Fund in 1978 helped to defray some of the research expenses I incurred along the way. I owe a special debt of gratitude, however, to the many students over the years who consistently showed an interest in the actions of ordinary rural people of nearly seven centuries ago.

Introduction: Peasant Unrest in Flanders and Europe

On 23 August 1328, near the small town of Cassel in southwestern Flanders, an army of Flemish peasants confronted a vastly superior military force advancing northward out of France. By the end of the day, more than three thousand of these peasants lay dead on the battlefield. Though they had fought bravely, in the end they simply had been outnumbered and out-maneuvered by one of the largest and best equipped forces to be assembled in years. The carnage of the Battle of Cassel, along with the reign of terror that followed, effectively ended the peasant revolt of Flanders, or, as the anonymous author of the *Chronicon comitum Flandrensium* described it, "this plague of people rebelling against their superiors."[1]

The author of the *Chronicon* was a monk at Clairmarais Abbey near Saint-Omer in the county of Artois, just across the southwestern boundary of Flanders. A Fleming by birth,[2] he was familiar with the land and people of Flanders, while his close vantage point gave him easy access to the events affecting his homeland. What he observed there between 1323 and 1328 disturbed him profoundly. At a loss to find any other explanation for the apparent madness that had descended on Flanders, he ascribed it to an outbreak of disease. The infection was at times so severe, he wrote, that many of those afflicted were driven by its fever into performing acts that were grotesquely horrible and inhumane; in the end, the rebels seemed to have lost all respect for life itself.[3] As we shall see later, the disease metaphor offers little by way of explaining peasant revolt in Flanders, but there is no denying its powerful descriptive qualities. The events of the 1320s were unprecedented and, at close range and without the advantage of hindsight, difficult to fathom. It seemed to some contemporaries, at least, that a "plague of insurrection" had indeed engulfed the land.

In fact, for nearly five years leading up to the Battle of Cassel, peasant in-surrection had completely dominated public affairs in Flanders.[4] Beginning as a series of scattered rural disturbances in late 1323, it quickly escalated and coalesced into a full-scale rebellion that spread to most of the rural districts of the principality. Following their own popularly chosen leaders, peasants defied the authority of the count of Flanders in the rural districts by driving his officials and their aristocratic allies into exile. They seized the accumulated property of some of these exiles and redistributed it within the rural communities from which it had been extracted. They organized their own armies, which effectively contended with most forces sent against them. For several years, in fact, no one in a position of authority seemed able to assemble sufficient military might to reverse the rebels' success. By the middle of 1325, peasant leaders had replaced the officials of the count of Flanders in ten of fourteen rural districts; they collected taxes, convened courts, issued verdicts, made disbursements of public funds, and much more.

The full impact of peasant rebellion was not confined to the countryside of Flanders. Even though it began as an exclusively rural movement, many ordinary urban people sympathized with peasant rebels from the beginning, and the eventual collapse of the count's authority in the countryside acted as a powerful stimulant to urban rebellion. Beginning in early 1325 and under the cover of rural insurrection, popular regimes achieved power in most of the cities and towns within the rebel rural districts and allied themselves with the rural rebellion. Also, a series of rumors from late 1327 reported that ordinary people in portions of the kingdom of France had begun to mobilize and move more forcefully onto the political stage, purportedly in imitation of Flemish rebels.

That the peasant revolt of Flanders and its associated urban movements constituted a significant episode in the history of northwestern Europe is shown by the scale and the character of the response that it provoked. The triumphant force at Cassel in 1328 was an international one, designed to restore the authority of the count of Flanders over his rebellious subjects. Though personally commanded by the king of France, it was generously supplemented by personnel, materiel, and money from kingdoms and principalities throughout northwestern Europe, including, among others, Artois, Brittany, Burgundy, Hainaut, Lorraine, and Navarre. Indeed, popular insurrection in Flanders had caused such a fright in the region that rival rulers temporarily put aside their differences and participated with papal blessing in a grim crusade designed to stop an evil that had threatened to spread to neighboring lands as well. Finally, the reign of terror that followed was meant to discourage other peasants from contemplating any insurrectionary activity of their own.

The peasant revolt of Flanders during the 1320s was neither the first nor the last time that European peasants engaged in armed struggle against those who dominated their lives. It was, however, the first and the most significant of the massive peasant movements of the fourteenth century. It far surpassed both the French Jacquerie of 1358 and the English revolt of 1381 in terms of scale, organization, duration, and impact on domestic and external affairs. Indeed, nothing matched it before the German Peasants' War of 1525.

Curiously, however, neither the unmatched quality of the Flemish revolt nor the obvious importance attached to it by many observers during the fourteenth century has earned it a prominent place in the modern historical literature on the late Middle Ages. Today, it remains virtually unknown outside the Dutch or Flemish-speaking world. General histories of the late Middle Ages simply never mention it,[5] and the specialized historical literature is not much better. An examination of the most commonly available studies of late medieval popular protest to appear in English during the last two decades shows that, while both the French and English revolts enjoyed major billing, the Flemish revolt received only token treatment.[6] Even within the Dutch-speaking world the Flemish revolt has never attracted the kind of attention it deserves. Despite an occasional review of the major events in a general history of the Low Countries as well as a series of excellent detailed studies on certain of its features or participants, the peasant revolt of Flanders has never been the subject of a full and critical study in any language.[7] An examination of some of the reasons for such neglect will help to define the present study.

The Flemish peasant revolt remains largely unknown today partly because ordinary people simply have never figured very prominently in the historical literature of the late Middle Ages. This is particularly the case with the most elusive of ordinary people, the majority that continued to live in the countryside, namely peasants.

Flemish peasants of the early fourteenth century, like medieval peasants generally,[8] were rural dwellers who possessed, even if they did not always own, the means of agricultural production. Such production, resulting from a combination of crop-raising and livestock-keeping, formed the basis of their subsistence. They lived in family units which provided most of the labor used to work their holdings, but they also associated in larger components, such as villages, hamlets, or parishes characterized by some degree of common property, communal rights, and collective activity—forming, in other words, rural communities.[9] Those who worked as agricultural laborers or artisans but were closely affiliated with other peasants through kinship ties, common residence, and shared experiences, formed an integral part of such communities. An essential, distinguishing feature of all peasants, regardless of time and place, is that they also sustain superimposed classes and institutions which dominate them politically and extract their surplus production.[10] In Flanders at the beginning of the fourteenth century, non-peasants lived from surplus peasant production that was extracted by means of various rents, tithes, taxes, tolls, labor services, and even outright theft or extortion.

Though the normal rigors of peasant existence and survival over the long term required great intelligence, immense practical knowledge, long suffering patience, and enormous skill, they did not require literacy. Medieval peasants were almost universally illiterate, and thus they left no direct, written record of their actions, aspirations, or intentions. Peasant culture, though doubtless rich and colorful, was transmitted orally from generation to generation, with the result that we remain largely ignorant of it today. This documentary silence of peasants is made even more deafening by the fact that those who did write during the Middle Ages were either unwilling or unable to write intelligently about ordinary rural people. Even though literate people, along with non-peasants generally, could not have survived without surplus peasant production, they showed an amazing lack of interest in or appreciation of this fundamental fact. At their best, medieval writers were condescending; at their worst, they were decidedly hostile to the supposed ignorance and brutishness of peasants. As a result, most narrative or expository sources reflect the knowledge and interests of their aristocratic, monastic, or governmental authors or patrons, and contain virtually nothing about peasant life.[11]

Non-narrative sources, less exclusionary in principle, do provide some essential information about peasant life, however.[12] Especially in administrative and judicial records of the late Middle Ages, individual peasants often appear as taxpayers, litigants, renters, or criminals while rural communities appear as possessors of or advocates for various rights and privileges. In a number of quarters, historians increasingly use non-narrative documentary sources to reveal some of the fundamental contours of peasant life. In Flanders, real progress has been made in the study of the late medieval rural economy and related issues.[13] Further, archaeology contributes significant amounts of new, incidental information about medieval rural life.[14] Still, much of the research based on non-narrative sources or archaeological reports deals primarily with the context of peasant life and often remains highly abstracted from the lives of real human beings. The most notable exception to this is the work done by social historians who have made painstaking and imaginative use of non-narrative sources to illuminate the lives of ordinary people confronted by large scale changes;[15] concerning peasants specifically, such work ranges from the use of inquisitorial records to reconstruct their mental universe[16] to the use of coroners' records to examine their family life.[17]

Traditional views of medieval life were set down long ago and, particularly when involving peasants, were informed by a sometimes uncritical reading of medieval narrative or expository sources. A long accepted view of medieval social relations, first propagated by medieval authors but adopted by many historians in the twentieth century, is the notion of a harmonious tripartite society supposedly consisting of those who prayed, those who fought, and those who worked, with each group functionally necessary for the other two.[18] Much new work based on non-narrative sources, however, shows this view was nothing more than myth—largely elite propaganda or wishful thinking. We now know, for example, that even though non-peasants needed peasants for elemental survival, the converse was not the case.[19] European peasants showed considerable ability to outsurvive numerous incarnations of those-who-prayed or those-who-fought, especially when it came to interacting with their natural surroundings.

A general scarcity of documentation relevant to the lives of peasants, however, does not by itself account for the almost total lack of attention to the Flemish revolt in the historiography of the late Middle Ages. In fact, when peasants engaged in mass collective actions such as demonstrations, riots, or rebellions, they often quite literally forced themselves into the historical record.[20] All the late medieval peasant revolts, including the Flemish one, produced considerably more information than normally would be available. Even the authors of narrative works could no longer totally ignore such lowly subjects.

The sudden appearance of peasants in the historical documentation associated with peasant revolts is something of a mixed blessing, however, because most of the sources that have survived, especially the contemporary chronicles, were written by individuals hostile to the movements they were describing. Not surprisingly, therefore, a dependence on sources created by a hostile, literate establishment can produce unbalanced accounts or conclusions. A single example illustrates my point. A European history textbook used in North American colleges and universities, depicting the French Jacquerie of 1358 as fairly typical of medieval peasant revolts, provides a number of examples of alleged peasant brutality taken straight from contemporary chronicles, along with the following example of aristocratic delusion: "The peasants' brutality deeply shocked the upper classes, *whose own violence was constrained within the bounds of the chivalric code*."[21] Detailed research by social historians in recent years has shown that especially the upper classes in the countryside, far from being constrained by some sort of chivalric code, were the most consistently violent social element during the late Middle Ages.[22] Fortunately for us, the attempts of rulers and their associates to oppose or contain revolts left unmistakable traces in non-narrative sources as well. As I will demonstrate below, non-narrative sources can provide important corrections to the sometimes distorted judgments found in the chronicles.

In some cases, at least, the fuller documentation produced by militant peasant action has been used to very good effect. For example, the English revolt of 1381 has long constituted an important area of research for British historians,[23] and this has helped to propel the state of late medieval peasant studies in Britain far beyond that found generally in Europe. Today, as a result, the English revolt is well enough known both inside and outside of Britain to serve as the quintessential, late medieval peasant revolt for many historians. In sharp contrast to this, however, the Flemish revolt has never been an important area of research for historians of Flanders. As a group, the latter have always preferred late medieval urban history over rural history.[24] My primary reason for writing this book, therefore, is to begin filling a major gap in our knowledge of ordinary people during the late Middle Ages by reconstructing an important series of events largely ignored today.

Besides being an interesting and important story in its own right, the Flemish revolt offers information that can help to correct some commonly held views about medieval peasant revolt in general. For example, in both the general and the specialized historical literature, mass peasant movements of the late Middle Ages are usually exemplified by the one that is best known today, the English revolt of 1381. But this revolt lasted about five weeks, compared to nearly five years for the Flemish one. As a result, English peasant rebels had much less opportunity than their Flemish counterparts to develop an organization for and gain experience in managing their own affairs. Indeed, without knowledge of the Flemish revolt, many historians have concluded that late medieval peasants would have been able to act more forcefully and effectively than previously thought possible,[25] but were simply incapable of building and sustaining a movement that might have established a new political order.[26] As we shall see, the Flemish revolt clearly illustrates what was only briefly glimpsed in the English case: planning, cohesion, organization, and self-direction.[27]

Popular Politics and Peasant Revolt

Until fairly recently, most explanations of medieval peasant revolts stressed what seemed to be their uniqueness or unusual character. As we saw earlier, for example, the author of the *Chronicon* used language that ascribed the Flemish peasant revolt to an exogenous evil force, a disease, that over-whelmed a normally healthy county of Flanders. But the metaphor of disease to explain revolts first of all oversimplifies; in assuming that all individuals in a given area constitute a unified social organism, it glosses over internal divisions such as parties, coalitions, and struggles for political control. In addition, it attributes revolt itself to external influences. Finally, it justifies brutal suppression of revolt as analogous to removing a diseased limb from a body.[28]

Many modern historians, meanwhile, suggest that economic depres-sion, famine, disease, warfare, or rapacious landlords, by making the always difficult lot of peasants even worse, drove otherwise docile people into taking desperate actions. Still others maintain that peasants engaged in rebellion only when more sophisticated city folk or renegade aristocrats incited them to do so.[29] What all such explanations share are two funda-mental assumptions: that revolt was uncommon, a rare departure from some normally peaceful condition, and that the causes of such unusual behavior were outside forces or influences impinging upon ordinarily pas-sive peasants. And indeed, as long as the total number of peasant rebellions remained relatively small and historians continued to believe that peasants were not themselves independent political actors, such assumptions seemed plausible. Recent research, however, has begun to call both assumptions into serious question and, by extension, the explanations based upon them.

Peasant revolt now appears to have been less rare during the Middle Ages than was previously thought. True, we still know only about scattered episodes of peasant militancy from the early and high Middle Ages, but that may well be a reflection of insufficient documentation. Peasant rebellion nevertheless became very common during the fourteenth and fifteenth centuries, affecting nearly all parts of Europe at one time or another.[30] In recent decades, systematic research based primarily on unpublished archival materials has uncovered so many late medieval peasant revolts, uprisings, and militant demonstrations as to validate Marc Bloch's proposition of more than a half century ago, that they were as natural to traditional Europe as strikes are today.[31] For the German lands alone, about sixty episodes of militant peasant unrest have been identified for the period 1336 to 1525, and the total number is likely to climb even further.[32]

Though recent research has clearly demonstrated that there were many more late medieval episodes of peasant militancy than were known just a generation ago, making them seem far less unnatural or abnormal than before, there is another and in some respects more profound sense in which they continue to be exceptional. This becomes clear when we abandon the notion that outside forces or influences were the primary causes of revolts and begin to see them instead as conceived, planned, and executed by peasants themselves.[33] Their exceptional character in such a view derives from the fact that they constituted but a small part of the larger category of popular political practice, ranging from routine acts of self-governance to armed resistance to external domination.

A wide chasm has always separated peasants from the elites who live from peasant labor without contributing to agricultural production in any significant way, and it is safe to say that peasants have always resented such social parasitism and found ways of resisting it.[34] Though social cleavages lie at the heart of peasant resistance to material domination, the means employed to mitigate domination has always been profoundly political. Until recently, however, most observers have considered as political only those actions that were openly declared and publicly performed. While such a definition might well include much of contemporary politics, it ignores the fact that open political expression was far too risky for most people to undertake until the modern achievement of the rights of free speech and association.[35] The unequal relations of power made open insubordination something that peasants simply had to avoid in most cases. But it has never been demonstrated that late medieval peasants were politically acquiescent when not engaging in revolt.[36]

To see revolt as the only form of political activity available to subordinate groups is to ignore the broad spectrum of possibilities between the one extreme of insurrection and the other extreme of passive acceptance of everything dominant groups might attempt to impose. Without cognizance of a broader spectrum of possible actions, popular revolts often appear suddenly, without warning or context, almost as though they were spontaneous, taking us by surprise much like the events of the 1320s took Flemish public officials by surprise. It is only when we define political action in such a way as to correspond more closely to pre-modern conditions[37] that we begin to see the proper context for late medieval peasant revolt.

Revolt was only the most visible of a whole range of actions that peasants might employ to resist domination. Indeed, for every known episode of outright peasant revolt there were many more peasant actions that often remained unrecorded, such as flight, boycotts, refusal to make payments of rents, tithes, or taxes, and various legal actions or appeals. And behind such acts of open defiance lay a whole assortment of semi-concealed forms of resistance, such as poaching, pilfering, delaying tactics, arson, sabotage, slander, feigned ignorance, dissimulation, and much more that made it into the documentary record only very sporadically.[38]

In most cases, revolt developed out of a lengthy process of escalation that started with semi-concealed, non-violent forms of resistance to domination that eventually gave way to more active and militant actions, and that finally developed into confrontations from which there was no easy turning back. Along the way, there would have been extensive thinking about, planning for, and considering of alternatives to revolt before it actually took place.[39] Indeed, because of the real risks associated with staging a revolt, less direct forms of resistance normally would have been preferred because they minimized risks and often were successful enough to eliminate the need for revolt. The problem for the historian is that most indirect forms of insubordination were actually played out behind closed doors, outside the purview of rulers and elites, deliberately concealed from those who dominated their lives. Because the latter also controlled the written record, such actions often are invisible to us as well.[40] Nevertheless, under certain kinds of circumstances, peasants could and did throw their traditional caution to the wind and actually engage in open revolt, either because authorities lacked the political skill or will to defuse potentially dangerous situations or because the social, economic, and political chasm separating peasants and rural elites simply became unbridgeable.[41] In short, a given revolt will have had a considerable prehistory, a principle clearly illustrated by the Flemish case.

Plan for This Work

This study is based exclusively on published materials that have been known for some time. What I have tried to do, however, is to bring together in one place what others uncovered separately and to ask questions of the material not previously asked. Specifically, I critically reread all the relevant sources, not so much for what they might tell us about the traditional concerns of political history, but rather for what they had to say about the rebels themselves, what specific actions they took, and why.

Despite my emphasis on placing medieval peasant revolt within the larger context of peasant politics, what follows is fundamentally social history. By taking peasant politics seriously and by considering it the primary means by which peasants defined themselves and interacted with those who dominated their lives, I have in fact undertaken an examination of part of a larger issue that lies at the heart of European social history—how ordinary people experienced the large structural changes of the late Middle Ages.[42] Peasant revolt in Flanders occurred at a time of social, political, and economic change represented by the rising importance of cities, the decline in the influence of traditional rural elites, and the growth of centralized governmental institutions.

Chapter 1 describes the county of Flanders and places it within the changing economic, social, and political structure of northwestern Europe at the beginning of the fourteenth century. After examining its dense population, high urbanization, and complex economic life, the chapter concludes with an exploration of the complicated political history of Flanders since the late thirteenth century. Particular attention is paid to the roles that ordinary people, including peasants, played in that history. Chapter 2 reconstructs the initial months of the revolt, from November 1323 to March 1324, links its origins to the count's inability or unwillingness to control the alleged corruption of his rural officials, examines the arbitrated settlement of April 1324, and concludes with an examination of the organizational structure and peasant leadership that made the revolt possible. Chapter 3 traces the revolt from its resumption in July 1324 to the Peace of Arques in April 1326, contrasts the rapid and surprisingly bloodless expansion of the revolt to the violent yet futile efforts of the count and his aristocratic allies to halt it, and examines the rebels' professed goal of ridding the countryside of all privilege. An important part of this chapter is an assessment of the effect that urban support had on the revolt between March and November 1325. Chapter 4 examines the reasons for the immediate failure of the Peace of Arques, treats the geographical stalemate that lasted until the Battle of Cassel in August 1328, and takes stock of the subsequent peace imposed by terror. Particular attention is paid to the traditional contention that the leaders may have lost the support of the rank and file peasantry during the last two years. Chapter 5 assesses the long term impact of the revolt on Flemish and external affairs, and considers how knowledge of the Flemish revolt changes our views of medieval peasant revolts generally.

Notes

1. Anonymous, *Chronicon comitum Flandrensium*, in *Corpus Chronicorum Flandriae sub auspiciis Leopold: primi serenissimi Belgarum regis: recueil des chroniques*

de Flandre, vol. 1, J. J. DeSmet, ed., Académie Royale de Belgique, Commission Royale d'Histoire, Mémoires en quarto (Brussels: H. Hayez, 1837) (hereafter cited as *Chronicon*) pp. 208–9: "haec pestis popularium contra superiores suos rebellantium. . . ." For the entire revolt, see pp. 184–209.

2. The continuation of this chronicle, from 1214 to 1328, is ascribed to Bernard of Ypres; see, for example, the literature referred to by Pierre Alexandre, *Le climat en Europe au moyen âge: contribution à l'histoire des variations climatiques de 1000 à 1425, d'après les sources narratives de l'Europe occidentale*, Recherches d'Histoire et de Sciences Sociales, no. 24 (Paris: École des Hautes Études en Sciences Sociales, 1987), p. 106, item 110.

3. *Chronicon*, p. 202: "et modo horribili et inhumano patriam perturbare"; "quod horrendum et inhumaninum est audire"; and "quod taederet homines vitae suae."

4. This initial brief description is based on the detailed reconstruction of events found in Chapters 2 through 4 below.

5. Even the otherwise richly detailed survey of medieval Flemish history by David Nicholas, *Medieval Flanders* (London and New York: Longmans, 1992), passes over the revolt in a perfunctory fashion; see pp. 212–17.

6. Guy Fourquin, *The Anatomy of Popular Rebellion in the Middle Ages*, trans. Anne Chesters, Europe in the Middle Ages, Selected Studies (Amsterdam: North Holland Publishing, 1978), devotes less than two pages to the Flemish peasant revolt. Michel Mollat and Philippe Wolff, *The Popular Revolutions of the Late Middle Ages*, trans. A. L. Lytton-Sells (London: Allen and Unwin, 1973), treat it in roughly four pages. Though Rodney H. Hilton, *Bond Men Made Free: Medieval Peasant Movements and the English Rising of 1381* (New York: Viking Press, 1973), makes frequent mention of Flemish matters, the total still amounts to only a handful of pages. All three works derive their information for the Flemish revolt solely from Henri Pirenne, ed., *Le soulèvement de la Flandre maritime, 1323–1328: documents inédites*, Académie Royale de Belgique, Commission Royale d'Histoire (Brussels: P. Imbreghts, 1900), pp. i–lxx; subsequently incorporated into his *Histoire de Belgique*, vol. 2, 3rd ed. (Brussels: Maurice Lamertin, 1922), pp. 75–100. Michael Mullett, *Popular Culture and Popular Protest in Late Medieval and Early Modern Europe* (London: Croom Helm, 1987), never mentions the Flemish revolt.

7. Jacques Sabbe, *Vlaanderen in opstand, 1323–1328: Nikolaas Zannekin, Zeger Janszone en Willem de Deken*, Genootschap voor Geschiedenis "Société d'Émulation" te Brugge, Vlaamse Historische Studies, VII (Bruges: Marc Van de Wiele, 1992), while providing a fine review of the urban side of the insurrection, especially the actions of Willem de Deken, assumes throughout that rural rebels simply followed the instructions of city dwellers and thus pays very little attention to them.

8. For basic definitions of medieval peasants, see Mullett, *Popular Culture and Popular Protest*, p. 2; Richard Wunderli, *Peasant Fires: The Drummer of Niklashausen* (Bloomington: Indiana University Press, 1992), pp. 29–30; Rodney H. Hilton, *The English Peasantry in the Later Middle Ages: The Ford Lectures for 1973 and Related Studies* (Oxford: Clarendon Press, 1975), pp. 3–19; and Barbara A. Hanawalt, *The Ties That Bound: Peasant Families in Medieval England* (New York: Oxford University Press, 1986), pp. 5–6.

9. See Susan Reynolds, *Kingdoms and Communities in Western Europe, 900–*

1300 (Oxford: Clarendon Press, 1984), p. 2; Gérard Sivéry, *Terroirs et communautés rurales dans l'Europe occidentale au moyen âge*, Économies et Sociétés (Villeneuve-d'Ascq: Presses Universitaires de Lille, 1990), pp. 71–78; and Léopold Genicot, *Rural Communities in the Medieval West*, Johns Hopkins Symposia in Comparative History (Baltimore: Johns Hopkins University Press, 1990).

10. Wunderli, *Peasant Fires*, pp. 30–31; Rodney H. Hilton, "Medieval Peasants: Any Lessons?" *Journal of Peasant Studies* 1 (1973–74), 209–10; idem, *The English Peasantry in the Later Middle Ages*, p. 13.

11. Wunderli, *Peasant Fires*, p. 32; Mullet, *Popular Culture and Popular Protest*, p. 72; Nicholas Brooks, "The Organization and Achievements of the Peasants of Kent and Essex in 1381," in *Studies in Medieval History Presented to R. H. C. Davies*, Henry Mayr-Harting and R. I. Moore, eds. (London and Ronceverte, WV: Hambledon Press, 1985), p. 249; J. A. Raftis, "Social Change Versus Revolution: New Interpretations of the Peasants' Revolt of 1381," in *Social Unrest in the Late Middle Ages: Papers of the Fifteenth Annual Conference of the Center for Medieval and Early Renaissance Studies*, Francis X. Newman, ed., Medieval and Renaissance Texts and Studies, vol. 39 (Binghamton, NY: Center for Medieval and Early Renaissance Studies, 1986), pp. 3, 18.

12. Genicot, *Rural Communities in the Medieval West*, pp. 5–11.

13. In particular, Adriaan Verhulst has led the way in this research, and his recent survey, *Précis d'histoire rurale de la Belgique* (Brussels: Éditions de l'Université de Bruxelles, 1990), offers a good starting point and bibliography. For an excellent example of detailed research into the context of peasant life, see Erik Thoen, *Landbouwekonomie en bevolking in Vlaanderen gedurende de late middeleeuwen en het begin van de moderne tijden; testregio: de kasselrijen van Oudenaarde en Aalst (eind 13de-eerste helft 16de eeuw)*, Belgisch Centrum voor Landelijke Geschiedenis, no. 90 (Ghent: Belgisch Centrum voor Landelijke Geschiedenis, 1988), 2 vols.

14. For example, the use of archaeological reports has made possible a much more comprehensive picture of early medieval rural settlement in Holland than was previously possible; see William H. TeBrake, *Medieval Frontier: Culture and Ecology in Rijnland*, Environmental History Series, no. 7 (College Station: Texas A & M University Press, 1985).

15. Charles Tilly, "Retrieving European Lives," in *Reliving the Past: The Worlds of Social History*, Olivier Zunz, ed. (Chapel Hill: University of North Carolina Press, 1985), pp. 11–52, argues that discovering how "ordinary people" lived the "big changes" is, in fact, the primary task of social history.

16. Emmanuel Le Roy Ladurie, *Montaillou: The Promised Land of Error*, Barbara Bray, trans. (New York: Random House, Vintage, 1979).

17. Hanawalt, *The Ties That Bound*.

18. For the history and use of this myth, see Georges Duby, *The Three Orders: Feudal Society Imagined*, Arthur Goldhammer, trans. (Chicago: University of Chicago Press, 1980).

19. See, for example, Rodney H. Hilton, "A Crisis of Feudalism," *Past and Present* 80 (1978), pp. 5–7; idem, "Medieval Peasants: Any Lessons?" pp. 211–12.

20. Genicot, *Rural Communities in the Medieval West*, pp. 79–80.

21. Mark Kishlansky, Patrick Geary, and Patricia O'Brien, *Civilization in the*

West (New York: HarperCollins, 1991), vol. I, p. 306 (italics mine). I single out this particular textbook not because it is worse than the others but because it is fairly typical in its treatment of peasant revolts. Indeed, in most respects, I consider it to be one of the best currently available and assign it in my own European Civilization course.

22. Mullett, *Popular Culture and Popular Protest*, p. 36, concludes that "despite the ideals of chivalry, there was indeed a good deal of brutality on the part of knights, nobles and their followers towards the lower orders, especially peasants, and above all in wartime." Barabara A. Hanawalt, *Crime and Conflict in English Communities, 1300–1348* (Cambridge, MA: Harvard University Press, 1979), pp. 177–80, 263, 265, while discussing the widespread and persistent violence of landed elites in early fourteenth-century England, described the perpetrators as a kind of "Mafia." There is little reason to believe that their equivalents in the remainder of Europe were much different. On violence in Flanders, see David Nicholas, "Of Poverty and Primacy: Demand, Liquidity, and the Flemish Economic Miracle, 1050–1200," *American Historical Review* 96 (1991), pp. 20–21.

23. Brooks, "The Organization and Achievements of the Peasants of Kent and Essex," pp. 247–48.

24. Thoen, *Landbouwekonomie en bevolking in Vlaanderen*, p. 2.

25. See, for example, Brooks, "The Organization and Achievements of the Peasants of Kent and Essex," pp. 247–70.

26. Genicot, *Rural Communities in the Medieval West*, p. 80.

27. W. P. Blockmans, "De ontwikkeling van een verstedelijkte samenleving (XIde–XVde eeuw)," in *Geschiedenis van Vlaanderen van de oorsprong tot heden*, Els Witte, ed. (Brussels: Historische Getuigen/La Renaissance du Livre, 1983), p. 93.

28. A version of this metaphor received scholarly justification in the twentieth century as part of a general model of revolutions that first appeared in 1938: see Crane Brinton, *The Anatomy of Revolution*, revised ed. (New York: Vintage, 1965), pp. 16–17; as well as the criticism of Charles Tilly, *Big Structures, Large Processes, Huge Comparisons* (New York: Russell Sage Foundation, 1984), p. 100.

29. See, for example, Fourquin, *The Anatomy of Popular Rebellion*, pp. 76, 129, 134; as well as the comments of J. Baerten, "Les mouvements paysans au moyen âge: reflexions sur deux ouvrages récents," *Le moyen âge* 87 (1981), pp. 455–64; James C. Scott, "Resistance Without Protest and Without Organization: Peasant Opposition to the Islamic *Zakat* and the Christian Tithe," *Comparative Studies in Society and History* 29 (1987), pp. 417–18; and David W. Miller, "Collective Violence in the Countryside," *Journal of Interdisciplinary History* 15, 3 (1985), pp. 501–2. In his comparative study of fourteenth-century revolts in Flanders, France, and England, F. W. N. Hugenholtz, *Drie boerenopstanden uit de veertiende eeuw: Vlaanderen 1323–1328, Frankrijk 1358, Engeland 1381; onderzoek naar het opstandig bewustzijn* (Haarlem: Tjeenk Willink, 1949), pp. 28–29, remarks that, in all three cases, contemporary observers, thoroughly convinced that peasants were irrational beings, insisted that the rural rebellions were instigated or at least led by city folk. See also Wunderli, *Peasant Fires*, pp. 144–47; Mullett, *Popular Culture and Popular Protest*, pp. 72–73; Sabbe, *Vlaanderen in opstand*.

30. Peter Blickle, "Peasant Revolts in the German Empire in the Late Middle

Ages," *Social History* 4 (1979), p. 223; Frantisek Graus, *Pest-Geissler-Judenmorde: Das 14. Jahrhundert als Krisenzeit*, Veröffentlichungen des Max-Planck-Instituts für Geschichte, no. 86 (Göttingen: Vandenhoeck und Ruprecht, 1987), pp. 391–96.

31. Marc Bloch, *French Rural History: An Essay in Its Basic Characteristics*, Janet Sondheimer, trans. (Berkeley: University of California Press, 1966), p. 170 (the first French edition was published in 1931). See also Genicot, *Rural Communities in the Medieval West*, pp. 79–80.

32. Peter Bierbrauer, "Bäuerliche Revolten im Alten Reich: ein Forschungs-bericht," in *Aufruhr und Empörung? Studien zum bäuerlichen Widerstand im Alten Reich* (Munich: H. Beck, 1980), pp. 1–8, 26, 62–65.

33. See, for example, Mullett, *Popular Culture and Popular Protest*, p. 71; Raftis, "Social Change Versus Revolution," pp. 6–14; and Samuel Cohn, Jr., "Florentine Insurrections, 1342–1385, in Comparative Perspective," in *The English Rising of 1381*, Rodney H. Hilton and T. H. Aston, eds., Past and Present Publications (Cambridge: Cambridge University Press, 1984), pp. 143, 151.

34. Hilton, "A Crisis of Feudalism," pp. 10–12.

35. On the ubiquity of resistance to domination, see James C. Scott, *Domination and the Arts of Resistance: Hidden Transcripts* (New Haven, CT: Yale University Press, 1990), throughout. On the risks of open political expression, ibid., pp. 198–99; and Mullett, *Popular Culture and Popular Protest*, pp. 4–5.

36. Sivéry, *Terroirs et communautés rurales*, pp. 189–90, points to the effectiveness of community solidarity against outside domination.

37. Wayne P. TeBrake, "Reconstructing the History of Popular Politics in Europe 1500–1850," paper presented at Netherlands Institute for Advanced Study, 1991, p. 2, provides an appropriate starting point by describing political action as "an on-going bargaining process between those who claim governmental authority in a given territory and those over whom that authority is said to extend."

38. See, for example, Bierbrauer, "Bäuerliche Revolten im Alten Reich," pp. 16–17; Genicot, *Rural Communities in the Medieval West*, p. 80; Raftis, "Social Change Versus Revolution," p. 9; Barbara A. Hanawalt, "Peasant Resistance to Royal and Seignorial Impositions," in *Social Unrest in the Late Middle Ages: Papers of the Fifteenth Annual Conference of the Center for Medieval and Early Renaissance Studies*, Francis X. Newman, ed., Medieval and Renaissance Texts and Studies, vol. 39 (Binghamton, NY: Center for Medieval and Early Renaissance Studies, 1986), pp. 30–37; Rodney H. Hilton, "Introduction," in *The English Rising of 1381*, Rodney H. Hilton and T. H. Aston, eds., Past and Present Publications (Cambridge: Cambridge University Press, 1984), pp. 3–4. Scott, *Domination and the Arts of Resistance*, p. 198, provides an extensive, categorized list.

39. Bierbrauer, "Bäuerliche Revolten im Alten Reich," p. 17. On the ability of peasants to plan, see Brooks, "The Organization and Achievements of the Peasants of Kent and Essex in 1381," pp. 247–70.

40. Brooks, "The Organization and Achievements of the Peasants of Kent and Essex in 1381," pp. 249–50; Genicot, *Rural Communities in the Medieval West*, pp. 79–80.

41. Bierbrauer, "Bäuerliche Revolten im Alten Reich," pp. 17–18.

42. See Tilly, "Retrieving European Lives," pp. 11–52.

1. Flanders and Its People on the Eve of Revolt

The geographical context of peasant revolt in the 1320s was the county of Flanders, occupying what is today the coastal lowland of Belgium and adjacent sections of France and the Netherlands. At the beginning of the fourteenth century, this principality stretched some 120 kilometers (75 miles) along the North Sea coast and extended roughly 80 kilometers (50 miles) inland. Despite its relatively compact size, however, the county of Flanders had an importance during the high and late Middle Ages that far outstripped many larger polities. Its dense population, high degree of urbanization, and advanced economy were unmatched in temperate Europe. Far from occurring in a backward area, the peasant revolt of Flanders took place in one of the wealthiest and most advanced regions of Europe. Only parts of Italy resembled Flanders in these respects.

The Territory of Flanders

Flanders first emerged as a distinct entity during the second half of the ninth century when members of a powerful local family became counts of and secured political control over a series of Carolingian *pagi* (cantons or districts) located in the North Sea coastal lowland, along or to the west of the Scheldt River. The new rulers were able to establish themselves in these districts largely because no one else was really interested in them, for what they acquired was nothing more than a few sparsely populated and widely separated clusters of settlements—a ring of villages around the central settlement of Ghent and some similar but smaller groupings around Bruges to the west and along the coast southwest of Bruges. The areas around and between these clusters of settlements were essentially unpopulated wilderness and remained so for some time to come.[1]

Through outright conquest combined with negotiations or the occupation of territories abandoned by other lords, the new rulers of Flanders were able to build on this meager base. Count Baldwin II (879–18), for example, consolidated his control over the lands from Ghent westward during the 880s and then gradually extended his influence southward along the coast during the next three decades. His successors added additional lands to the southwest during the tenth century and eventually ruled over the entire area within a triangle formed by the Canche River, the North Sea, and the Scheldt River. Finally, during the first half of the eleventh century, the counts of Flanders extended their political authority into the German Empire by annexing lands to the northeast and the southeast of Ghent, thereby pushing the eastern boundary of their principality to the Dender and lower Scheldt Rivers.[2]

The apparent ease with which the counts of Flanders expanded the territory under their control was a reflection not so much of their own initial strength as of the inability of anyone to prevent them from doing so. However, by the middle of the eleventh century, with their acquisition of all territory as far south as the Canche River and as far east as the Dender and lower Scheldt Rivers, they had become in fact quite powerful. Though technically the counts of Flanders were vassals of the West Frankish kings and their successors the Capetian kings of France,[3] in practice they behaved as autonomous princes. When Count Philip married Elisabeth of Vermandois in 1163 and thereby gained control over the county of Vermandois, south of the Somme River, he exercised political authority to within 25 kilometers (15 miles) of Paris. In fact, Philip ruled over a larger territory than the king of France did for the next two decades.[4] But the tide was beginning to turn. By the end of the twelfth century, the French monarchy was able to make considerable headway against some of its most powerful and independent vassals, including the counts of Flanders.

With the gradual increase in the political might of the Capetian kings of France during the twelfth and thirteenth centuries, the maintenance of total Flemish autonomy became ever more difficult to guarantee. The first result of heightened royal power was the loss of some of the southernmost territories. When Count Philip's wife died in 1182, he was forced by the king of France to relinquish his claim to Vermandois, and when Philip himself died in 1191, the king claimed the cities of Arras and Saint-Omer and all the land west and south of the Aa River as a dowry for his niece, thereby creating the county of Artois, which served as a buffer against future Flemish southward advances. This move created the southwestern border of Flanders that was to persist until early modern times.[5]

Further royal pressure at the beginning of the fourteenth century, as we shall see, alienated the territory of Walloon Flanders containing the important cities of Lille and Douai. Initially it was handed over as a temporary trusteeship designed to hold Flanders to the Peace of Athis-sur-Orge (1305), but in the following decade it was surrendered entirely to French control until it was finally returned to the Flemish counts in the second half of the fourteenth century. At the beginning of the revolt in 1323, therefore, the counts of Flanders controlled all the territory between the North Sea and the Scheldt River from just north of Lille to the river's mouth, as well as the land between the Scheldt and Dender Rivers from Geraardsbergen northward (see the map in Figure 1).

Though Flanders stood out as one of the most economically advanced territories in all of Europe at the early fourteenth century, it had not always been so. In fact, it had rather unpropitious beginnings. At the turn of the millennium much of Flanders was seriously underpopulated and considered extremely backward economically, and little changed in these respects until well into the eleventh century.[6]

The quality of the land that constituted the county of Flanders varied considerably. Much of the original territory was far too soggy for most people's tastes. West of the low sandy ridges that separated the Scheldt-Leie watershed from the sea were extensive coastal marshes and brackish or freshwater lagoons behind partially submerged sand bars. The coast itself was neither stable nor continuous, but segmented by a series of broad estuaries at the mouths of rivers and streams. The dunes guarding the coast today have developed only since the high Middle Ages. North of a line from approximately Dunkirk to Dendermonde, soils varied greatly, from low sandy ridges to salt marsh or backwater swamps of heavy clay, with virtually every other possibility in between. Because these soils could be made to produce crops only with great effort, most crop raising in the northern part of the county was practiced on a very small scale, with an actual preference for livestock raising. Population densities remained very sparse in the northern parts of Flanders until well into the eleventh century. Only in the lands to the south of the Dunkirk-Dendermonde line was there a gradual transition to sandy loam and loam soils that were naturally better drained and thus better suited to crop agriculture, and this was reflected in a greater density of population in this part of the county as well.[7] But even so, the lands in the south of Flanders were not as well suited to crop agriculture as were those further south, including the lands lost at the end of the twelfth century to form the new county of Artois.

Like much of Europe before the eleventh century, Flanders was se-

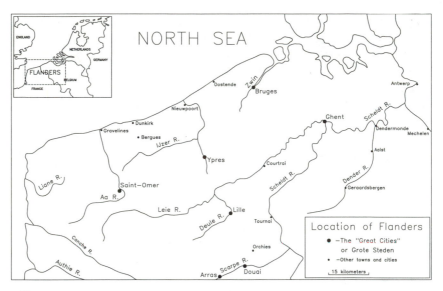

Figure 1

riously underpopulated, most significantly expressed in a severe scarcity of labor. When one considers that early medieval aristocrats attempted to control such labor to their own purposes, it is hard to avoid the image of crushing poverty that was at least in part a reflection of the few exploiting the many. However, from the second half of the tenth through the thirteenth century, all Europe saw more or less sustained population growth. Though it is impossible to come up with accurate global statistics, there is every reason to believe that Europe's overall population doubled, with some regions experiencing larger and others smaller increases. By the end of the thirteenth century, some parts of the continent saw rural population densities not reached again until the eighteenth century or later. Apparently growth in Flanders was on the high side, with at least a tripling of the population over the period, despite considerable emigration of Flemings to the British Isles, central Europe, and elsewhere.[8]

We are never likely to know exactly why population growth began when it did. We can only assume that there were a number of factors involved, all of which in one way or another contributed toward a reduction in mortality rates. The traditional explanations include climatic amelioration, an end to invasions by Scandinavians, and the development of new agricultural tools and techniques, but recent research has called such explanations into serious question.[9] In the end, it may well have been the gradual erosion of social parasitism that made the biggest difference. By the early eleventh century, for example, the classic manorial system developed by kings, aristocrats and religious landholders during the early Middle Ages had began to unravel in a number of places. In fact, serfdom had never been very important in Flanders, and most lingering signs of servitude disappeared entirely during the eleventh and twelfth centuries.[10] The weakening of the grip of elites on peasants represented by the gradual decline of labor services can only have released a tremendous amount of peasant energy that could then be directed toward activities that would raise standards of living and average life expectancies.[11]

Though it is still too early to give a definitive explanation of what actually caused population growth during the high Middle Ages, it is clear that it was closely associated throughout temperate Europe with a massive expansion of settlement and agriculture into previously unused lands. The growing population of Flanders participated fully in this movement to an impressive degree by wresting additional living space from woods, bogs, salt marshes, and moors. The earliest stages of land reclamation in the tenth and eleventh centuries seem to have been inspired primarily by population growth, and systematic reclamation on a large scale beginning in the twelfth century may well have encouraged further growth. By the thirteenth century, population growth became a significant cause of further land reclamation once again. In particular, the rapid rise in land taxes during the first half of the thirteenth century suggests a certain amount of population pressure.[12]

When the expansion came to an end during the second half of the thirteenth century, Flanders had roughly three times more settlements than the same territory had three centuries earlier, and they were considerably larger on average as well. At the same time, wooded lands, peat bogs and salt marshes had been reclaimed, parts of the coast were protected by dikes, and the regime of waters was regularized and brought under human control. Wilderness, for the most part, had ceased to exist in Flanders—the natural landscape had been extensively humanized.[13]

The Cities of Flanders

The most striking feature of Flanders at the beginning of the fourteenth century was its high degree of urbanization. Ghent, with approximately 64,000 people, was the second largest city of Europe north of the Mediterranean. Only Paris was larger. Bruges, meanwhile, had 46,000 inhabitants and Ypres slightly fewer than 30,000. Because the three cities lay scarcely 50 kilometers (30 miles) apart from each other, they represented a compact urban concentration virtually unparalleled in Europe in the first half of the fourteenth century.[14] In addition, a number of smaller cities and towns may have accounted for almost as many inhabitants as the three great cities together. Finally, Saint-Omer and Arras in Artois, Lille and Douai in Walloon Flanders, and the cities along the Scheldt as far south as Cambrai continued to be bound in numerous ways to the network of cities in Flanders proper. So too were the cities of western Brabant, including Antwerp and Mechelen.[15] As a result, Flanders was not only highly urbanized itself, but also lay at the heart of a network of cities not seen elsewhere in Europe.[16]

From the time of their first appearance, the cities of Flanders were closely tied to their rural hinterlands, which always included important grain-growing areas upstream along the Leie and Scheldt rivers in Artois, Picardy, and Hainaut. Regular and reliable trade in agricultural products was a prerequisite for urban life, while urbanites provided manufactured products or various services to the rural population. By the early fourteenth century, however, the cities of Flanders had developed connections that reached far beyond their rural hinterlands. During the preceding three centuries, many cities had become important textile-manufacturing centers, and the trade dedicated to provisioning them drew from a base extending far beyond their immediate surroundings. In fact, a significant proportion of trading capacity was dedicated not only to providing for the basic alimentary needs of the cities but also to supplying the raw materials or marketing the finished products of the textile industry.[17]

Some twenty cities and towns within Flanders produced cloth for export by the second half of the thirteenth century, and, within these cities and towns, the many stages of cloth production employed substantial numbers of people. Around the middle of the fourteenth century, for example, roughly 60 percent of Ghent's population was employed in some aspect of textile production. Similar proportions would have been found in Ypres and in many of the smaller cloth-making cities as well. Another group of cities, meanwhile, specialized in the trade associated with textile production: supplying the raw wool and distributing the finished cloth. While initially much of the wool came from sheep grazed on the extensive grasslands of coastal Flanders, imported English wool had outstripped the still significant quantities of domestically produced wool by the beginning of the fourteenth century. In particular, merchants in the city of Bruges specialized in the English wool trade, but so too did merchants from the smaller Flemish ports of Bergues, Dunkirk, Gravelines, Nieuwpoort, and Oostende.[18]

The huge textile industry of Flanders and the extensive commerce associated with it generated considerable wealth for those who owned or controlled the means of production. And wealth had become the key to achieving political power and influence in the cities by the second half of the thirteenth century. In Ghent, for example, a group of prominent, wealthy families controlled the city administration by dominating the Council of Thirty-Nine that provided access to city offices, and similar oligarchies dominated in most of the other cities of Flanders as well.

The concentration of people and capital within cities, meanwhile, turned the three largest cities, Ghent, Bruges, and Ypres, into important players on the political stage of Flanders. In fact, they often were referred to collectively as the *drie steden* (three cities) because of their special political relationship to the counts and to the rest of the county.[19] Both independently and in concert, the *drie steden* could pursue their own objectives, which might or might not coincide with the policies of the counts of Flanders; for example, they were not afraid of sending delegations to Paris or London to seek protection of their interests. In general, cities introduced a complexity to the political, social, and economic life of Flanders that was lacking in less urbanized regions of Europe.

The Countryside of Flanders

Unfortunately, the danger exists that observers today might be blinded to certain realities by the brilliance of Flemish urban life. First of all, despite the multitude of changes that cities introduced to Flanders, it remained an overwhelmingly rural and agrarian principality through the fourteenth century and beyond. The fortunes of the great urban patrician families derived largely from the buying and selling of agricultural products such as grain, wool, and livestock, while most ordinary urban people were employed in industries that processed agricultural products. In short, the rural sector, represented by the production of food and fiber through the practice of crop raising and livestock keeping, remained the most important sector of the Flemish economy.[20]

In addition, while the extensive urban development of Flanders certainly received much stimulus from industrial concentration and widening trade contacts from the eleventh and twelfth centuries onward, the primary enabling factor for the appearance of cities in the first place must be sought in the countryside. Without the dynamism of local, agrarian communities, urban development never could have followed the course that it did. The factors that produced initial structural change in Flanders, as we saw above, appeared in the countryside. Sustained rural population growth provided the vitality, and the expansion of settlement and agriculture into vacant lands provided the structure that made urban life possible.[21]

Finally, regardless of the large numbers of people inhabiting Flemish cities by the beginning of the fourteenth century, most Flemings still lived in the countryside. There is insufficient demographic data to make accurate estimates of rural population for the early fourteenth century, but the more extensive information available for the late fifteenth century suggests that two out of every three Flemings continued to reside in the countryside. Since there is little reason to believe that this situation differed greatly a century-and-a-half earlier, it seems safe to assume that every urbanite will have represented at least two country-dwellers in Flanders during the early fourteenth-century as well.[22] And even though some inhabitants of the countryside happened to be nobles or even citizens of cities, the vast majority of Flemish rural people were peasants, that is, small-scale agricul-turalists who provided for their own subsistence and whose surplus pro-duction was essential to the survival of nearly everyone else.[23]

To administer the countryside, the counts of Flanders divided the entire county into a number of castelries (Dutch, *kasselrijen*; French, *châtellenies*), based originally on a system of military districts and associated castles dating from the Carolingian era. From the late twelfth century onward, however, the castelries lost their military character and became simply administrative districts attached to the count's central administra-tion (from here onward, I will use the terms rural district or simply district to refer to the Flemish castelries). Their once powerful military heads, the castellans, were reduced to the possession of certain feudal revenues and honorific rights and replaced by bailiffs, civilian officials who reported directly to the count.[24] Colleges of magistrates (Latin, *curatores*; Dutch, *keurheren*; French, *keuriers*) formed courts of justice as well as administra-tive councils with certain fiscal responsibilities, such as authorizing and apportioning the collection of taxes. Eventually, all rural districts became essentially territorial communes with relationships to the count that were similar to those enjoyed by the large cities of the county. By the beginning of the fourteenth century Flanders had seventeen rural districts, three of which, constituting Walloon Flanders, were ceded until the 1360s to the French monarchy by the treaty of Athis-sur-Orge in 1305 (see the map in Figure 2). All had their own sets of laws, privileges, and tribunals, had considerable autonomy, and existed as corporations recognized and guaranteed by public law. In addition, as in the cities, the magistracies of the rural districts had come to be dominated by oligarchies, small, closed groups of the most powerful families.[25]

While the Flemish rural districts were tied directly to the central administration of the counts, they also grouped together under their jurisdiction varying numbers of rural communities. By far the largest, with roughly 100 rural communities, was Bruges. It combined eight districts formed individually during the period of land reclamation into a single one, though it was often divided for administrative purposes into western, northern, and eastern sectors.[26] Most of the remaining rural districts grouped smaller numbers, usually several dozen or so. Each rural community had its own council of aldermen (Dutch, *schepenen*; French *échevins*) which was attached to the colleges of magistrates at the district level, and alongside the aldermen stood the counts' local representative, the *amman*, an official resembling a sheriff. Rural communities thus had direct links to both the rural districts and the counts' central administration. Most important for our purposes, however, they provided the immediate context of peasant life in Flanders.[27]

Flemish peasants lived in rural communities that not only defined territorial units but bound them together by various collective concerns.[28] In theory, rural communities could be defined geographically in various ways—by a manor, a village, an ecclesiastical parish, an administrative or taxing unit, or a set of shared public works (dikes and drainage ditches, for example), to name just a few.[29] Those of Flanders in the early fourteenth century corresponded most closely to the territories described by ecclesiastical parishes ("parish" used here in an exclusively secular sense, to describe a territory devoid of any specific religious content) and their associated villages. This is not to suggest that parishes provided the only geographical parameters for collective concern in Flanders. In fact, multiple rural communities might be linked together in drainage districts or *wateringen*, which could be important frameworks for collective peasant activity. Parishes could also be grouped into *ambachten*, local administrative units varying in size from one to several parishes or parts of parishes.[30] Despite the potential importance of larger entities in providing communication and

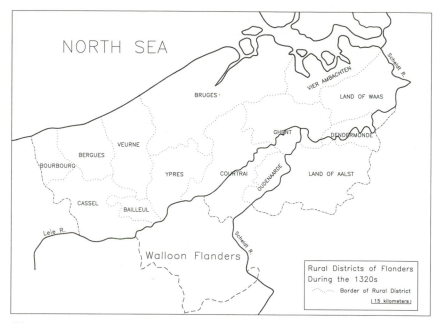

Figure 2

coordination between parishes, however, the territory of the parish corresponded most closely to the basic residential unit of those who lived and
worked together and constituted the rural community.[31]

The rural communities of Flanders differed from those found elsewhere by exhibiting very little if any communal agricultural exploitation.
The colonization of land during the eleventh through thirteenth centuries,
an early liberalization of property laws, and the extension of a monetized,
market-oriented economy throughout the countryside encouraged the in-
dividualistic exploitation of land.[32] Instead, community was most commonly expressed in rituals aimed at maintaining custom, in the joint stew-
ardship of common property, and in coming to each other's aid in times of
trouble.

In the normal course of events, a rural community periodically congre-
gated in a general assembly of its members—usually defined as those with a
minimal amount of property and thus a stake in the community—and one
of the primary issues addressed at such gatherings was the maintenance of
custom. Custom consisted of the rules and regulations based on past
collective decisions or bylaws (*keuren* in Dutch) which, whether written
down or part of oral tradition, provided the basis for orderly life within

individual communities. Custom also defined membership in the rural community and enumerated the rights and obligations that came with it.[33] A rural community also convened meetings or assemblies in order to make decisions concerning the usage and upkeep of common or community property, such as the church, roads, woods, and pastures, and to choose a whole range of wardens, caretakers, and inspectors to look after the community's assets. A significant addition to the list of common property in the lowest lying portions of the Low Countries were the hydraulic works such as dikes, dams, drainage canals, and sluices that needed constant care and attention. In Flanders, this factor was particularly important in the rural districts along the coast, that is Bourbourg, Bergues, Veurne, and Bruges. Finally, meetings or assemblies were used to decide on cooperative agricultural activities, to establish procedures for providing mutual aid in time of emergency, such as fire, flood, or warfare,[34] and, as we shall see below, to organize insurrection.

Who actually called meetings or assemblies, who attended them, and what rules for decision making, if any, were followed varied widely from one place to the next. For example, some decisions might be arrived at by general consensus, but others might be made by a subgroup of the whole, perhaps a jury or a council of elders chosen to represent the interests of the entire community. Similarly, a given rural community might routinely use meetings or assemblies to select special agents or proxies to represent the entire community in other settings—to larger political jurisdictions, such as the Flemish rural districts, or to neighboring rural communities or nearby towns or cities.[35]

Generally, those chosen to make decisions for a particular community or to represent the community in another political jurisdiction came from the most prominent peasant families of that community, those who already had influence within the community.[36] It is important to recognize in this regard that Flemish rural communities of the early fourteenth century, like their counterparts in Europe generally, were not homogeneous but combined multiple status groups. Research into the makeup of individual medieval rural communities has progressed the furthest in England, where it now is commonplace for historians to speak of at least three groups of peasants (using terms such as primary peasants, secondary or middling peasants, and tertiary peasants or cottars), differentiated not only by wealth but also by the holding of community offices or the practice of certain village trades.[37] Though comparable research has not yet been done for late medieval Flanders, it is possible to get an idea of differentiation within rural

communities by looking at the ranges of peasant wealth that some documents illustrate for a number of places in the southern Low Countries. On
the basis of such information, it seems reasonable to suggest that small
peasant holdings usually amounted to no more than 2 or 3 hectares (1
hectare equals 2.47 acres) or less, that medium-sized holdings ranged from
this threshold up to 10 hectares or so, and that large peasant holdings were
10 to 20 hectares in size and even larger.[38] The lists of property drawn up for
the purposes of confiscation at the end of the revolt show just such a range
of peasant wealth (see Appendix A, below).

Despite sometimes significant differences in wealth, there was in fact
widespread solidarity among the Flemish peasants who lived and worked
together in the rural communities. Such solidarity may have been expressed
in a general way by popular rhymes that have survived since the fourteenth
century contrasting the honesty and integrity of ordinary people to the
greed and corruption of lords and public officials.[39] Solidarity within rural
communities was expressed most forcefully, however, in the swearing of
oaths of mutual aid and support. At times such solidarity was formalized in
sworn associations to combat fire and guard against the loss of cattle, for
example.[40] Indeed, an extensive system of mutual pledging and reciprocal
obligations is what created a community and made survival over the long
term possible.[41] As we shall see, it also helps to explain the resilience of rural
rebellion in Flanders during the 1320s.

City, Count, and Countryside

When cities first appeared in Flanders during the tenth and eleventh centuries, the counts patronized and protected them because they promised to
bring tangible benefits to city dweller and prince alike. The counts and
urbanites also shared a preference for law and order which led to alliances
against the violence traditionally practiced by landed aristocrats and their
private armies.[42] Such cooperation along with changes taking place in the
countryside, especially labor services and other marks of serfdom being
replaced by money rents, gradually weakened the position of aristocrats.
Cities themselves began to develop an importance of their own along with
considerable autonomy from the authority and influence of the counts (the
locations of the most important cities are indicated on the map in Figure 3).

The cities of Bruges, Ghent, Ypres, Lille, and Douai controlled a
significant proportion of the wealth of the principality—by 1300, for exam-

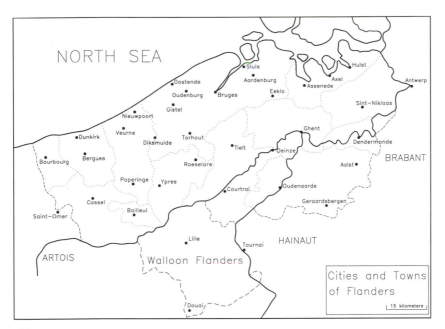

NORTH SEA

• Sluis
Hulst
• Oostende   Aardenburg   Axel   Antwerp
Oudenburg   •Bruges   •Assenede   Eeklo
Gistel   Sint–Niklaas
Nieuwpoort
Dunkirk   Veurne   Torhout
Diksmuide   •Tielt   Ghent   Dendermonde
Bourbourg Bergues   Roeselare   •Deinze   BRABANT
                                        Aalst •
Poperinge Ypres
•Courtrai   Oudenaarde
Cassel   Geraardsbergen
Bailleul
Saint–Omer
• Lille   HAINAUT
Tournai
ARTOIS   Walloon Flanders
                                Cities and Towns
                                of Flanders
                                   15 kilometers
Douai

Figure 3

ple, the city of Ghent alone could command public revenue that equalled or surpassed the normal income available to the counts.[43] Both singly and in various combinations, they could and often did apply political pressures within Flanders that the counts simply could not ignore. By the late thirteenth century the great cities had replaced the nobility as the most potent rivals to the power of the counts. By that time, political power within the cities had become concentrated in the hands of narrow sub-groups of wealthy citizens or patricians, many of whom were descended from some of the first residents and had become wealthy because they controlled important tracts of urban real estate. More or less characteristic of such groups of patricians were the great families that controlled the Thirty-Nine of Ghent and formed a closed oligarchy that was able to monopolize positions on the court of aldermen or *schepenbank* of the city through a system of cooptation. By monopolizing the aldermanate they controlled access to all administrative and judicial offices in Ghent, and anyone not associated with their select, inner circle was automatically excluded from consideration for such positions. Similar situations also pertained in other Flemish cities.[44]

Though the combination of count and cities had effectively limited the influence of aristocrats at the county level, aristocrats nevertheless continued to have considerable influence within the rural districts. Instead of commanding the labor of a semi-servile peasantry, as their equivalents still did in some parts of Europe, the traditional rural elites of Flanders had been forced to adapt to changed economic, social, and political conditions. Their incomes, by the end of the thirteenth century, derived primarily from the rents of peasants who leased land from them, supplemented by whatever wealth might come their way as magistrates of the rural districts with control over the public purse.[45]

Aristocrats did not control the colleges of magistrates by themselves, but were assisted by another group of great proprietors living from land rents as opposed to the actual labor of crop raising and livestock keeping, whose position and status was based not on aristocratic blood lines but on fortunes acquired through successful agricultural, industrial, or commercial activities or service in the central administration. A good example of a non-noble great proprietor, even though he never held public office, was Simon de Rikelike, a prominent landowner in Bruges district during the 1320s and 1330s. According to his account book, he owned lands and houses scattered over 11 parishes in the district, most of which were managed for him by agents who oversaw the collection of substantial rents, tithes, and payments in kind.[46] Together, the two groups of great proprietors were able to form an effective oligarchy, a closed group of the most powerful families, and dominate the political life of the rural districts just as the oligarchies of the cities did. By extension, individual great proprietors played important political roles in many rural communities as well, though in this venue they were seriously outnumbered and often neutralized by the concerted efforts of ordinary peasants to resist dominance.[47] Even though rural elites would have been very sensitive to distinctions of nobility and non-nobility—non-noble great proprietors were aspirants to the privileged status of the nobles who frequently blocked such upward mobility—peasants often tended to see them as a single group and referred to all of them simply as "lords." This was particularly the case during the peasant rebellion of the 1320s, as we shall see.

The relationships between the cities and the countryside were not always clearly delineated. There were times, both before and during the revolt of the 1320s, when the oligarchies of both joined together in conflict against coalitions of peasants and members of certain craft guilds from the cities. But there also were times when coalitions of urbanites came to blows with coalitions of country dwellers, especially over questions of rural textile manufacturing or control of the wool or grain trade. Most often, however, town and country relations were much more subtle and nuanced.[48]

The cities of Flanders provided important central-place functions for nearby rural populations, which in turn helped to produce a rural population density in their immediate hinterlands that was considerably greater than normally found in less urbanized areas. The most obvious central-place function was a market for the surplus agricultural production of nearby rural communities. High rates of urbanization in Flanders, therefore, were paired with high rural population densities, while a significant proportion of the country dwellers at the beginning of the fourteenth century not only sold their agricultural products in the nearby cities but also purchased many necessities there.

It is impossible to calculate the quantity of foods brought into the cities on a daily or weekly basis, but it must have been very significant. So, too, was the flow of surplus people who took up residence in the cities. And, despite English imports, Flemish peasants continued to produce large quantities of wool for the urban textile industries. All roads, canals, and paths converged on the cities.[49] As a result, to a far greater degree than in most parts of Europe, a market-oriented, monetized economy characterized significant segments of the rural sector as well. Though production for urban markets introduced elements of economic risk beyond the control of ordinary individuals, many Flemish peasants profited greatly from the opportunity to specialize in the production of products that had high value on urban markets.

War with France and the Mobilization of Ordinary People

At the beginning of the fourteenth century, Flanders ceased to exist as an independent principality. A French army occupied the entire land by the end of May 1300, and the count, imprisoned in a French castle, was replaced by a governor who reported directly to the king of France. Scarcely two years later, however, a force of ordinary Flemings, including many from the countryside, began a successful campaign that drove the occupying force from the land and set the stage for the reestablishment of the county of Flanders. The conquest, the war of independence, and the two decades of troubled French-Flemish relations that followed dramatically changed the lives of peasants.

Surviving twenty-five years of on and off war with France, along with
the internal political discord that it inevitably produced, meant choosing
sides, defining interests, and learning to cooperate with others who shared
their goals. In short, Flemish peasants, learning quickly from their more
experienced compatriots in the urban craft guilds, became public political
actors for the first time, and this experience constituted much of the prehistory to the peasant revolt of the 1320s. This is not to suggest that they
became politically active only during the first quarter of the fourteenth
century. What changed around 1300 was that it became possible—or,
perhaps more accurately, necessary—for peasants to use open, declared
forms of resistance at a time when preferred, concealed, undeclared forms
of resistance to domination no longer seemed effective.[50]

The French conquest and the popular liberation of Flanders, which
first drew peasants onto the public political stage, grew out of the political
turmoil and party strife that initially erupted in Flemish cities during the
last quarter of the thirteenth century. By that time, the oligarchies dominating political affairs of the cities were being increasingly challenged by other
wealthy citizens, often referred to as the second patriciate—in many cases
entrepreneurs who had profited from the economic flowering since the
twelfth century. The latter had for some time been making a claim for a role
in urban decision-making, though the oligarchs still managed to hold on to
their monopolies of political office. And, alongside the rival groups of
patricians vying for political influence were ordinary urban people who had
begun to formulate a series of grievances against the management of the
cities, particularly the handling of taxes levied on daily provisions, the so-
called *ongeld* that weighed most heavily on those of modest or meager
means. Organized by the craft guilds but driven by economic hard times,
they began asking for the right to oversee public finances as well as for
places on the courts of aldermen.[51]

When Guy of Dampierre became count of Flanders in 1278, he began
almost immediately to meddle in the political and economic affairs of the
cities in an attempt to extend his own political power at the expense of the
urban oligarchies. As early as 1279, for example, he supported the demand
of the ordinary people of Ghent for the right to inspect city finances, and in
September 1280 he temporarily removed the Thirty-Nine of Ghent from
power. The second patriciate, those wealthy citizens thus far excluded from
real involvement in public affairs, benefited from such actions against the
traditional oligarchs. But Guy's moves, along with a growing economic

crisis, caused serious divisions and rivalries which eventually degenerated into bitter quarrels between oligarchs and political outsiders, and some of these quarrels resulted in bloody street fighting and prolonged and bitter feuds.[52]

This already tense situation escalated considerably after 1285 when King Philip IV, the Fair, began to intervene directly in Flemish political affairs. His opportunity to do so actually grew out of the political animosity that already existed between the urban oligarchies and Count Guy—the oligarchs of Ghent actually asked for royal intervention. Believing that the surest way to gain control over Flanders was by undermining the authority of the count, Philip announced his support for the ruling oligarchies of the cities against the centralizing pressures of Count Guy. The result of this was the gradual formation of two major parties or coalitions. The pro-French urban oligarchs and their associates became known as *leliaarts*, so-called because they chose the French lily or *fleur-de-lis* (Dutch, *lelie*) as their symbol. Their anti-French opponents, the second patriciate along with significant numbers of craft guild members, became known as *klauwaarts* because they chose the claw (Dutch, *klauw*) of the lion of Flanders as their symbol.[53] From the 1290s into the 1320s, *leliaart* fortunes rose when the king gained advantage over the count, and *klauwaart* fortunes rose when the count gained advantage over the king.

Many times before, French kings had looked enviously at this wealthy and industrious principality to the north and sought ways of increasing their influence over it. But the pressures applied by Philip were much more aggressive and authoritarian than any that had come before. While his predecessors seemed content with acting as arbiters within the feudal structure of mutual rights and obligations, Philip shamelessly embarked on an attempt systematically to remove all prerogatives of the count of Flanders. Royal agents operated openly in Flanders, stirring up discontent, countering every move of the count, offering rewards to those who would assist in undermining the count's authority, and much more.[54]

For a long time Count Guy remained a loyal vassal to the king, but the incessant royal harassment finally forced him to renounce his allegiance to King Philip in January 1297 and to seek an alliance with England. His English allies, however, proved to be unfaithful, while most of his own nobles, forced to choose between honoring the oaths of allegiance they had sworn to both the king and count, decided to side with the French king.[55] And because he had always been so much more concerned with his own welfare than that of his ordinary subjects, Count Guy had lost the loyalty and trust that might have allowed him to forge a united front of ordinary people and second patriciate against the ever more aggressive king. The expected invasion began during the summer of 1297, with French forces seizing much of Walloon Flanders and the districts of Bourbourg and Bergues along the coast; the anonymous annalist of Ghent specifically blamed the loss of the coastal districts and the burning of the city of Veurne on the treason of the nobility of west Flanders.[56] A series of truces arrived at through papal mediation maintained the status quo for two years, but when they expired in January 1300, Philip simply resumed the invasion. By the end of May 1300, all Flanders was occupied and quickly incorporated into the royal domain.[57]

Through much of the political turmoil of the 1280s and 1290s, the peasants of Flanders remained essentially spectators. The attempts by Count Guy to use urban unrest as a means of extending his political authority over the cities was not an issue that bothered most country dwellers very seriously. Indeed, some may well have approved of the count's actions, since cities literally dominated the economic life of the countryside, occasionally in quite unfavorable ways. Similarly, the increasing involvement of the king of France in the political fray after 1285 did not immediately alarm most peasants as long as it remained a problem for the count and his urban followers alone. It was only after the king's actions became ever more clearly directed against the authority of Count Guy, and particularly after nobles sided with the king and delivered the westernmost coastal districts to their patron, that peasants were drawn into the maelstrom. No longer able to stay aloof, they joined the pro-count *klauwaart* party and the losing side. As a result, the conquest and French occupation weighed very heavily on them.[58]

The attachment of the county of Flanders to the royal domain brought hard times to ordinary Flemings. According to the anonymous author of the *Chronicon comitum Flandrensium*, the royal governor of Flanders, Jacques de Châtillon, imposed a generally oppressive regime designed to consolidate the king's hold on Flanders.[59] The property of *klauwaarts* and many of their supporters was confiscated and redistributed to anti-count backers of the king, or *leliaarts*.[60] In the countryside specifically, many peasants saw their possessions transferred to those *leliaart* nobles who had welcomed the conquest. Meanwhile, the pressure of increased taxation hurt ordinary people in both city and countryside, and many complained that those who had sided with the *klauwaarts* bore a much heavier share of the tax burden than did their *leliaart* opponents.[61] And some of the uses to which new taxes were put, especially the construction of new fortresses, made a particularly unpopular impression.[62] In addition, *leliaarts* prospered politically under de Châtillon's administration. In the cities conservative oligarchies once again dominated, while in the countryside great proprietors, especially those who were nobles, used French support to impose a feudal reaction against the free rural population, a reaction that seemed aimed at restoring their long-lost ascendancy.[63] As a result, many ordinary people, including peasants, became convinced that the royal governor intended to destroy the traditional liberties of Flanders and reduce the entire land to slavery, and they consequently developed a deep hatred for him and his *leliaart* supporters.[64]

Despite the authoritarian control exercised by de Châtillon's regime and its *leliaart* allies, an active opposition gradually developed throughout the principality. Discontent was widespread, erupting into a series of bloody street confrontations in Bruges and Ghent during 1301 and 1302. Elsewhere, resistance to domination remained semi-concealed for the moment, seething just below the surface.[65] As a result, what was by itself a rather insignificant event, the so-called "Matins of Bruges"—an early-morning attack by *klauwaarts* on 18 May 1302—signaled the start of a massive popular rebellion against de Châtillon and his *leliaart* clients that resulted in the total liberation of Flanders and the eventual release of the imprisoned count.[66]

The high point of the war of independence was the battle fought outside the walls of Courtrai on 11 July 1302 in which 8,000 to 10,000 Flemish foot soldiers, almost all of them drawn from the ranks of ordinary people, including 3,000 peasants, inflicted a humiliating defeat on the forces of the king and his allies. The latter consisted of perhaps 7,500 warriors, fully one-third of which were French and Flemish nobles in cavalry units, who, according to contemporary beliefs, should have been the equal of 25,000 infantry. When the battle was over, however, a thousand knights lay dead as opposed to a few hundred Flemish infantry.[67] In the wake of this battle, the French military and administration and many *leliaarts* fled in haste, bringing an end to the rule of the conservative oligarchies in both city and countryside. By the end of September 1302, the people had triumphed. Additional military engagements during 1303 and 1304 produced little change, although ordinary Flemings felt confident in the knowledge that they effectively warded off all attempts by the king and the nobles to achieve revenge for their defeat at Courtrai. A peace concluded at Athis-sur-Orge in June 1305 finally restored Flanders as a semi-autonomous principality, and Count Guy's son, Robert of Béthune, was invested with the countship.[68]

The events of 1302 to 1305 changed the political life of ordinary Flemish people. Immediately after the Battle of Courtrai, new coalitions swept into power in most Flemish cities, coalitions that included members of craft guilds. The war of independence was also an important turning point for Flemish peasants. First of all, it introduced them to the more fully developed political experience of urban people, including traditions of direct political action when other types of resistance to domination proved ineffective. In addition, it helped to radicalize them by showing them more clearly than ever before who were their friends and who were their enemies. Further, it showed what they could do when they mobilized, when they asserted themselves, particularly when they made common cause with others beyond their local communities. Finally, it provided practical lessons in political action. Nobles were virtually eliminated from power in the coastal rural districts from 1302 to 1305 and suffered significant setbacks elsewhere, while peasants themselves learned to control their own affairs within their rural communities and participated as well in the governance of the rural districts.[69] During the 1320s, the peasant rebels of Flanders drew on these experiences as they made their own rebellion, and they used their contacts of two decades earlier to gain the support of many urban people. Previous cooperation made later cooperation easier to arrange.

The People Betrayed

Although popular Flemish forces, including sizable contingents from the rural districts, had defeated the best that the king of France and his allies in Flanders could assemble, the Peace of Athis-sur-Orge of 1305 contained provisions that treated the victors in the Battle of Courtrai and the war of independence as though they actually had lost. The Peace did reestablish Flanders as a semi-autonomous principality ruled directly by its restored counts, but it exacted a tremendously heavy price from its inhabitants. First of all, to compensate the king for his loss of revenue, he was promised an annual income of 20,000 lbs. as well as an additional sum of 400,000 lbs. to be paid in four installments from 1306 to 1309—and, as everyone knew, such sums would derive largely from taxes paid by ordinary people, the liberators of Flanders. Additional clauses provided special punishment for the city of Bruges because of its role in the "Matins of Bruges" and the unhindered return of all exiles who had been expelled for their association with the French occupation. Finally, the king maintained temporary control over the cities and rural districts of Lille, Douai, and Orchies, all of Walloon Flanders, as a guarantee that the Flemings would live up to the provisions of the Peace.[70]

It is easy to understand the hatred of the ordinary people of Flanders and their fellow *klauwaarts* toward the Peace of Athis-sur-Orge. Not only were they required to pay the huge indemnities to the king of France, they also had to stand aside as *leliaart* nobles and patricians returned in force, arrogantly demanding subsidies for every penny they had lost during the war. They failed to understand the political considerations that had forced Count Robert to accept the treaty, seeing it instead as just another example of betrayal by the nobles and patricians who had negotiated the peace. However, the provisions of the Peace were poorly enforced, resulting in a series of long drawn out negotiations to work out points of dispute, such as what currency the indemnities would be reckoned in. When attempts to collect taxes to pay the indemnities provoked widespread opposition, Count Robert simply stopped or delayed them, moves that gained him considerable popular support, and the fact that he could stretch things out for such a long time indicates how weak the French king apparently felt himself to be diplomatically. The cities of Flanders refused to accept the Peace of Athis-sur-Orge until 1309, and until then very little of the promised indemnity was paid.[71]

When Count Robert made a serious effort to collect taxes to pay the indemnity promised the king, it provoked violent opposition in the countryside in 1309. In particular, peasants in the Land of Waas district, northeast of Ghent, publicly declared their opposition and organized a substantial resistance. In a manner that became commonplace during the 1320s, they placed themselves under the leadership of their own *hoofdmannen* or captains. The count had to appeal to the nobility to suppress this outburst, and it did so only with the application of overwhelming force. After a bloody conflict, twenty-five peasant captains were banned, while another five were tortured and put to death.[72] Violence also erupted in the cities of Aardenburg and Ghent in 1311 over collection of indemnity taxes.[73]

Further negotiations between the French and Flemings led to the Treaty of Pontoise in June 1312. In exchange for the final relinquishment of Walloon Flanders, Count Robert was offered one-half of the 20,000 lb. annual income provided for in the Treaty of Athis-sur-Orge but which in reality had rarely been paid. Such an agreement could be rationalized from both sides. The king had received very little of his indemnity, not only because of popular Flemish opposition to collections but also because Robert kept dragging his heels. Robert would now doubtless be inclined to help collect the indemnity. For his part, Robert may have been willing to agree to the definitive loss of Flemish territory not only because he needed money but also because he had in fact already lost control over the territory in question. The so-called "Transport of Flanders" was devised to spread the payments over all Flemish cities and rural districts, clearly spelling out just how much each city or rural district was required to pay each year. As a result of this agreement, however, Robert now began to bear some of the displeasure his Flemish subjects previously had reserved exclusively for the king.[74]

Even though many ordinary Flemings opposed the Treaty of Pontoise with as much fervor as the Treaty of Athis-sur-Orge, Count Robert continued to enjoy reasonably good relations with his subjects, particularly with members of craft guilds and with peasants, thanks to his suspension of the indemnity collections, the confiscation of *leliaart* possessions, and a renewed offensive against the king in 1314.[75] In fact, some jurisdictions began to accept the modifications of the Treaty of Pontoise. For example, Veurne district paid its share until 1322, and the rural district of Ypres paid its portion until 1323. The rural district of Ghent, meanwhile, continued to pay as late as 1325, but others were less willing to give in so easily. At best, collections for the count's "Transport of Flanders" were sporadic.[76] And, when magistrates attempted once again to levy taxes for the king's indemnity in 1315 and 1316, violence broke out in the district of Bergues. Peasants of the district marched under their own banner against the count's captain and bailiff of Bergues, freed prisoners, and threatened to kill the magistrates. They charged that the magistrates unfairly placed the entire tax burden for the indemnities on the backs of ordinary people.[77]

Nevertheless, by 1320 the will to continue resisting all French designs had begun to wane considerably in some quarters. Count Robert was becoming increasingly preoccupied with the discord between his sons, Louis and Robert, at a time when a French expedition against Flanders seemed ever more likely. Meanwhile, warfare or the threat of warfare over a period of two decades had seriously eroded the commercial and industrial strength of Flanders. In Ypres, for example, cloth production dropped sharply during the years following the Peace of Athis-sur-Orge. The wealthy citizens of Flanders, therefore, were becoming increasingly interested in peace, so much so that the magistrates of the city of Ghent refused to allow the city's militia to assist Robert in a campaign against Lille in 1319. Left in the lurch, all Robert could do was offer homage to Philip V, the second son of Philip the Fair, who had become king of France in 1316.[78] Recognizing the growing desire for peace among his subjects, and perhaps fearing that the cities of Flanders might seek their own peace with France if he did not act himself, Robert undertook negotiations in Paris in 1320. The peace that finally emerged closed a long period of tension and warfare and included a succession agreement whereby Robert's grandson, not his son, would succeed him as count. The peace left intact the still unpopular indemnities for the king from earlier treaties, however. Any hope that the count might once again support popular opposition to these hated payments was dashed when Count Robert died in 1322.[79]

Notes

1. Adriaan Verhulst, "Occupatiegeschiedenis en landbouweconomie in het Zuiden circa 1000–1300," in *Algemene geschiedenis der Nederlanden*, vol. 2 (Haarlem: Fibula-van Dishoeck, 1982), pp. 83–85.

2. David Nicholas, *Medieval Flanders* (London: Longmans, 1992), pp. 13–20, 39–55; Jean Dunbabin, *France in the Making, 843–1180* (New York: Oxford University Press, 1985), pp. 70–71.

3. Though the move into the lands to the northeast and southeast of Ghent during the eleventh century had complicated the political situation of Flanders because its counts thereby became vassals to the emperor as well, the ties to the French king were always the strongest and most direct, bringing aid to the counts on more than one occasion, but also bringing increasing royal involvement in internal Flemish affairs; see D. Lambrecht and J. van Rompaey, "De staatsinstellingen in het Zuiden van de 11de tot de 14de eeuw," in *Algemene geschiedenis der Nederlanden*, vol. 2 (Haarlem: Fibula-van Dishoeck, 1982), p. 77.

4. David Nicholas, "Of Poverty and Primacy: Demand, Liquidity, and the Flemish Economic Miracle," *American Historical Review* 96 (1991), p. 17; idem, *Medieval Flanders*, pp. 39–74; W. P. Blockmans, "De ontwikkeling van een verstedelijkte samenleving (XIe–XVde eeuw)," in *Geschiedenis van Vlaanderen van de oorsprong tot heden*, Els Witte, ed. (Brussels: Historische getuigen/La Renaissance du livre, 1983), p. 64.

5. Nicholas, *Medieval Flanders*, pp. 73–74; Blockmans, "De ontwikkeling van een verstedelijkte samenleving," p. 65; Karen S. Nicholas, "The Role of Feudal Relationships in the Consolidation of Power in the Principalities of the Low Countries, 1000–1300," in *Law, Custom, and the Social Fabric in Medieval Europe*, Bernard S. Bachrach and David Nicholas, eds., Studies in Medieval Culture, XXVIII (Kalamazoo: Western Michigan University-Medieval Institute Publication, 1990), p. 116.

6. Nicholas, "Of Poverty and Primacy: Demand, Liquidity, and the Flemish Economic Miracle," pp. 17–33.

7. Adriaan Verhulst, *Histoire du paysage rural en Flandre de l'époque romaine au XVIIIe siècle*, Collection "Notre Passé" (Brussels: La Renaissance du Livre, 1966), pp. 15–24; idem and D. P. Blok, "Het natuurlandschap," in *Algemene geschiedenis der Nederlanden*, vol. 1 (Haarlem: Fibula-van Dishoeck, 1981), pp. 116–35.

8. Verhulst, "Occupatiegeschiedenis en landbouweconomie," p. 93–94. For the general patterns, see Georges Duby, *Rural Economy and Country Life in the Medieval West*, Cynthia Postan, trans. (Columbia: University of South Carolina Press, 1968), pp. 119–25; William H. TeBrake, *Medieval Frontier: Culture and Ecology in Rijnland*, Environmental History Series, no. 7 (College Station: Texas A & M University Press, 1985), pp. 5–6; Norman J. G. Pounds, *An Historical Geography of Europe* (New York: Cambridge University Press, 1990), pp. 119–23.

9. See, in particular, the important observations of Adriaan Verhulst, "The 'Agricultural Revolution' of the Middle Ages Reconsidered," in *Law, Custom, and the Social Fabric in Medieval Europe*, Bernard S. Bachrach and David Nicholas, eds. Studies in Medieval Culture, XXVIII (Kalamazoo: Western Michigan University-Medieval Institute Publication, 1990), pp. 17–28.

10. Nicholas, "Of Poverty and Primacy: Demand, Liquidity, and the Flemish Economic Miracle," pp. 26–27; idem, *Medieval Flanders*, pp. 23–9, 104–7; W. P. Blockmans, J. Mertens, and A. Verhulst, "Les communautés rurales d'ancien régime en Flandre: caractéristiques et essai d'interprétation comparative," in *Europe occidentale et Amerique—Western Europe and America*, vol 5 of *Les communautés rurales—Rural Communities*, Recueils de la Société Jean Bodin pour l'Histoire Comparative des Institutions, XLIV (Paris: Dessain et Tolra, 1987), p. 233; Henri Pirenne, ed., *Le soulèvement de la Flandre maritime, 1323–1328, documents inédites*, Académie Royale de Belgique, Commission Royale d'Histoire, Publications in-octavo (Brussels: P. Imbreghts, 1900), pp. v–vi.

11. See Verhulst, "Occupatiegeschiedenis en landbouweconomie," pp. 83, 95; the discussions in TeBrake, *Medieval Frontier*, pp. 41–52; as well as Rodney H. Hilton, "Medieval Peasants: Any Lessons?" *Journal of Peasant Studies* 1 (1973–4), p. 214.

12. Verhulst, "Occupatiegeschiedenis en landbouweconomie," p. 93.

13. Nicholas, "Of Poverty and Primacy: Demand, Liquidity, and the Flemish Economic Miracle," p. 26; Pirenne, ed., *Le soulèvement*, pp. vi–vii.

14. See Walter Prevenier, "La démographie des villes du comté de Flandre aux XIIIe et XIVe siècles: état de la question, essai d'interprétation," *Revue du Nord* 65 (1983), pp. 255–75; and W. Simons, *Stad en apostolaat: de vestiging van de bedelorden in het graafschap Vlaanderen (ca. 1225–ca. 1350)*, Verhandelingen van de Koninklijke Academie voor Wetenschappen, Letteren en Schone Kunsten van België, Klasse der Letteren, 49, nr. 121 (Brussels: Paleis der Academiën, 1987), p. 89.

15. By the early fourteenth century, Saint-Omer had roughly 35,000 inhabitants, Arras between 20,000 and 30,000, Lille around 26,000, Douai between 21,000 and 26,000, and Tournai between 19,000 and 23,000—see Simons, *Stad en apostolat*, pp. 92–93, 98; Alain Derville, "Le nombre d'habitants des villes d'Artois et de

la Flandre Wallonne (1300–1450)," *Revue du Nord* 65 (1983), pp. 277–99; and Blockmans, "De ontwikkeling van een verstedelijkte samenleving," p. 58.

16. Graphically illustrated by the map in Pounds, *An Historical Geography of
Europe*, p. 164. Nicholas, *Medieval Flanders*, p. 117, says that Flanders succeeded in
"surpassing even Italy" in its degree of urbanization.

17. For an important reconsideration of this transformation, see Nicholas,
"Of Poverty and Primacy: Demand, Liquidity, and the Flemish Economic Miracle,"
pp. 17–41; and idem, *Medieval Flanders*, pp. 21–38, 97–149.

18. R. van Uytven, "Stadsgeschiedenis in het Noorden en Zuiden," *Algemene
geschiedenis der Nederlanden*, vol. 2 (Haarlem: Fibula-van Dishoeck, 1982), pp. 194,
198; Jacques Toussaert, *Le sentiment religieux en Flandre à la fin du moyen âge*,
Civilisations d'Hier et d'Aujourd'hui (Paris: Plon, 1963), p. 35. On the continuing
importance of domestically produced wool in the Flemish textile industry, see
Nicholas, "Of Poverty and Primacy: Demand, Liquidity, and the Flemish Economic Miracle," pp. 35–36.

19. Earlier there had been a certain amount of political cooperation on occasion between the great cities of Saint-Omer, Arras, Ghent, Ypres, Bruges, Douai,
and Lille, but the first two were incorporated into the county of Artois in 1191, while
the last two came into the hands of the king of France when he acquired Walloon
Flanders in 1305.

20. Blockmans, Mertens, and Verhulst, "Les communautés rurales d'ancien
régime en Flandre," pp. 238–39.

21. Blockmans, "De ontwikkeling van een verstedelijkte samenleving (XIde–
XVde eeuw)," pp. 43–48; Nicholas, "Of Poverty and Primacy: Demand, Liquidity,
and the Flemish Economic Miracle," pp. 17–41.

22. Prevenier, "La démographie des villes du comté de Flandre aux XIIIe et
XIVe siècles," p. 270. There is some evidence to suggest that Flemish cities reached
their medieval maxima shortly after 1300—see Walter Prevenier and W. P. Blockmans, *The Burgundian Netherlands*, trans. Peter King and Yvette Mead (Cambridge: Cambridge University Press, 1986), pp. 37, 40, 45, 48; W. P. Blockmans, G.
Pieters, W. Prevenier, and R. W. M. van Schaik, "Tussen crisis en welvaart: sociale
veranderingen 1300–1500," in *Algemene geschiedenis der Nederlanden*, vol. 4.
(Haarlem: Fibula-van Dishoeck, 1980), p. 49. See also Léopold Genicot, *Rural
Communities in the Medieval West*, Johns Hopkins Symposia in Comparative History (Baltimore: Johns Hopkins University Press, 1990), p. 32. Rodney H. Hilton,
"A Crisis of Feudalism," *Past and Present* 80 (1978), p. 5, suggests that peasants still
constituted three-quarters or more of the total population in much of Europe.

23. Blockmans, Mertens, and Verhulst, "Les communautés rurales d'ancien
régime en Flandre," p. 233. See as well my discussion in the introduction, above.

24. L. M. de Gryse, "Some Observations on the Origin of the Flemish Bailiff
(bailli): The Reign of Philip of Alsace," *Viator: Medieval and Renaissance Studies* 7
(1976), pp. 143–94; Ellen E. Kittell, *From Ad Hoc to Routine: A Case Study in
Medieval Bureaucracy*, Middle Ages Series (Philadelphia: University of Pennsylvania
Press, 1991), pp. 6, 19; and Nicholas, *Medieval Flanders*, pp. 82–85.

25. Blockmans, Mertens, and Verhulst, "Les communautés rurales d'ancien
régime en Flandre," pp. 234–35; Pirenne, ed., *Le soulèvement*, pp. viii–ix.

26. Ernest Warlop, "De vorming van de grote schepenbank van het Brugse Vrije (11de–13de eeuw)," *Anciens Pays et Assemblées d'États/Standen en landen* 44 (1968), p. 15, describes these as follows: eastern, east of the Zwin; northern, north of a line between Oostende-Oudenburg to the sea and the Zwin; western, southwest of the same line.

27. Blockmans, Mertens, and Verhulst, "Les communautés rurales d'ancien régime en Flandre," p. 235; Pirenne, ed., *Le soulèvement*, pp. viii–ix; Warlop, "De vorming van de grote schepenbank van het Brugse Vrije," pp. 1–28.

28. According to Susan Reynolds, *Kingdoms and Communities in Western Europe, 900–1300* (Oxford: Clarendon Press, 1984), p. 2, a community is a group "which defines itself by engaging in collective activities—activities which are characteristically determined and controlled less by formal regulations than by shared values and norms, while the relationships between members of the community are characteristically reciprocal, many-sided, and direct, rather than being mediated through officials or rulers."

29. Rural communities could be defined in various ways that were not necessarily mutually exclusive. In fact, most peasants were likely to be members of multiple, overlapping communities: see Genicot, *Rural Communities in the Medieval West*, throughout; Gérard Sivéry, *Terroirs et communautés rurales dans l'Europe occidentale au moyen âge*, Économies et Sociétés (Villeneuve-d'Ascq: Presses Universitaires de Lille, 1990), p. 139.

30. In the district of Bruges, for example, about 100 parishes were grouped into 35 *ambachten* at the end of the thirteenth century; see Warlop, "De vorming van de grote schepenbank van het Brugse Vrije," p. 4.

31. Blockmans, Mertens, and Verhulst, "Les communautés rurales d'ancien régime en Flandre," pp. 233–35.

32. Nicholas, "Of Poverty and Primacy: Demand, Liquidity, and the Flemish Economic Miracle," pp. 37–40; Blockmans, Mertens, and Verhulst, "Les communautés rurales d'ancien régime en Flandre," pp. 225–31.

33. Sivéry, *Terroirs et communautés*, pp. 85–86, 125–26; Blockmans, Mertens, and Verhulst, "Les communautés rurales d'ancien régime en Flandre," p. 233. Reynolds, *Kingdoms and Communities in Western Europe*, pp. 151–52, maintains that any group that deserved to be called a community held meetings to regulate matters of common concern "through collective counsel and collective judgment." See also Richard Wunderli, *Peasant Fires: The Drummer of Niklashausen* (Bloomington: Indiana University Press, 1992), p. 34; J. A. Raftis, "Social Change Versus Revolution: New Interpretations of the Peasants' Revolt of 1381," in *Social Unrest in the Late Middle Ages: Papers of the Fifteenth Annual Conference of the Center for Medieval and Early Renaissance Studies*, Francis X. Newman, ed., Medieval and Renaissance Texts and Studies, vol. 39 (Binghamton, NY: Center for Medieval and Early Renaissance Studies, 1986), p. 10.

34. Blockmans, Mertens, and Verhulst, "Les communautés rurales d'ancien régime en Flandre," p. 232; Reynolds, *Kingdoms and Communities in Western Europe*, pp. 150–51; Genicot, *Rural Communities in the Medieval West*, pp. 82–89.

35. See Genicot, *Rural Communities in the Medieval West*, p. 84.

36. Often referred to as the *probi viri, consules, preud'hommes*; see Genicot,

Rural Communities in the Medieval West, pp. 83–84, 87; Reynolds, *Kingdoms and Communities in Western Europe*, p. 152; and Hilton, "A Crisis of Feudalism," p. 9.

37. This line of research is particularly associated with the work of J. Ambrose Raftis, starting with his "Social Structures in five East Midland Villages: A Study of Possibilities in the Use of Court Roll Data," *Economic History Review* 18 (1965), pp. 83–100; and "The Concentration of Responsibility in Five Villages," *Mediaeval Studies* 28 (1966), pp. 92–118. This work has been carried on by him and his students largely through painstaking family reconstruction based on linking vast ranges of court and manorial material. Barbara A. Hanawalt, *The Ties That Bound: Peasant Families in Medieval England* (New York and Oxford: Oxford University Press, 1986), pp. 6, 275 (note 4), reviews the essential literature.

38. See, for example, Adriaan Verhulst, *Précis d'histoire rurale de la Belgique* (Brussels: Éditions de l'Université de Bruxelles, 1990), pp. 84–85, 115–16. These should not be taken as hard and fast categories but as general ones that would have varied considerably from one locale to another.

39. F. W. N. Hugenholtz, *Drie boerenopstanden uit de veertiende eeuw: Vlaanderen 1323–1328, Frankrijk 1358, Engeland 1381; onderzoek naar het opstandig bewustzijn* (Haarlem: Tjeenk Willink, 1949), p. 140, reproduces the following:

"Langhe arme ende wide hande
    Hebben de heren van de lande;"
"Wie in officien comt in heren hove
    Seker hi leeft meest bi rove."

40. Pirenne, ed., *Le soulèvement*, pp. ix–x.

41. See Reynolds, *Kingdoms and Communities in Western Europe*, p. 174; and Raftis, "Social Change Versus Revolution," pp. 8–9.

42. The alliance between counts and cities was especially strengthened by the turmoil and civil war resulting from the assasination of count Charles the Good by the Erembald clan and its allies in 1127. See the contemporary account by Galbert of Bruges, *The Murder of Charles the Good, Count of Flanders*, James Bruce Ross, trans. and ed. (New York: Harper, 1967); as well as R. C. van Caenegem, "De Gentse februari-opstand van het jaar 1128," *Spiegel historiael*, 13 (1978), pp. 478–83.

43. W. P. Blockmans, *Een middeleeuwse vendetta: Gent 1300* (Houten, NL: Unieboek-De Haan, 1987), p. 65. See also Nicholas, *Medieval Flanders*, p. 211.

44. Blockmans, "De ontwikkeling van een verstedelijkte samenleving (XIe–XVde eeuw)," pp. 65–66; Nicholas, *Medieval Flanders*, pp. 132–35.

45. Nicholas, *Medieval Flanders*, pp. 104–7, 158–61; Jacques Sabbe, *Vlaanderen in opstand, 1323–328: Nikolaas Zannekin, Zeger Janszone en Willem de Deken*, Genootschap voor Geschiedenis "Société d'Émulation" te Brugge, Vlaamse Historische Studies, VII (Bruges: Marc Van de Wiele, 1992), pp. 11, 13.

46. See J. De Smet, ed., *Het memoriaal van Simon de Rikelike, vrijlaat te St. Pieters-op-den-dijk, 1323–1336*, Koninklijke Commissie voor Geschiedenis (Brussels: Maurice Lamertin, 1933).

47. Sivéry, *Terroirs et communautés*, pp. 182, 189–90; Nicholas, "Of Poverty and Primacy: Demand, Liquidity, and the Flemish Economic Miracle," pp. 16–41;

Blockmans, Mertens, and Verhulst, "Les communautés rurales d'ancien régime en Flandre," pp. 233–35; Hilton, "A Crisis of Feudalism," pp. 8–9. See as well the general discussion of peasant resistance to domination in the introduction, above.

48. David Nicholas, *Town and Countryside: Social, Economic, and Political Tensions in Fourteenth-Century Flanders*, Rijksuniversiteit te Gent, Werken uitgegeven door de faculteit van de letteren en wijsbegeerte, 152 (Bruges: De Tempel, 1971), pp. 51–172.

49. Van Uytven, "Stadsgeschiedenis in het noorden en zuiden," pp. 188–253. Charles Tilly, *Coercion, Capital, and European States, AD 990–1990*, Studies in Social Discontinuity (Cambridge, MA: Basil Blackwell, 1990), pp. 17–19, speaks of the "spiral of change" that cities worked on their hinterlands, though most of it, including networks of navigible canals and streams, was in place in Flanders a full two centuries before the sixteenth century as he suggests; see Nicholas, "Of Poverty and Primacy: Demand, Liquidity, and the Flemish Economic Miracle," p. 33.

50. According to Genicot, *Rural Communities in the Medieval West*, p. 79, "the peasants had always resisted," though the form that resistance might take could vary considerably. See the discussion of resistance to domination in the previous chapter.

51. M. Vandermaesen, "Vlaanderen en Henegouwen onder het huis van Dampierre 1244–1384," in *Algemene geschiedenis der Nederlanden*, vol. 2 (Haarlem: Fibula-van Dishoeck, 1982), pp. 403–4.

52. Blockmans, *Een middeleeuwse vendetta*, pp. 15–63; Nicholas, *Medieval Flanders*, pp. 181–86.

53. Walter Prevenier, "Motieven voor leliaardsgezindheid in Vlaanderen," *De Leiegouw*, 19 (1977), pp. 273–88; Nicholas, *Medieval Flanders*, pp. 190–91; Blockmans, *Een middeleeuwse vendetta*, pp. 64–84.

54. Vandermaesen, "Vlaanderen en Henegouwen onder het huis van Dampierre," pp. 403–19; Blockmans, *Een middeleeuwse vendetta*, pp. 64–133; Kittell, *From Ad Hoc to Routine*, p. 41; and Joseph R. Strayer, *The Reign of Philip the Fair* (Princeton, NJ: Princeton University Press, 1980), pp. 326–33.

55. According to Vandermaesen, "Vlaanderen en Henegouwen onder het huis van Dampierre," p. 408, the defecting nobles decided to cooperate with the highest bidder. Refusal to collaborate with the king meant the certain confiscation of their possessions after the expected French invasion was completed. Confiscations by the count constituted only a temporary threat, since the king would offset such losses by giving them the confiscated goods of the count's partisans. See also Prevenier, "Motieven voor leliaardsgezindheid in Vlaanderen," pp. 273–88; Nicholas, *Medieval Flanders*, pp. 186–91.

56. Anonymous, *Annales gandenses*, Hilda Johnstone, trans. and ed., Medieval Classics (London: Thomas Nelson and Sons, 1951), p. 4.

57. Vandermaesen, "Vlaanderen en Henegouwen onder het huis van Dampierre," pp. 405–9; Nicholas, *Medieval Flanders*, p. 191.

58. According to the *Annales gandenses*, p. 10, when French forces were unable to seize a number of well-fortified cities in the districts of Ypres, Ghent, and Bruges during the spring of 1300, they unleashed a wave of violence against the unprotected rural communities nearby instead.

59. Anonymous, *Chronicon comitum Flandrensium*, in *Corpus chronicorum*

Flandriae, sub auspiciis Leopoldi primi, serenissimi Belgarum regis: recueil des chroniques de Flandre, vol. 1, J. J. DeSmet, ed., Académie Royale de Belgique, Commission Royale d'Histoire, Mémoires en quarto (Brussels: H. Hayez, 1837) (hereafter cited as *Chronicon*) p. 165.

60. See Strayer, *The Reign of Philip the Fair*, p. 332.

61. *Chronicon*, p. 165; Nicholas, *Medieval Flanders*, p. 212.

62. Hugenholtz, *Drie boerenopstanden*, p. 18; T. De Limburg-Stirum, ed., *Codex diplomaticus Flandriae ab anno 1296 ad usque 1327, ou recueil de documents relatifs aux guerres et dissensions suscitées par Philippe-le-Bel, roi de France, contre Gui de Dampierre, comte de Flandre*, Société d'Émulation pour l'Étude de l'Histoire et des Antiquités de la Flandre (Bruges: De Plancke, 1889), vol. II, p. 152; Pirenne, ed., *Le soulèvement*, p. x.

63. Hugenholtz, *Drie boerenopstanden*, p. 18. According to *Annales gandenses*, p. 26, the peasants of the rural districts of Ypres, Veurne, Bergues, and Bourbourg were reduced almost to slavery by French and *leliaart* actions—"qui a Francis et Liliardis suis fuerant oppressi et quasi ad servilitatem redacti."

64. *Annales gandenses*, p. 11: "totam terram redigere in maximam servitutem, et omnes adnihillare libertates; unde factus es populo terre invisus et odiosus."

65. Blockmans, *Een middeleeuwse vendetta*, pp. 110–16; Vandermaesen, "Vlaanderen en Henegouwen onder het huis van Dampierre," pp. 409, 412; Hugenholtz, *Drie boerenopstanden*, p. 18; Pirenne, ed., *Le soulèvement*, p. x.

66. Blockmans, *Een middeleeuwse vendetta*, pp. 119–33; Vandermaesen, "Vlaanderen en Henegouwen onder het huis van Dampierre," pp. 409–14; Nicholas, *Medieval Flanders*, pp. 191–92.

67. See J. F. Verbruggen, *The Art of Warfare in Western Europe During the Middle Ages: From the Eighth Century to 1340*, Sumner Willard and S. C. M. Southern, trans., Europe in the Middle Ages: Selected Studies, 1 (Amsterdam and New York: North Holland Publishing, 1977), pp. 166–73; Nicholas, *Medieval Flanders*, pp. 192–94; Blockmans, *Een middeleeuwse vendetta*, pp. 124–29.

68. Vandermaesen, "Vlaanderen en Henegouwen onder het huis van Dampierre," pp. 414–15.

69. Hugenholz, *Drie boerenopstanden*, pp. 19–20.

70. H. van Werveke, "Les charges financières issues du traité d'Athis (1305)," *Revue du Nord* 32 (1950), pp. 81–93; Nicholas, *Medieval Flanders*, p. 195; Hugenholtz, *Drie boerenopstanden*, p. 19; Vandermaesen, "Vlaanderen en Henegouwen onder het huis van Dampierre," p. 414.

71. *Annales Gandenses*, pp 85–86, 89–90, 93–97; Nicholas, *Medieval Flanders*, pp. 195–96; Sabbe, *Vlaanderen in opstand*, p. 14; Hugenholtz, *Drie boerenopstanden*, pp. 20–21; Pirenne, ed., *Le soulèvement*, pp. xii–xiii; J. van Rompaey, "De opstand in het Vlaamse kustland van 1323 tot 1328 en de figuur van Nikolaas Zannekin," in *Nikolaas Zannekin en de Slag bij Kassel, 1328–1978: bijdrage tot de studie van de 14de eeuw en de landelijke geschiedenis van de Westhoek* (Diksmuide, Belgium: Kulturele Raad van Diksmuide, 1978), p. 104.

72. *Annales Gandenses*, p. 97; Kittell, *From Ad Hoc to Routine*, p. 128; Pirenne, ed., *Le soulèvement*, p. xiii; Hugenholtz, *Drie boerenopstanden*, p. 22; Sabbe, *Vlaanderen in opstand*, p. 15.

73. See C. Wyffels, "De oudste rekening der stad Aardenburg (1309–1310) en de opstand van 1311," *Archief: vroegere en latere mededelingen voornamelijk in betrekking tot Zeeland* (1949–1950), pp. 10–52, though in Aardenburg, it seems, members of the conservative oligarchy actually opposed the tax collections for the king's indemnity. See also F. Blockmans, "De bestraffing van den opstand van Brugge en Westelijk-Vlaanderen in 1328," *Beknopte Handelingen, XVe Vlaamsche Filologencongress* (1940), p. 39.

74. Nicholas, *Medieval Flanders*, pp. 186, 196; Van Rompaey, "De opstand in het Vlaamse kustland," p. 108; Sabbe, *Vlaanderen in opstand*, p. 15; Vandermaesen, "Vlaanderen en Henegouwen onder het huis van Dampierre," pp. 415–16.

75. Pirenne, ed., *Le soulèvement*, p. xiv; Blockmans, "De bestraffing van den opstand van Brugge en Westelijk-Vlaanderen in 1328," pp. 39–40.

76. See Kittell, *From Ad Hoc to Routine*, table 2, pp. 115–17; van Rompaey, "De opstand in het Vlaamse kustland," p. 108.

77. Quoted and dated by Pirenne, ed., *Le soulèvement*, pp. xiv–xv. See as well Blockmans, "De bestraffing van den opstand van Brugge en Westelijk-Vlaanderen in 1328," p. 40.

78. Hugenholtz, *Drie boerenopstanden*, p. 21; van Rompaey, "De opstand in het Vlaamse kustland," p. 104.

79. Hugenholtz, *Drie boerenopstanden*, pp. 21–22; Sabbe, *Vlaanderen in opstand*, p. 15.

2. For a World Without Corruption

When Count Louis II of Nevers inherited the countship of Flanders on 17 September 1322, thereby becoming Count Louis I of Flanders, he acquired one of the wealthiest, most densely populated, and most highly urbanized states in all of Europe. At only eighteen, he seemed to be a fortunate young man indeed. Not only did Flanders complement an already sizable inheritance in the counties of Rethel and Nevers, in northern and central France, but his marriage to a French princess two years earlier had provided him with truly enviable family connections. On the other hand, by inheriting Flanders, Louis also acquired an enormous amount of trouble. In early January 1324, less than sixteen months after coming to power, he complained that Flanders had provided him with nothing but difficulty thus far.[1] By that time, in fact, a large proportion of his rural subjects were in open revolt against his authority.

The Flemish peasant revolt actually grew out of a situation that Louis of Nevers played little role in creating. The revolt was first and foremost the public expression of a popular political culture that had been developing for some time. Flemings were accustomed by the 1320s to joining together or associating in factions and parties that often transcended family, neighborhood, class, or locality, and they regularly took direct political action, ranging from riots and demonstrations to armed struggle. At one end of the political spectrum were the traditional, privileged elites and their associates who continued to behave as though they were accountable to no one but themselves for their actions. At the other end were many ordinary people, including even some peasants, who were presumptuous enough to suggest that rulers and their agents should act in the interests of the ruled, reflecting, perhaps, embryonic forms of popular sovereignty. Between these two extremes lay a variety of intermediate positions and combinations. In short, Flanders possessed a political culture that was more complex and in certain respects much more sophisticated than that found elsewhere north of Italy, and this complexity formed the background or prehistory of the Flemish peasant revolt of the 1320s as it did for a whole series of popular urban revolts before, during, and after this time. Nevertheless, even though the popular political culture of Flanders had developed over an extended period of time, it was a specific series of events since the beginning of the fourteenth century that set the stage for the expression of that culture in the open, defiant manner that it assumed during the 1320s.

The Tangled Web of Elite Politics

Although the complex political culture of Flanders provided the background or prehistory for peasant revolt in the 1320s, Count Louis himself, by virtue of his inexperience, temperament, and political orientation, was an important additive to the political cauldron of Flanders. Certainly he was not himself solely responsible for its outbreak, but his presence directly affected the timing and helped to shape the character of the revolt. Nothing in his previous experience had prepared him for the task that lay ahead of him. He had been raised in a world totally isolated from any form of popular politics. As a result, he was ineffective as the ruler of Flanders. Politically speaking, things seemed to happen to him, a point clearly illustrated when we examine the circumstances of his coming to power and review the events of his first year as count of Flanders.

Louis' accession itself had a powerfully destabilizing effect on elite politics within Flanders. During the quarter of a century leading up to that day, as we saw in the previous chapter, the counts themselves had led resistance to French royal designs on Flanders that included several episodes of full-blown warfare and numerous armed skirmishes. The new count, however, declared himself a loyal vassal of the king of France and announced his readiness to honor all French claims against Flanders, moves that threatened to alter political fortunes and alignments drastically. Presumably, fear of increasing French intrusion into Flemish affairs inspired the discussions between officials of the rural district of Bruges and the cities of Bruges and Ghent at the end of September 1322 concerning how best to maintain the principality's liberties or privileges.[2]

That Count Louis should be pro-French is not surprising. He had spent most of his childhood and youth either in the county of Nevers, approximately 200 kilometers (125 miles) south of Paris in central France, or at the royal court in Paris.[3] He was in virtually every respect a product of the social environment of the French royal court, a world in which princes such as himself were the dominant political actors. His close ties to the French court were further reinforced in July 1320 when he married Margaret, a daughter of King Philip V of France (and niece of King Philip's successor, Charles IV, 1322–1328), in what can only be described as an alliance of dynastic convenience: he was sixteen years old at the time, while she was only ten.[4] In addition, Louis had depended on royal assistance to ward off the claims of close relatives to the throne of Flanders. Indeed, only an enforceable claim to the countship, stipulated in a succession agreement of June 1320, earned him the right to marry the king's daughter seven weeks later.

Louis' grandfather and predecessor, Count Robert, with the active involvement of the French royal administration, had drawn up a succession agreement designed to secure once and for all the independence he so desired for Flanders, or at least the independence of the countship. According to that agreement, grandson Louis would become count of a Flanders closely allied to France, sealed by his marriage into the royal family. Toward the end of his reign, Count Robert had found himself increasingly isolated within Flanders and constantly quarreling with various coalitions of his own subjects. A close relationship to the royal court seemed the only way to protect the prerogatives of the count. But by making young Louis the designated heir, he had sacrificed the claims of other members of the comital house in the process. Louis' chief rival was his uncle Robert who, after being compensated with a large *apanage* or lordship in southwestern Flanders centered on the town and district of Cassel, was henceforth known as Robert of Cassel.

When Louis of Nevers suddenly became count of Flanders in September 1322, then, he was young and largely unacquainted with the kinds of demands that being a ruler placed on an individual. Besides, he was a total stranger to Flanders, a principality that challenged even the most experienced of rulers. He did not seem to be aware of the efforts of his grandfather and immediate predecessor, Robert of Béthune, or the efforts of his own father, Louis I of Nevers, who had risked both possessions and reputation in opposing French designs on Flanders.[5] In short, the difficulties that Louis had inherited were aggravated before long by his own inexperience and lack of sophistication.

Count Louis' troubles did not begin immediately, however. Despite a last-minute effort by his uncle, Robert of Cassel, to oppose Louis' succession by seizing some castles in Flanders and by asking the Parlement of Paris to overturn the succession agreement of 1320, most Flemings seemed willing to accept the new count. The almost constant threat of warfare with France had taken a heavy toll over the preceding quarter of a century, and many welcomed the prospect of external peace under any conditions. Others, remembering how a series of bitter disputes over fiscal and trade policy had seriously disrupted internal Flemish affairs during the last years of Count Robert's reign, hoped that Louis, who had played no part in these disputes, might be able to inaugurate a period of domestic peace and tranquility.

In fact, some of Louis' initial actions as count only encouraged those hoping for a period of calm and order. First of all, he agreed to long-standing demands by magistrates of the cities of Bruges and Ypres for greater economic control over their hinterlands, the source of a number of rancorous quarrels between the former count and especially Bruges in recent years. As early as October 1322, both cities acquired a monopoly over the production of textiles within their respective rural districts.[6] In foreign affairs as well he showed some signs of accommodation to the wishes of many within Flanders. In particular he backed away from a prolonged quarrel with the Avesnes dynasty, rulers of the county of Hainaut to the southeast and the counties of Zeeland and Holland to the north of Flanders. He refused to pursue the old Flemish claim to Zeeland and in fact made overtures that resulted in peace with Hainaut-Holland-Zeeland the following year, thus changing political alignments in northwestern Europe significantly. Because of such widely-approved actions, Louis' first few months in office passed without major incident.

Not everyone was satisfied with Louis, however. Perhaps viewing the peace overtures to Hainaut, Holland, and Zeeland as a sign of too much independence, King Charles IV summoned the young count to Paris around the end of 1322 for a quick lesson in docility. A brief imprisonment inside the Louvre followed by a period of restricted movement around the city and its suburbs was sufficient to bring the lesson home. On 19 January 1323, the Parlement of Paris reconfirmed the succession arrangement of 1320 that gave Louis the countship of Flanders, thereby denying the challenge to his rule by his uncle, Robert of Cassel. In return, Louis had no choice but to reaffirm his homage to the king by endorsing all French claims against Flanders and promising their immediate implementation.[7] From then onward, however, he appeared in the eyes of many Flemings to be nothing but a pawn of the French king, despite the fact that a peace agreement with the rulers of Hainaut, Holland, and Zeeland was concluded in early 1323.[8]

Count Louis returned to Flanders during March 1323 with the intention of recruiting representatives from the Flemish cities who might accompany him to Paris so that they might show homage to the king as well. But the magistrates of the cities were beginning to have some second thoughts about the intentions of their new count and stated their unwillingness to accompany him. Louis, therefore, returned to Paris by himself, and shortly thereafter purged the *raad* or council that aided him in the governance of Flanders of all anti-French partisans.

The political situation in Flanders began to change considerably over the next several months. At a special meeting at Ypres at the beginning of July 1323, the representatives of 27 large and small cities bluntly complained to some of the count's advisers about a number of important issues. One area of concern was the maintenance of good commercial relations between Flanders and England at a time of increasing English-French tensions. Urban magistrates wanted guarantees that trade with England would not be sacrificed to political expediency. Another major issue was the plan to resume collection of the annual assessment of 10,000 lbs. apportioned over the cities and districts according to the "Transport of Flanders," a payment long opposed by the ordinary people of Flanders and rarely collected since first instituted.[9]

During the first half of 1323, Louis also came increasingly under the influence of his great uncle John, who, besides being the patriarch of the family and the lord of some strategic Flemish towns, was count of Namur and consistently pro-French.[10] John of Namur had been an early supporter of Louis' claim to the Flemish throne, but Louis soon realized that support from his great uncle could prove to be as problematic as it was helpful. John of Namur always had an agenda of his own and had made a host of enemies over the years. Before long, Louis' close association with John of Namur introduced the young prince to that morass of Flemish politics in which he became stuck on more than one occasion over the next two decades.

The first clear indication of trouble for Louis appeared in the form of the Sluis affair. On 13 July 1323, Louis awarded jurisdiction over the Zwin waterway that linked Bruges to the North Sea to his great uncle, John of Namur.[11] While he may have seen this simply as a reward for John's valuable support during the succession challenges, it is more likely that he was responding to various political pressures, not only from John of Namur but also from the king of France. Whoever controlled the Zwin controlled access to the port of Bruges, and Bruges had in the past offended both John of Namur and the king of France by its independent policies. Since John had been trying for some time to make the town of Sluis into a major commercial center, the magistrates of Bruges viewed Louis' act as a direct threat to their city's future. Though they protested, the decision stood.

John of Namur quickly rushed a substantial armed force to Sluis to enforce his new jurisdiction, but such hostile actions only heightened tensions.[12] On 31 July, therefore, the magistrates of Bruges began making preparations for armed action against him and the town of Sluis. Louis, hearing of the preparations for conflict, rushed to the scene from Courtrai in an attempt to calm the situation, but all he could do was watch as the Bruges militia marched on Sluis. The battle, on 1 August, was bloody and decisive. Sluis was plundered and burned while John of Namur was taken prisoner and locked up in the city of Bruges; in fact, he escaped death only because of Louis' personal intervention on his behalf.[13]

The Bruges militia had quickly and decisively removed any immediate threat of a blockade of the Zwin by John of Namur and the city of Sluis, but it was a terribly humiliating experience for Count Louis. By comparison to the actions of his subjects, his own reaction to the Sluis affair appeared extremely ineffective. He could do nothing about this flagrant defiance of his authority. His appeals for the release of his great uncle were unavailing, and he appeared even more inept by having to beg his subjects in the first place. Negotiations at Saint-Omer mediated by the countess of Artois, meanwhile, brought no results. Only John of Namur's escape in late September pushed this particular problem into the background, but Louis could derive little comfort from this turn of events. Young, inexperienced, and naive, he was beginning to realize what his predecessors had learned long before, that Flemish cities were prepared to take armed action on their own behalf if peaceful entreaties were ineffective. He found it safer and much more congenial, therefore, to retreat for a time to the friendlier confines of Nevers. Such a response, however, did nothing to restore his authority in Flanders, and it may well have offered encouragement to further challenges to his authority.[14]

The Sluis affair was a very public crisis for Count Louis, but he survived it and became perhaps a bit wiser in the bargain. What had been going on meanwhile behind the scenes proved to be a much more serious problem. The effects of Louis' pro-French orientation and his promises to honor obligations to France began to change the political situation in a much more profound way than the Sluis affair ever did. And if Louis had not anticipated the reaction of the city of Bruges to his granting of jurisdiction over the Zwin to John of Namur in the summer of 1323, he was even less prepared for the crisis that appeared a few months later.

Elite/Popular Coalitions

While many ordinary Flemings had been willing to give the new count a chance to prove himself, there were also those who viewed the accession of Louis from the very beginning with considerable apprehension, perhaps even dread. As we saw in the previous chapter, Flemish politics for decades had been framed by the external opposition between France and Flanders, as *leliaart* (pro-French) and *klauwaart* (anti-French) parties[15] developed in both city and countryside and competed for advantage. Ghent, Bruges, and Ypres all saw considerable unrest in the past because of the strong rivalry between these two groups. During the reign of Robert of Béthune, *klauwaarts* had benefited the most while many *leliaarts* fled or had been banished from the county. With the accession of Louis to the Flemish throne, *leliaart* partisans were made to feel welcome by the new prince, including many exiles who now returned to take up their previous roles often with revenge in mind, while the *klauwaarts* began to ponder their political futures.

It was the vast majority of Flemings, the ordinary people of both countryside and city, who had the most to lose from Louis' promises to honor all treaties with France. First of all, *leliaart* nobles and patricians, returning with the approval of the central government, inaugurated a wave of revenge aimed at the ordinary people of city and countryside who had helped to drive them into exile.[16] By Christmas 1322, returning *leliaarts* in the district of Veurne apparently had regained some of their former posts as *curatores* or magistrates, and from then onward began using these positions to reward their friends and punish their enemies. Peasants loudly objected to and challenged such actions.[17] Both in Veurne district and elsewhere, the return of the *leliaarts* opened many old wounds.[18]

In addition, these same former exiles now began to use their influence on the colleges of magistrates to force the rural districts into full compliance with the central government's order to resume tax collections for the payments associated with the various French treaties. In particular, the 1305 treaty of Athis-sur-Orge was supposed to provide the king with an annual indemnity to compensate him for his loss of direct control over Flanders because of the Flemish war of independence between 1302 and 1305. As we saw in the previous chapter, from the very beginning there was considerable popular resistance against taxes aimed at raising these sums because ordinary people of both city and countryside believed they had won that war. The fact that modifying treaties since then had turned over part of the payments to the count of Flanders made them no more palatable.

Those who bore the primary burden of taxation, the ordinary people of the cities and the countryside, could expect to pay much higher taxes as the sums owed by virtue of the French treaties were levied once again. To make matters even worse, however, Count Louis, and presumably Robert of Cassel within his apanage, apparently decided to collect not only the normal amounts due in the current year but also all arrears.[19] Whatever the case, there were widespread and bitter complaints among the rural population of Flanders by late 1323 that magistrates and tax collectors were raising more taxes in the districts than they had been authorized to take in. The author of the *Chronicon* saw this as related to Count Louis' need for increased income, since he appeared to be living beyond his means. When no one in authority seemed prepared to look into their complaints, however, peasants took action themselves to stop the offending collections.[20]

The Beginnings of Peasant Revolt

The very first signs of public protest in the Flemish countryside appeared in the form of widely scattered riots and demonstrations during late October and November 1323,[21] while Count Louis was visiting his ancestral land of Nevers in central France. Though representatives from the three great cities of Flanders had asked Louis to delay his departure, perhaps fearing that trouble was at hand, he was not dissuaded and set off on 15 October after placing the government of the county in the hands of a regent, the lord of Aspremont. The early disorders apparently caught the regent, a nobleman from Nevers and a total stranger to Flanders, by complete surprise, for the initial response of the central government was to do absolutely nothing.[22]

Some of the earliest militant peasant activity seems to have occurred in both the northern and western sections of the district of Bruges, but in the absence of a meaningful response from the central government the cities of Ghent and Bruges sent out their militias and apparently were able to contain the disorders, at least temporarily.[23] In southwestern Flanders, in contrast, public demonstrations escalated and coalesced into a general movement. In defiance of the bailiffs, the count's chief administrative officers in the rural districts,[24] peasants began organizing a systematic obstruction of any further collection of taxes. Specifically, they seized and detained the members of the colleges of magistrates and judicial and administrative councils in the districts responsible for authorizing the tax collections, along with their supporters, the great proprietors or lords.[25] The image we should have in mind here is that of large numbers of people assembling, chanting, milling about, and shouting threats in front of or around one or more of the intended victims. This essentially is the scene that was presented to Ghis du Boos, a magistrate in the district of Bergues and the owner of substantial property just outside the town of Dunkirk. In testimony he gave some years later, he described how the ordinary people of the district of Bergues and their captain came to his house on 6 December 1323 and forced him and his companions to spend the next 21 weeks in the prison of the town of Bergues, all the while fearing for their lives.[26] Though the details of the release of du Boos and his companions around 1 May 1324 remain obscure, we know that many others who were detained fled the districts immediately upon their release, as did most of those who had avoided detainment. Finally, peasant rebels attacked the property of fleeing or detained officials and lords, in particular destroying the houses of noble families from which magistrates had been recruited.[27]

By the end of 1323, governmental authority had collapsed completely in the districts of Veurne, Bergues, and Bourbourg, and, despite the efforts of the militias from the cities of Bruges and Ghent, in Bruges district as well, while tensions remained very high elsewhere in the county. In the face of such sharply focused rebellion, the response of the lord of Aspremont was ineffective. He called on the three great cities of Ghent, Bruges, and Ypres for assistance,[28] but it soon became apparent that the defiance was so widespread that only a massive show of strength would be effective, and such a response would take much too long to organize. The situation was made even more serious by the circulation of a rumor that Count Louis had no intention of ever returning to Flanders, that he was negotiating with the king of France to trade the county for a more pleasing principality to the south, presumably the county of Poitou.[29] Initial discussions produced no results, since the rebels showed little willingness to listen to the appeals of a regent whose term of office might soon expire. The lord of Aspremont could only plead with the count to return.

Count Louis seemed at first reluctant to return to Flanders. Because the rebellion continued with no end in sight, however, he decided in early 1324 to observe the situation for himself. He stated his intention to return in a letter of 7 January to the lord of Aspremont, while categorically denying the rumor that he wished to trade Flanders for Poitou. At the same time he expressed his impatience with his headstrong subjects by suggesting that he would be justified in trading the county away if such in fact were his desire.[30]

Having returned to Flanders by 2 February 1324, Count Louis showed little intention of launching a punitive expedition against the rebellious peasants. In fact, he probably could not have done so even if he had wanted to, because the rebels were well organized and firmly in control of the coastal districts. Besides, as became apparent in the months to come, the rebellion had struck a sympathetic chord among many non-peasants who thought that the count himself was at least partially responsible for the rebellion by not sufficiently supervising the actions of his officials in the districts and by underestimating the potential seriousness of the crisis.[31] Under such circumstances, Louis, after authorizing the execution of a number of rebels for treason,[32] quickly temporized by promising to consider the validity of peasant complaints against his officials in the rebel districts. This strategy worked for the moment. Under the protection of a general truce that would last until 1 October 1324, the rebels agreed to suspend all direct action while a permanent settlement was worked out.[33]

Airing Peasant Grievances

The means used to arrive at a permanent settlement varied considerably from place to place, leaving an uneven documentary record. Despite such unevenness, however, the sources revealing the settlement processes also provide the first real glimpses of peasant grievances. While the disorders of late 1323 and early 1324 appeared initially to have been attempts aimed primarily at preventing tax collections, the inquiries and arbitrations of early 1324 clearly show that the rebels were much more concerned with how the tax burden was apportioned and how the monies collected as taxes were disbursed than they were with the issue of tax collection itself. They complained most vigorously about the arrogance, arbitrariness, corruption, and favoritism of rural officials and their supporters, the lords or great proprietors.[34]

In the district of Bruges, Count Louis himself set out to resolve the crisis with the aid of his trusted councilor and keeper of the seal, Artaud Flote, abbot of the monastery of Vézelay in Burgundy.[35] Presumably there was some sort of formal inquiry involved, but the documents that have survived do not reveal it very clearly. Louis seems to have dealt with the rural revolt at the same time that he addressed the problems he had encountered with the city of Bruges during the previous year, specifically the Sluis affair examined above.[36] Contemporaries referred to an agreement between the count and the city and district of Bruges known as the Peace of Sint-Andries, apparently drawn up on 8 April 1324 at Sint-Andries just outside Bruges.[37] All that survives, however, is a series of related acts that reveal only certain aspects of that agreement.

Despite a lack of documentation concerning the arbitration process for the district of Bruges, the acts that resulted from the process give some idea not only of the kinds of grievances that peasants had articulated but also of the kinds of actions they had taken in support of their grievances. Apparently because the rebels were particularly angry with the arbitrary behavior of rural officials, Louis issued new procedures on 10 April 1324 that were designed to provide better judicial and financial management for Bruges district. Among other things, he placed limits on the authority of the district's magistrates to raise fees and collect expenses, thereby lending credence to the complaint that they had been enriching themselves at public expense.[38] In another act of the same day, Louis granted an amnesty to the inhabitants of the district of Bruges for all the actions they had taken during the rebellion. Though many had been accused of terrible wrongdoings, all would be forgiven. Specifically, rebels were said to have attacked and destroyed houses, seized and destroyed movable goods and possessions, and injured individuals, some of whom died as a result. Nobles and others of privilege in the countryside appear to have been the primary victims of such peasant violence.[39]

A series of additional acts from 12 April 1324 formed an integral part of the settlement for Bruges district. For example, one of these addressed the behavior of rural officials. Because some had been accused of corruption, Count Louis ordered his bailiffs and other judicial officers in Flanders to begin investigating those individuals who in one way or another had received payments of public funds from the district. If any could not produce appropriate authorization for pocketing the sums in question, they should be forced to make restitution.[40] He also granted permission to the ordinary people of the district to institute legal proceedings against officials who had misbehaved or acted with contempt during the recent disorders.[41] And, as a warning against future corruption, he ordered that all functionaries convicted of betraying their oaths of office and violating the law of the district be punished in an exemplary fashion.[42]

A somewhat different picture emerges from the steps taken in the district of Veurne. Here Count Louis' uncle, Robert of Cassel, presided over the process because he governed southwestern Flanders as a vassal to the count.[43] Robert carried out an investigation in his apanage by presiding over a commission of arbitration, consisting of two representatives from the city of Ghent and three each from the cities of Bruges and Ypres.[44] On 20 March 1324 the rebels in the district of Veurne agreed to abide by any decision that the arbitration commission might reach.[45] As part of the process, the commission asked for advice from the aldermen of the city of Ypres. The latter charged that a major share of the blame for the disturbances lay with Count Louis and his top officials because of their failure to take seriously earlier complaints concerning official corruption by the residents of the district. The aldermen of Ypres specifically referred to a series of unauthorized loans, gifts, and payments from public funds by the magistrates of Veurne district, to the unlawful return of a number of individuals banished by the former count for their *leliaart* or pro-French sympathies, and to the capriciousness of local tax assessors who used their authority to punish their enemies and reward their friends. Because of the broad range of official corruption and the validity of peasant complaints, they advised the commission to punish the corrupt officials of Veurne district and their supporters and to forgive the rebellious actions of the rural population.[46]

The findings of the arbitration commission were announced on 28 April at St. Nicholas Abbey at Veurne. If peasants would now put their rebellion behind them, the commission declared, they would receive a general amnesty as well as a redress of most of their grievances concerning the assessment and collection of taxes and the choice of individuals for public office. Among other things, peasants, the taxpaying public in the district, would be excused from having to pay the monies assessed by officials to cover the costs of managing the district. In the future, officials would pay such expenses out of their own pockets to be reimbursed at the next assessments, but then only for expenses incurred while actually traveling on official business. The only regular income authorized for officials was their share of the fines collected in the courts of justice. Nor would taxpayers, that is, the peasant population, be required to pay for several sums not authorized at official assessments, such as the payments by former magistrates to various unnamed individuals for unspecified purposes or the sums turned over to 18 named individuals as either loans or gifts. In fact, such expenditures henceforth would be charged to the officials themselves. Further, the accounts of the financial administration would be examined from then onward by two representatives from each parish and one from the count before new assessments could be decided upon. Finally, virtually all former officials who had been banished by Count Louis' predecessor would remain exiles, while a number of currently active magistrates would be removed permanently from their positions because of their corrupt activities.[47] In short, the arbitration commission for the district of Veurne found that virtually all rebel complaints about official arrogance, arbitrariness, corruption, and favoritism had been justified.

The arbitration commission that addressed peasant complaints in the district of Veurne apparently held additional hearings and issued verdicts in the remaining districts of southwestern Flanders as well. For example, according to a plaintiff appearing before a commission convened some years later, Robert of Cassel and representatives from the cities of Bruges, Ghent, and Ypres held an investigation in the district of Bergues around 1 May 1324. Unfortunately, neither the details of such proceedings nor their verdicts have survived.[48]

By the beginning of May, 1324, the first phase of the revolt had come to a conclusion and, officially at least, domestic peace was supposed to return to the county of Flanders. Not only the commission of arbitration under Robert of Cassel but even the count himself had recognized the basic justice of peasant complaints concerning the behavior of county officials. Direct peasant action had extracted promises of punishment for past official wrongdoing and of better oversight to prevent the same in the future. Many now believed that the crisis had been resolved, though, as we shall see in the next chapter, they were seriously mistaken. Count Louis felt confident enough to return to Nevers around the beginning of July, entrusting the governance of Flanders once again to one of his councilors. This time he chose the lord of Axel, who had the advantage over the former regent of being himself a Fleming and presumably somewhat more attuned to the mood of the county's inhabitants.[49]

Patterns of Peasant Mobilization

Though the surviving documentation does not provide as much detail as we would like, it does contain the clues necessary to reconstruct in broad outline how Flemish peasants mobilized in late 1323 and early 1324. The author of the *Chronicon* said simply that rebels made or chose captains in each rural district,[50] without explaining how the selections were actually made. The arbitration verdict of 28 April 1324 for the district of Veurne was slightly more expansive. Specifically, it ordered peasants to dissolve their alliances, oaths, and promises, to quit ringing bells to convene gatherings of the people, and to remove all popular captains.[51] It seems clear, in fact, that peasants on their own initiative called local meetings or popular assemblies to which all were summoned by the ringing of church bells. Such meetings constituted the forum within which they then chose their own captains or leaders.

Calling meetings was not by itself a subversive activity. Such assemblies were a regular part of rural life, routinely convened without the participation of rural elites. We should remember that one of the primary tasks of such gatherings was to reiterate and reaffirm the customary rules and regulations that provided the basis for orderly life within individual communities. But custom, by defining membership in the rural community and by enumerating the rights and obligations that came with it, also provided the foundation for a sense of peasant justice, while a violation of custom by outside officials or others of privilege might set the stage for communal resistance to domination.[52] The meetings convened by Flemish rural communities to organize a rebellion in late 1323 fit completely within this tradition.

As we saw earlier, the territory of the ecclesiastical parish corresponded most closely to the local rural community in Flanders, and it was at this same scale that the groundwork for peasant rebellion was laid. For example, when the arbitration commission of 1324 asked peasants to discontinue the ringing of bells to summon people to meetings, it was referring to the use of parish-church bells; it also offered the right to inspect the official's accounts to representatives of the parishes. Some later evidence suggests that the parish churches themselves may have served on occasion as meeting places,[53] while the lists of those who participated in the Battle of Cassel, drawn up for the purpose of confiscating their property, grouped the rebels according to the parishes in which they lived.[54] This is not to suggest that the rebellion was religiously inspired or that priests played a role in it. In fact, it remained throughout a decidedly non-religious movement with goals that were always mundane and, perhaps most frightening to their opponents, seemingly attainable. The population of the parish, not its clergy, was recognized by officials as the group that had made the revolt. The community of those who lived and worked together and sprang to each other's aid in times of trouble also swore the rebel oaths of solidarity, while the clergy sat on the sidelines or joined the opposition.[55]

It was normal practice for rural communities to select proxies or special agents to represent the entire community in other settings—to larger political jurisdictions, such as the rural districts, or to neighboring rural communities or nearby towns. The two representatives chosen from each parish, called for in the arbitration verdict of 28 April 1324 to journey to the city of Veurne and there to examine the accounts of the parish, essentially were proxies.[56] In most cases, those chosen to make decisions for a particular community or to represent the community in another political jurisdiction came from the most prominent peasant families of that community, those who already had influence because of their wealth. Choosing captains to plan and lead the rebellion in 1323 should be seen as an extension of the practice of choosing proxies. And those that can be identified for later phases of the rebellion in Flanders were clearly wealthier than the average for the communities they represented.[57]

If the convening of popular assemblies for the purposes of choosing captains and swearing oaths of solidarity laid the groundwork for rebellion in 1323, these actions by themselves do not account for the high degree of cohesiveness and coordination that peasant rebels achieved from the very beginning. The problem is illustrated by examining some details of what happened in the district of Veurne. During the 1320s, Veurne district comprised an area of roughly 15 by 40 kilometers (10 by 25 miles), containing about 40 individual villages or parishes,[58] and these rural communities together may have accounted for as many as 25,000 inhabitants.[59] Yet the arbitration proceedings for Veurne district from the spring of 1324 clearly show that the commissioners were dealing with a single, unified rebellion, not forty separate ones. For example, on 20 March 1324 a group of peasant leaders described as the "companions of the rebellion and the commons of the territory of Veurne" journeyed outside the bounds of Veurne district to the city of Ypres, where it promised compliance with any eventual verdict of the arbitration commission. This "commons" of Veurne district was accompanied on this expedition by its allies, "those from the cities of Veurne, Nieuwpoort, and Lombardsijde [across the IJzer River from Nieuwpoort], as sworn-ones with those of the said territory."[60] Apparently the forty rural communities of Veurne district had forged a single, corporate entity to which others could ally themselves. In a similar fashion, aldermen of the city of Veurne, in their advice to the commissioners on the same day, also spoke of a single commons or community of Veurne territory,[61] while the verdict itself, of 28 April 1324, referred on several occasions to a single community of Veurne district.[62]

Though our sources do not explain exactly how a single commons or community was developed in the district of Veurne in 1323, we can be certain that it was not done in a single mass assembly but in some venue of more moderate size. Seeing how it was done at another time and in another place is very instructive. For example, in the duchy of Normandy, in or around the year 996, peasants launched a sizable and highly coordinated rebellion by first meeting in local *conventicula* or assemblies throughout the duchy. Each *conventicula* in turn sent two representatives or proxies to a *conventus* or central assembly which coordinated the movement.[63] Since we already know that rural communities could and often did choose sworn delegates or proxies to represent them in other settings, we will not go far wrong in assuming that the forty separate rural communities of Veurne district did much the same as their Norman counterparts did more than three centuries earlier: sent proxies or delegates to a district-wide assembly which then formed a single sworn-association or commons in 1323. Evidence for such a two-tiered organization in fact appears in testimony given before a later commission that referred to a two-tiered leadership structure—in the neighboring district of Bergues, at least in 1327, there were some captains who represented individual communities and other captains who represented the entire district.[64]

In short, peasants in the rebel districts developed an organization closely patterned after the count's administration. The bailiffs were replaced in each district by one or more general captains, while the flight or neutralization of the notables, such as Ghis du Boos in Bergues district, who had dominated the colleges of magistrates, provided new opportunities to those traditionally excluded from positions of authority. Though the details remain obscure, it may well have been groups of proxies from individual rural communities that provided the new candidates to the colleges of magistrates. At the local level, the count's *ammans* or sheriffs were replaced by the local captains, while the assemblies of rural communities simply would chose new candidates for the local governing council of aldermen.[65]

The ability of Flemish peasants effectively to adapt commonplace institutions and conventions such as assemblies and sworn associations to new and subversive ends helps to explain their rapid and complete mobilization in 1323, catching most public authorities by complete surprise. No single element was totally new. Even the announcement of meetings by ringing church bells, especially at unusual times of the day or in an unusual fashion, was an adaptation of the traditional manner of sounding an alarm, of getting people's attention.[66] Not surprisingly, what worked so effectively in 1323 and 1324 became characteristic of the remaining years of the revolt.

Notes

1. See Count Louis' letter of 7 January 1323 to the lord of Aspremont, published in Henri Pirenne, ed., *Le soulèvement de la Flandre maritime, 1323–328, documents inédites*, Commission Royale d'Histoire, Académie Royale de Belgique, Publications in-octavo (Brussels: Hayez, 1900), pp. 163–65.

2. L. Gilliodts-van Severen, *Inventaire des archives de la ville de Bruges, section première, inventaire des chartes*, Publié sous les auspices de l'administration comunale (Bruges: E. Gailliard, 1871), vol. 1, pp. 335–36, no. 28; A. Schouteet, *Regesten op de oorkonden van het stadsarchief van Brugge (1089–1500)*, vol. 2, *1301–1339*, Brugse geschiedbronnen uitgegeven door het Genootschap voor Geschiedenis "Société d'Émulation" te Brugge met steun van het Gemeentebestuur van Brugge, V (Bruges: Stadsarchief van Brugge, 1978), p. 143, no. 385. Both refer to a document, dated 30 September 1322, authorizing representatives from the district of Bruges to confer with representatives of the cities of Bruges and Ghent on this question.

3. Louis spent part of his youth at the royal court in Paris as a hostage or surety, presumably to guarantee Flemish adherence to Flemish-French agreements; see David Nicholas, *Medieval Flanders* (London and New York: Longmans, 1992), pp. 209–10; I. H. Gosses, *Handboek tot de staatkundige geschiedenis der Nederlanden*: vol. 1, *De middeleeuwen*, Post, R. R., ed. (The Hague: Martinus Nijhoff, 1959), p. 156.

4. For the early life of Louis of Nevers, before he became count of Flanders, see M. Vandermaesen, "Lodewijk II van Nevers," in *Nationaal biografisch woordenboek*, vol. 5, Koninklijke Académiën van België (Brussels: Paleis der Académiën, 1972), cols. 523–24. The French royal family apparently kept Margaret in protective custody until she was released to Louis' wardship in 1327; see ibid., p. 528.

5. Ellen E. Kittell, *From Ad Hoc to Routine: A Case Study in Medieval Bureaucracy*, Middle Ages Series (Philadelphia: University of Pennsylvania Press, 1991), pp. 138–39, 161.

6. David Nicholas, *Town and Countryside: Social, Economic, and Political Tensions in Fourteenth-Century Flanders*, Rijksuniversiteit te Gent, Werken uitgegeven door de faculteit van de letteren en wijsbegeerte, 152 (Bruges: De Tempel, 1971), pp. 98, 105; idem, *Medieval Flanders*, pp. 280–81; Jacques Sabbe, *Vlaanderen in opstand, 1323–1328: Nikolaas Zannekin, Zeger Janszone en Willem de Deken*, Genootschap voor Geschiedenis "Société d'Émulation" te Brugge, Vlaamse Historische Studies, VII (Bruges: Marc Van de Wiele, 1992), p. 16. Louis' grant to Bruges, dated 27 October 1322, is published in Gilliodts-van Severen, *Inventaire des archives de la ville de Bruges*, vol. 1, pp. 337–39, no. 287.

7. Sabbe, *Vlaanderen in opstand*, p. 16; Nicholas, *Medieval Flanders*, pp. 209–10.

8. Published in Frans van Mieris, ed., *Groot charterboek der graaven van Holland, van Zeeland en heeren van Friesland* (Leiden: Pieter van der Eyk, 1754), vol. 2, p. 52. See also Gilliodts-van Severen, *Inventaire des archives de la ville de Bruges*, vol. 1, pp. 340–41, no. 290; Schouteet, *Regesten op de oorkonden van het stadsarchief van Brugge*, vol. 2, p. 146, no. 392, 396.

9. M. Vandermaesen, "Vlaanderen en Henegouwen onder het huis van

Dampierre 1244–1384," in *Algemene geschiedenis der Nederlanden*, vol. 2 (Haarlem: Fibula-van Dishoeck, 1982), p. 420; Sabbe, *Vlaanderen in opstand*, p. 18.

10. Actually, John of Namur started out as an anti-French partisan in the war of independence of 1302 to 1305. After he made peace with the king and married into the royal family, however, he became a devoted defender of French interests in Flanders; see Sabbe, *Vlaanderen in opstand*, p. 20.

11. Jean Bovesse, "Notes sur l'Écluse et la maison comtale namuroise à la fin du XIIIe et au début du XIVe siècle," in G. Despy, ed., *Hommage au professeur Paul Bonnenfant (1899–1965): études d'histoire médiévale dédiées à sa mémoire par les anciens élèves de son séminaire à l'Université Libre de Bruxelles* (Brussels: Universa, 1965), pp. 242–45, and p. 253 for the document itself. See also Sabbe, *Vlaanderen in opstand*, p. 20; Nicholas, *Medieval Flanders*, p. 213.

12. See Sabbe, *Vlaanderen in opstand*, p. 20; H. van Werveke, "Vlaanderen en Brabant, 1305–1346: de sociaal-economische achtergrond," in *De late middeleeuwen, 1305–1477*, vol. 3 of *Algemene geschiedenis der Nederlanden* (Utrecht and Antwerp: De Haan and Standaard Boekhandel, 1951), 28.

13. Anonymous, *Chronicon comitum Flandrensium*, in *Corpus chronicorum Flandriae, sub auspiciis Leopoldi primi, serenissimi Belgarum regis: recueil des chroniques de Flandre*, vol. 1, J. J. DeSmet, ed., Académie Royale de Belgique, Commission Royale d'Histoire, Mémoires en quarto (Brussels: H. Hayez, 1837) (hereafter cited as *Chronicon*), p. 185. See also Bovesse, "Notes sur l'Écluse et la maison comtale namuroise," pp. 244–45; Sabbe, *Vlaanderen in opstand*, p. 20.

14. Van Werveke, "Vlaanderen en Brabant," p. 28. As James C. Scott suggests, in *Domination and the Arts of Resistance: Hidden Transcripts* (New Haven, CT: Yale University Press, 1990), p. 196, acts of insubordination that go unpunished are "likely to encourage others to venture further."

15. For an explanation of the terms *leliaart* and *klauwaart*, see the previous chapter.

16. Pirenne, ed., *Le soulèvement*, p. xv; F. W. N. Hugenholtz, *Drie boerenopstanden uit de veertiende eeuw: Vlaanderen 1323–328, Frankrijk 1358, Engeland 1381; onderzoek naar het opstandig bewustzijn* (Haarlem: Tjeenk Willink, 1949), p. 22.

17. See the documents associated with an arbitration commission of March and April 1324, published in Pirenne, ed., *Le soulèvement*: appendix 2, p. 166, "toutes demandes, calainges, entreprisures et mesprisures, que lidit compaignon et commun . . . ont demandé ou poent demander sur les coriers, sur les pointeurs et sur tous autres dudit terroir, qui ont esté puis le Noël l'an de grâce M. CCC. et XXII jusques aujourdewy;" appendix 4, p. 172, "van al den debaten ende van allen den claghen, dat die meentucht . . . hem beclaghen of doleren mochten van eneghen mescripe jof van enegher mesdaet, dat die wethouders van Vorneambachte, die cueriers ende lanthouders waren van der tijt van daghe van Kersdaghe, doe men screef M.CCC. ende XXII, tote in 't jaer dat men screef M. CCC. ende XXIII."

18. Vandermaesen, "Vlaanderen en Henegouwen onder het huis van Dampierre," p. 421.

19. Vandermaesen, "Vlaanderen en Henegouwen onder het huis van Dampierre," p. 421. Kittell, *From Ad Hoc to Routine*, p. 151, makes clear not only that Count Louis' receivers were more "proficient in extracting payments of the Trans-

port of Flanders" than were their predecessors during Count Robert's reign, but also that agents of the French king operated freely within Flanders collecting taxes for the king's indemnities.

20. *Chronicon*, pp. 186–87: "Comes autem Flandriae videns se sumptuosum in expensis, ultra quam reditus sui se possent extendere, procuravit sibi quaedam donaria promissa per villas et castellanias Flandriae . . . exiit murmur permaximus inter populares, quod scabini et curatores castellaniarum majores summas pecuniarum eis imponerent in duplo, quam essent summae promissae comiti gratiose, non de jure. Et cum haec credebantur murmura . . . rebellavit populus contra curatores, scabinos et dominos. . . ."

21. Vandermaesen, "Vlaanderen en Henegouwen onder het huis van Dampierre," p. 421.

22. J. van Rompaey, "De opstand in het Vlaamse kustland van 1323 tot 1328 en de figuur van Nikolaas Zannekin," *Nikolaas Zannekin en de Slag bij Kassel, 1328–1978: bijdrage tot de studie van de 14de eeuw en de landelijke geschiedenis van de Westhoek* (Diksmuide, Belgium: Kulturele Raad van Diksmuide, 1978), p. 107; Sabbe, *Vlaanderen in opstand*, p. 21.

23. Vandermaesen, "Vlaanderen en Henegouwen onder het huis van Dampierre," p. 421.

24. Count Louis referred to defiance of his bailiffs in a letter of 7 January 1324 to the lord of Aspremont, published in Pirenne, ed., *Le soulèvement*, appendix 1, p. 164.

25. *Chronicon*, p. 187: "Et rebellavit populus contra curatores, scabinos et dominos in territoriis Brugburgensi, Brugensi, Furnensi, Bergensi et alibi." The lords referred to by the word "dominos" were both noble and non-noble great proprietors, as we saw in Chapter 1, above.

26. See the report of a damages commission, convened sometime after 1328, published in Pirenne, ed., *Le soulèvement*, appendix 16, pp. 211–12: "vienrent li commun et li hoefman de le castelrie de Berghes . . . et ajournèrent ledt Ghis. es ses compaingnons qui adont furent coriers, de venir en prison à Berghes ens le piere. sour perdre cors et avoir. Là mirent ledit Ghis. et ses compaingnons vint et un semaines en grant péril de leur vie du commun de le castelrie."

27. *Chronicon*, p. 187: "incedebant per turmas contumaces, et captivabant omnes praedictos curatores, scabinos, et dominos et impositores summarum praedictarum, fugientiumque dominorum domos illico destruebant." See also Pirenne, ed., *Le soulèvement*, pp. xvi–xvii; van Rompaey, "De opstand in het Vlaamse kustland," pp. 107–8; Sabbe, *Vlaanderen in opstand*, p. 21.

28. *Chronicon*, p. 187: "Nec potuit hunc sedare tumultum dominus de Aspero Monte cum adjutorio trium Flandriae villarum, licet ad hoc plurimum laboraret."

29. Pirenne, ed., *Le soulèvement*, pp. xvi–xvii; Sabbe, *Vlaanderen in opstand*, p. 25.

30. Published in Pirenne, ed., *Le soulèvement*, appendix 1, pp. 163–65

31. See, for example, the advice of the *schepenen* of Ypres to an arbitration commission on 20 March 1323, published in Pirenne, ed., *Le soulèvement*, appendix 3, pp. 168–70; as well as Hugenholtz, *Drie boerenopstanden*, p. 25. According to Sabbe, *Vlaanderen in opstand*, p. 25, ordinary people from the city of Bruges, aided by allies

from the small cities and the rural communities of Bruges district, conspired to kill a number of rich citizens of the city, officials of the count, and nobles on 21 February 1324.

32. Pirenne, ed., *Le soulèvement*, p. xvii.

33. Sabbe, *Vlaanderen in opstand*, p. 28; Vandermaesen, "Vlaanderen en Henegouwen onder het huis van Dampierre," p. 421.

34. Van Rompaey, "De opstand in het Vlaamse kustland," p. 108.

35. Concerning Flote, see M. Vandermaesen, "Flote, Artaud," *Nationaal biografisch woordenboek*, vol. 8, Koninklijke Academiën van België (Brussels: Paleis der Academiën, 1979), cols. 317–21; Sabbe, *Vlaanderen in opstand*, pp. 16–18.

36. Bovesse, "Notes sur l'Écluse," p. 245; van Rompaey, "De opstand in het Vlaamse kustland," pp. 108–9.

37. See Gilliodts-van Severen, *Inventaire des archives de la ville de Bruges*, vol. 1, p. 350, no. 304, who quotes from an original document of 24 June 1324 referring to the agreement of 8 April. See also van Rompaey, "De opstand in het Vlaamse kustland," p. 110.

38. Published in Gilliodts-van Severen, *Inventaire des archives de la ville de Bruges*, vol. 1, pp. 342–46, no. 294.

39. Van Rompaey, "De opstand in het Vlaamse kustland," pp. 108–09, 130, notes 11–12, reviews the provisions of this anmesty. See also Gilliodts-van Severen, *Inventaire des archives de la ville de Bruges*, vol. 1, pp. 346–47, no. 295; and Schouteet, *Regesten op de oorkonden van het stadsarchief van Brugge*, vol. 2, p. 154, no. 414.

40. Schouteet, *Regesten op de oorkonden van het stadsarchief van Brugge*, vol. 2, p. 154, no. 416; Sabbe, *Vlaanderen in opstand*, p. 27, provides a photograph of the original act.

41. Schouteet, *Regesten op de oorkonden van het stadsarchief van Brugge*, vol. 2, p. 155, no. 417, quoting from the original: "qui ont mespris ou fait tort ou griez envers autrui."

42. Gilliodts-van Severen, *Inventaire des archives de la ville de Bruges*, vol. 1, p. 302, who quotes from the original: "soient condempnez en maniere que touz autres y puissent prendre exemple." See also Schouteet, *Regesten op de oorkonden van het stadsarchief van Brugge*, vol. 2, p. 156, no. 421.

43. Besides the city and district of Cassel, which gave Robert of Cassel his name, this apanage included the rural districts of Veurne, Bergues, Bourbourg, and Bailleul; see M. Vandermaesen, "Cassel, Robrecht, heer van," *Nationaal biografisch woordenboek*, vol. 6, Koninklijke Academiën van België (Brussels: Paleis der Academiën, 1974), cols. 83–86.

44. The accounts of the city of Ypres, published by G. Des Marez and E. de Sagher, eds., *Comptes de la ville d'Ypres de 1297 à 1329*, Académie Royale de Belgique, Commission Royale d'Histoire (Brussels: P. Imbreghts, 1913), vol. II, p. 379, show that the city paid some of the expenses of its three representatives on 17 and 31 March 1324.

45. This agreement is published in Pirenne, ed., *Le soulèvement*, appendix 2, pp. 165–68.

46. The recommendations of the aldermen of Ypres are published in Pirenne, ed., *Le soulèvement*, appendix 3, pp. 168–70.

47. The verdict is published in Pirenne, ed., *Le soulèvement*, appendix 4, pp. 171–78.

48. See the report of a commission on damages, dating from sometime after 1328, in Pirenne, ed., *Le soulèvement*, appendix 16, pp. 211–12. The representatives from the city of Ypres on the arbitration commission for Veurne district also traveled to Bergues—perhaps in conjunction with additional hearings—see Des Marez and de Sagher, eds., *Comptes de la ville d'Ypres*, vol. II, p. 380 (dated 31 March 1324): "A Lambert Morin, Jehan de la Clite et Crestien Hanewas pour 1 voiage fait à Furnes et à Berghes, demourans par 6 jours: 22 lb. 16 s."

49. Sabbe, *Vlaanderen in opstand*, p. 33; Van Rompaey, "De opstand in het Vlaamse kustland," pp. 110–11. The accounts of the city of Ypres for the second half of July, dated 28 July 1324, published by Des Marez and de Sagher, eds, *Comptes de la ville d'Ypres*, vol. II, p. 389, include the following entry: "A 1 garchon, qui aporta lettres de monsingneur de Axele, lieutenant monsingneur de Flandres: 4 s."

50. *Chronicon*, p. 187: "et facientes capitaneos in suis castellaniis."

51. Published in Pirenne, ed., *Le soulèvement*, appendix 4, p. 179: "dat alle aleyanchen, alle ede, alle ghelove ende alle clocken te ludene omme vergaderinghe van den volk to makene ende alle hooftmanne in Vorneambacht of zijn ghedaen ende te niete." Frantisek Graus, *Pest-Geissler-Judenmorde: Das 14. Jahrhundert als Krisenzeit*, Veröffentlichungen des Max-Planck-Instituts für Geschichte, no. 86 (Göttingen: Vandenhoeck und Ruprecht, 1987), pp. 448–54, has classified such activities as characteristic of late medieval rebellions.

52. Reynolds, *Kingdoms and Communities in Western Europe*, pp. 151–52; Michael Mullett, *Popular Culture and Popular Protest in Late Medieval and Early Modern Europe* (London: Croom Helm, 1987), p. 74. For this, and for the remainder of this section, see as well the discussion of rural communities in the previous chapter.

53. From testimony given before a damages commission convened after 1328, but referring in this case to 1326 or 1327, published in Pirenne, ed., *Le soulèvement*, appendix 16, p. 217: "Item, Pierin Boid ende H. Boid zeiden voren 't commun in de carke van Honscote. . . ."

54. Pirenne, ed., *Le soulèvement*, pp. 1–162.

55. W. P. Blockmans, J. Mertens, and A. Verhulst, "Les communautés rurales d'ancien régime en Flandre: caractéristiques et essai d'interprétation comparative," in *Europe occidentale et Amerique—Western Europe and America*, vol. 5 of *Les communautés rurales—Rural Communities*, Recueils de la Société Jean Bodin pour l'Histoire Comparative des Institutions, XLIV (Paris: Dessain et Tolra, 1987), p. 247, aptly speak of an "esprit de clocher", a parochial spirit, as an identifying characteristic of local rural communities. The primarily secular nature of the Flemish revolt stands in sharp contrast to the strong religious overtones that some historians have identified in other late-medieval peasant uprisings—see, for example, Richard Wunderli, *Peasant Fires: The Drummer of Niklashausen* (Bloomington: Indiana University Press, 1992); and Mullett, *Popular Culture and Popular Protest*.

56. See Genicot, *Rural Communities in the Medieval West*, p. 84. Pirenne, ed., *Le soulèvement*, appendix 4, p. 179: "ende ute elker prochije van Vorneambacht twe man" and "die ute elker prochie ghenomen zullen zijn, zullen wesen up den cost elc van sire prochie."

57. See, for example, J. Mertens, "Het Brugse Vrije en de opstand van kust-Vlaanderen," *Spieghel historiael* 6 (1971), pp. 306–7; as well as Appendix B, below.
58. See the list in Pirenne, ed., *Le soulèvement*, pp. li–lii.
59. W. P. Blockmans, G. Pieters, Walter Prevenier, and R. W. M. van Schaïk, "Tussen crisis en welvaart: sociale veranderingen 1300–1500," in *Algemene geschiedenis der Nederlanden*, vol. 4 (Haarlem: Fibula-van Dishoeck, 1980), pp. 45–46, estimate a rural population density of 44.9 people per square kilometer for Flanders in 1469. It may have been just as high in the 1320s, before the bubonic plague and other demographically depressing problems of the late fourteenth and fifteenth centuries; see Walter Prevenier and W. P. Blockmans, *The Burgundian Netherlands*, trans. Peter King and Yvette Mead (Cambridge: Cambridge University Press, 1986), pp. 37, 40.
60. Published in Pirenne, ed., *Le soulèvement*, appendix 2: p. 166, "compaignon de l'esmeute et le commun dou terroir de Furnes et chil des villes de Furnes, de Neufport et de Lombardie" and "compaignon et commun dudit terroir de Furnes"; p. 167, "dessusdis compaignons, communalté dudit terroir de Furnes et villes desusdites aveuc eaus sermentés." I disagree here with Sabbe, *Vlaanderen in opstand*, p. 24, who suggests that phrases such as "compaignon de l'esmeute" refer to a hard core of radicals who incited others to rebellion.
61. Published in Pirenne, ed., *Le soulèvement*, appendix 3, p. 168: "cheus dou terroir de Furnes dou commun" and "à tous cheus dou commun, hofmans, capitains et autres."
62. Published in Pirenne, ed, *Le soulèvement*, appendix 4, p. 172: "die meentucht van Vorneambacht" and "der meentucht"; p. 173, "der meentucht"—*meentucht* is Middle Dutch for commons or community.
63. See Rodney H. Hilton, *Bond Men Made Free: Medieval Peasant Movements and the English Rising of 1381* (New York, Viking Press, 1973), pp. 70–71; idem, "Medieval Peasants: Any Lessons?" *Journal of Peasant Studies* 1 (1973–74), p. 216; and Reynolds, *Kingdoms and Communities*, p. 120—all referring to the only reliable source for this episode, the chronicle of William of Jumièges. Peasants were angered by attempts to restrict their access to woods, pasture land, and fishing waters—they were acting in defence of their custom. The movement eventually was crushed militarily.
64. See, for example, Pirenne, ed., *Le soulèvement*, appendix 16, p. 215: "Winnoc le Fiere adonc hoofman de Berghes et Jehan le Valewe hoofman de Hondescote [Hondschoote, a community within the rural district of Bergues]"; and "Winnoc le Fiere, hoofman de le castelerie de Berghes et de tout le commun." Winnoc le Fiere, who died in the Battle of Cassel, was particularly active in the years 1326 to 1328 and was *hoofdman* or captain of the entire district from late 1327 onward. See Appendix B, below.
65. Pirenne, ed., *Le soulèvement*, p. xxv.
66. For example, peasants in parts of the County of Hainaut were summoned to work on the drainage canal of the common marsh by the ringing of the parish bell, according to Gérard Sivéry, *Terroirs et communautés rurales dans l'Europe occidentale au moyen âge*, Économies et Sociétés (Villeneuve-d'Ascq: Presses Universitaires de Lille, 1990), p. 198. See also Graus, *Pest-Geissler-Judenmorde: Das 14. Jahrhundert als Krisenzeit*, pp. 470–71, 492–93; Sabbe, *Vlaanderen in opstand*, p. 25.

3. For a World Without Privilege

When Count Louis returned to his ancestral home of Nevers around the beginning of July, 1324, leaving the governance of Flanders in the hands of the lord of Axel, he apparently did so in the firm belief that any further threat of peasant revolt had been eliminated. Unlike his experience with the Sluis affair of the previous year, he seemed to have survived this crisis without serious humiliation. By personally overseeing the settlement process for the district of Bruges, he actually improved his image as ruler. After all, the revolt had been leveled against his officials, not directly against himself, and his promise to punish past official wrongdoing and his establishment of measures to improve oversight of financial and judicial officers in Bruges district created the impression at least that he was now in command of the political infrastructure of Flanders. But nothing could be further from the truth. Almost immediately, peasants reconvened their assemblies and reaffirmed their oaths of solidarity, if indeed they had ever disbanded at all, and they drove returning officials into exile once again.

Far from gaining control of the political infrastructure of Flanders, Louis soon saw his situation deteriorate far beyond anything he had experienced before. There were some warnings that he might have heeded. In a letter of 16 May 1324 to both Count Louis and Robert of Cassel, Pope John XXII expressed his pleasure at the restoration of peace to Flanders, but also warned both against being unrealistically optimistic about its permanence.[1] Once again, Louis' own inexperience and the manipulative counsel of his advisers led not only to an unfortunate miscalculation of his own political circumstances but also to a serious underestimation of the perceptiveness and determination of ordinary Flemings. Within a year, in fact, the rural rebellion became formally allied to a number of cities, including Bruges and Ypres, and Louis spent the second half of 1325 as a prisoner of a general insurrection that had both rural and urban components.

By late summer of 1324, organized peasant rebellion reappeared in full force in the district of Bruges. The author of the *Chronicon*, a monk of

Clairmarais Abbey near Saint-Omer, attributed this to a conscious decision on the part of peasants to build on their recent success by pushing for additional change. He saw the vindication of rebel complaints by both the count and the arbitration commission at Veurne as constituting a significant turning point. According to him, many peasants now acquired an audacity that they had not displayed initially. Some of their captains began to question publicly whether nobles or others of privilege should even be allowed to live among them in their fortified houses, and such questioning, he maintained, soon led many peasants to resume their revolt with greater impunity than ever before.[2] Indeed, the logic of resistance to domination suggests that there was an element of truth here. Flemish peasants had tested the limits of the possible and achieved considerable success. Doubtless some now began to advocate openly what until then had seemed too dangerous to consider, the permanent removal of all privileged orders from the countryside.[3]

But attributing the resumption of revolt exclusively to the willfulness of Flemish peasants—almost as though they were spoiled children—does not fit well with all the surviving evidence. In fact, an attempt to drive those of privilege from the countryside can be credited just as easily to a defensive posture inspired by the simple need for self-preservation as to any offensive posture encouraged by recent successes. After all, the rural population had every reason to fear a reaction of lords and rural officials who, having fled the districts during the first stage of the revolt, were now preparing to return and assume their privileged positions with vengeance on their minds. More than any others, peasants had first-hand experience with the violence that propped up privilege even during the most placid of times; they were regularly exposed to the violence of rural elites who, with their bands of armed retainers, formed the most disruptive segment of the entire population. Indeed, a close examination of the surviving documentation suggests that it was the treachery of elites rather than the audacity of peasants that was primarily responsible for the resumption of revolt during the summer of 1324.

It is important to understand at this juncture that revolt initially resumed in Bruges district alone and only somewhat later in those districts that constituted the apanage of Robert of Cassel. This apparent anomaly can best be explained by the ways in which the first phase of the revolt had been resolved. As we saw earlier, a settlement was brought about in Veurne district, as well as the other territories to the southwest of Bruges, by a commission of arbitration that not only solicited the advice of third parties, such as the magistrates of the city of Ypres, but listened to the testimony of rebels themselves. In addition, the verdict for Veurne district not only gave rural communities a measure of political standing by granting them the right to inspect local tax assessments, but it also held out the possibility that the commission could be reconvened to discuss complaints that ordinary rural people might have about the implementation of the settlement.[4] And there can be little doubt that peasants viewed the presence of urban magistrates on the arbitration commission as an assurance that the settlement would not easily be weakened later by rural elites. Because they had confidence in the process that had produced it and the guarantees that were built into it, the peasants of southwestern Flanders were inclined to honor the settlement.

Such confidence, however, was minimal in the district of Bruges, where Count Louis and his advisers presided over the resolution of the revolt. After assessing the situation at close range, Louis simply imposed rather than negotiated a settlement designed to end the insurrection and to reinstate order by restoring all exiled officials and lords to their former positions. He offered an amnesty, made provisions to reform the financial and judicial administration of the district, and promised to punish corrupt officials. But peasants were excluded from the entire process and thus acquired neither the right to inspect local accounts nor the semblance of political standing. No impartial commission was convened to gather testimony, to solicit advice from third parties, or to arbitrate the issues involved. No provisions were made to ensure an equitable implementation of the settlement. Despite all this, however, there is every reason to believe that the first reaction of the peasants of Bruges district was to accept Louis' amnesty and promises at face value and hope for the best. But such hope evaporated as Louis began to undermine the promises he had made and as spiteful lords and officials began returning to the countryside.

Whatever good will the peasants of Bruges district might have held for Louis disappeared after he began issuing a series of modifying acts that had the effect of seriously crippling the concessions he had made to the rebels. For example, Louis issued his amnesty and the orders to reform the administration of Bruges district on 10 April while in the city of Bruges, entirely surrounded by rebel territory and with broad sympathy among its citizens for the rebellion. The only conditions attached to the amnesty appear to have been the requirements that the rebels end their rebellion, set aside their captains, and dissolve their oaths. But two days later, by which time he was safely ensconced within the much less intimidating surroundings of loyal Ter Duinen Abbey, Louis refashioned the entire character of the amnesty by attaching a stiff fine to it. The rural rebels, along with supporters from the nearby towns and cities, were now ordered to assist the city of Bruges in paying a fine of 66,000 lbs., presumably levied in connection with the Sluis affair of the previous summer.[5] Louis issued other qualifying measures on 12 April as well. The same act that gave permission for the people of Bruges district to institute legal proceedings against officials who had misbehaved or acted with contempt during the recent disorders specifically exempted magistrates and lords from legal prosecution, the very people whom the rebels had accused of wrongdoing. Another charter, in fact, gave magistrates and lords who had fled the district the right to return and institute their own legal proceedings against those who had driven them out.[6]

Either Louis had realized or his advisers had pointed out to him that the reestablishment of his authority in the countryside depended entirely on getting his officials and their supporters back into place in Bruges district. To do so, he employed a familiar tactic: making public promises to buy time but then doing little to keep such promises. Indeed, most of the conditions and qualifications that Louis attached to the settlement on 12 April 1324 were issued as instructions to his bailiffs and legal officers in the county of Flanders, and it is unlikely that most peasants were aware of their existence until some time later. But he and his advisers were naive in believing that they could fool anyone for very long.

When it became clear that Louis was not prepared to carry out his public promises to the letter—and particularly after lords and officials began to return seeking revenge for their recent exile, while nothing came of peasant attempts to bring legal proceedings against them—the peasants of Bruges district took action once again on their own behalf. And, once again, their collective actions brought results. This is clear from a document of 24 June 1324 in which Louis extended an amnesty to those rebels who had continued or resumed acts of insurrection during the six weeks since the settlement of early April known as the Peace of Sint-Andries. Specifically forgiven were such acts as ringing bells to convene popular assemblies without permission of the count's bailiff and appointing their own captains, marshals, and others in place of the count's officials. While no fines were mentioned, all acts of rebellion were to be abandoned immediately, or the amnesty would be canceled.[7] On the same day, he established a commission of representatives from both the district and the city to decide the cases of those who had fled the district during the recent disorders. He ordered all of them to return within a month to answer charges of wrongdoing. Apparently these included some lords and officials, for he promised to return all public funds embezzled or otherwise improperly diverted by fugitives to the inhabitants of the district.[8] But such measures amounted to too little too late, and the district of Bruges became engulfed once again in full peasant rebellion by late summer 1324.

Peasant Revolt Resumes

Whereas the first stage of the Flemish peasant revolt had begun as widely scattered rioting in a number of districts before it became an organized movement, this time it resumed with immediate, full force, especially in the countryside north of Bruges. And those holding political authority in Flanders were no better prepared for revolt in 1324 than they had been the year before.[9] In contrast to the first phase of the revolt, which was ostensibly aimed at ending the corrupt activities of county officials, especially the district magistrates and the tax officials who were collecting more than they were supposed to, beginning in the late summer of 1324 rebels began to take action not only against officials who often happened to be nobles but also against nobles as such. Presumably acting on the conviction ascribed to them by the author of the *Chronicon*, that lords should not be living among them in their castles and fortified country houses, the rebels began to attack these symbols of power and privilege. This time as their opening move, rebels stormed castles and fortified chateaux, set them on fire, and seized those occupants who had not already fled.[10]

At the same time, the other group of powerful great proprietors, the great monasteries, came into increasing difficulty when some rebels began refusing to pay the tithes, a percentage of agricultural production claimed by such religious establishments. That Flemish peasants might turn against monastic houses in their neighborhoods in this fashion should not surprise us. To most, the tithe constituted just another demand alongside many others made on their own limited resources and for which they received very little in return. Indeed, at popular assemblies held at both Oostburg and Yzendijke in the northern part of Bruges district, peasants demanded that grain, collected as tithes by some of the great abbeys, be redistributed as bread for the poor in the same communities from which it had been collected,[11] suggesting dissatisfaction with the uses made of these ecclesiastical exactions.

Rebel opposition to the great monasteries was more profound, how-ever, than displeasure with the collection and management of the tithe. Some of the abbeys were perceived as enemies of the people. Such was the case, for example, with Ter Duinen Abbey, headquartered in the coastal dunes at Koksijde near Veurne. During the French conquest and war of independence at the beginning of the fourteenth century, this abbey had joined others in the area in siding with the pro-French or *leliaart* partisans, and it apparently continued to back the enemies of the local peasantry in the 1320s.[12] In any case, Ter Duinen Abbey suffered significant property dam-age at the hands of peasant rebels during the 1320s.[13] One of the provisions of an unsuccessful treaty negotiated in early 1326 demanded compensation for damages done to abbeys since the resumption of the revolt in 1324.[14]

Peasant captains seized the reins of public authority in much of the district of Bruges by once again assuming the functions of the count's bailiffs at the district level, convening courts and rendering justice, and collecting public revenues. They levied, provisioned and placed garrisons in some of the small cities of the district to discourage exiled magistrates or their associates from trying to return. Meanwhile, the local captains once again replaced the count's local officials, the *ammans* or sheriffs.[15] Though Robert of Cassel tried to organize a force that might counter rebel actions, he discontinued his efforts when they proved ineffective in the face of the quick and decisive actions by the rebels. By the end of 1324 he had joined his nephew in France, while rebels controlled most of the district of Bruges.[16]

This time, in fact, we know the names of some of the peasant captains. Segher Janssone was a peasant from Bredene, fifteen kilometers west of the city of Bruges, near the town of Oostende, while Lambert Bonin most likely was a peasant from Westkapelle, about twelve kilometers north of the city of Bruges. Both were well-to-do peasants, with a considerable stake in the communities within which they resided.[17] However, by the end of 1324, both had also acquired a responsibility that far transcended their native communities. Janssone was described as the captain for the entire northern part of the district of Bruges, while Bonin served as a captain for the eastern part of the same district. Presumably they had been chosen by assemblies of sworn delegates from the individual rebel communities to coordinate and lead the movement.[18]

Faced with a dangerous and spreading conflagration, and actually ordered by King Charles IV to do something about the situation, Count Louis, attended by Robert of Cassel, returned to Flanders in late December 1324 intent on ending the rebellion.[19] Louis went first to Courtrai to meet with representatives from Ghent, Ypres, and a number of smaller cities and rural districts and to develop a strategy to contain the rebellion raging in Bruges district. He began by reinforcing outposts within the district of Bruges at Aardenburg and Gistel, to the northeast and the southwest of Bruges respectively, but these contingents soon found themselves under attack. Peasant forces from the northern and western parts of the district, led by Segher Janssone, laid siege to Gistel, while Lambert Bonin and his associates from the eastern part of the district besieged Aardenburg.[20]

Realizing that he could not restore authority by himself, Count Louis asked Robert of Cassel to help him in suppressing the rebellion. In a letter of 21 January 1325, he gave his uncle license to attack rebels and their property in any fashion he desired, whether burning down their houses, murdering or killing them, flooding their lands or property, or any other manner that might produce results.[21] Consequently, Robert of Cassel stationed his force in the district of Veurne[22] apparently with the intention of keeping his apanage (the districts of Veurne, Bergues, Bourbourg, Cassel, and Bailleul) free of rebellion; Veurne also could serve as a staging area for raids into the district of Bruges.

Finally, Count Louis gave a free hand to aristocrats forced to flee their burning castles and abandon their possessions within the district of Bruges in seeking revenge on their own. From out of the eastern half of Flanders, but especially from Ghent where many had sought safety, exiled aristocrats and their bands of armed retainers set out on raids with permission from the count to burn peasant houses and seize their occupants and, regardless whether they put up a fight, or whether they actually were rebels, to decapitate them or break them on the wheel.[23] There was to be no quarter given.

Urban Involvement

Despite the execution of a number of rebel captains and an aristocratic reign of terror, Count Louis and his supporters could make no headway against the rebellion. Rising levels of loyalist violence were simply met by increased rebel violence. In fact, the rebellion was threatening to spread once again to the districts of southwestern Flanders despite Robert of Cassel's actions in that quarter. The loyalist position was further aggravated by the increasingly rebellious mood of craft guild members, especially weavers, in the largest cities of Flanders. In the heavily industrialized centers of Ghent and Ypres, only the stepped up vigilance of the city magistrates kept matters under control.[24]

In Bruges, however, the political tide ran in the opposite direction.

First of all, there is some reason to believe that relations between the city and district of Bruges in general were more cordial than they were between the other great cities of Flanders and their hinterlands.[25] Many artisans and craftspeople in the overwhelmingly commercial center of Bruges openly sympathized with the rebellion raging in the surrounding countryside. Indeed, many such individuals may well have participated in the rebellion ever since 1323. Others, meanwhile, including even merchants who were not otherwise perceived as political radicals, simply saw Count Louis' discomfort as serving both their own interests and the interests of the city.[26] Such a position had long helped to shape the political stance of the city of Bruges. It lay, for example, behind the city's bitter quarrel over trade policy with the former count in 1321 as well as its preemptive strike against the city of Sluis during the summer of 1323.[27] In any case, by the beginning of 1325 there apparently was a growing suspicion that Count Louis was not fully committed to maintaining good commercial relations with England, while many in the craft guilds were pressuring the city magistrates into joining the rural rebellion. Still, as late as 21 January 1325 Count Louis continued to see the city of Bruges as, if not exactly a devoted follower, at least not an open enemy.[28]

Two months later, however, the situation had changed considerably. Count Louis now began to see the city of Bruges as part of the rebellion itself, and on 14 March 1325 he rescinded the privileges he had granted the city a year earlier regarding control over the Zwin in the wake of the Sluis affair.[29] Indeed, for the remainder of 1325, the city played an extremely important, at times even a leading, role in the continuing rural rebellion.[30] Even after the city magistrates made peace with the count in early 1326, individuals from the city continued to participate in the rebellion. Not only did the city's organized and disciplined craft organizations help provide experience and leadership, but, at least until the end of 1325, they brought the might of the well trained and highly disciplined city militia as well.

This does not mean, as the author of the *Chronicon* and most historians following him have suggested, that the city of Bruges now began to dominate or take over what had been until then a predominately rural movement.[31] The bulk of the information, including that supplied by the *Chronicon*, simply does not allow such a conclusion. Rather, it was a matter of two independent movements converging to make common cause.[32] But such cooperation began to make a significant difference in early 1325. With the city of Bruges officially joining the revolt, the movement acquired the critical mass it needed to expand in the face of the concerted efforts of the count and the nobility. In addition, the support of the city of Bruges gave the movement an aura of semi-respectability for a time.

While the city of Bruges allied itself with the rebellious rural population of Flanders, the city of Ghent for reasons of its own remained firmly in the loyalist camp. The loyal magistrates of Ghent during the 1320s were dominated by the guild of fullers, rivals of the more prosperous and often more "revolutionary" weavers' guild which tended to favor the rural rebellion.[33] As a result, Ghent increasingly served as the base of operations for the count and the nobility. Such loyalty may well have been reinforced by the count's decision on 18 February 1325 to absolve the city, its suburbs, and its rural district from having to pay a series of unpopular exactions.[34] Even at the best of times, however, relations between the two cities could be stormy, especially when Bruges' desires for tariff-free commerce conflicted with Ghent's desires to protect its textile industries. This rivalry soon began to express itself in a series of violent clashes. By choosing sides in what had been thus far an exclusively rural struggle, the two most important cities of Flanders now added an additional dimension to the rebellion already dominating public life.[35]

Insurrection Spreads

At the same time that the cities of Bruges and Ghent were becoming increasingly involved, the rural rebellion itself began to expand. Probably during February 1325, Segher Janssone and his peasant forces defeated the count's contingent at Gistel in the western part of Bruges district. The author of the *Chronicon* described the situation with a popular proverb to the effect that nothing seemed secure any longer, that the natural order of things had been inverted. When the battle was over, Janssone's contingent had killed fifteen of the count's forces and turned over another fifteen to the now friendly city of Bruges for imprisonment.[36] Indeed, accepting the prisoners from Gistel seems to have been the first act by the city in direct support of the rural rebellion.

The capture of Gistel marked a real turning point in the progress of the revolt by showing that a force primarily of peasants could defeat the forces at the disposal of the count. And this lesson was not lost on peasants in other rural districts. With much of the district of Bruges in their hands and a friendly city of Bruges at their backs, Segher Janssone and company set off immediately in the direction of Veurne and the other districts of southwestern Flanders that had played such important roles in the first stage of the revolt. In quick succession these districts joined the rebellion, in most cases without a real fight. Janssone was joined in this venture by another peasant captain, Nikolaas Zannekin.

Although little is known about his early career, Zannekin appears to have been a well-to-do peasant from Lampernisse in the district of Veurne, who first served as a captain for Veurne district in late 1323 and early 1324.[37] By early 1325, however, he had developed very close ties to both the city and the district of Bruges. In a letter of 21 January 1325 in which Count Louis asked his uncle for assistance in suppressing the rebellion, Zannekin was listed as an ally of the rebels of Bruges district.[38] But he continued to maintain very close ties to the districts of southwestern Flanders, most likely as their proxy or representative in temporary exile. His continuing leadership role in southwestern Flanders proved to be invaluable in the rebel push outside of the district of Bruges during the early months of 1325.

While Lambert Bonin and rebel contingents from the eastern half of Bruges district maintained their pressure on Aardenburg, and while allies from the city of Bruges watched Ghent and Count Louis, the peasant forces led by Segher Janssone and Nikolaas Zannekin began the liberation of southwestern Flanders from loyalist control. This immediately brought them into conflict with Robert of Cassel who, since 21 January 1325, had primary responsibility for organizing an aristocratic force capable of preventing the further spread of the rebellion. Apparently, the repression he and his warriors imposed on the districts of southwestern Flanders— Robert, we must remember, had been told to use whatever means he saw fit, including fire, flood, and murder[39]—had been sufficient to maintain a veneer of loyalty in that quarter. But that veneer soon proved to be paper thin.

The peasant force from Bruges district, jointly led by Janssone and Zannekin, encountered its first resistance at Nieuwpoort, about 15 kilometers west of Gistel, just across the IJzer River in the district of Veurne. Robert of Cassel was waiting there with an armed contingent whose task was to stop any peasant advance out of rebel Bruges district, but they were unable to mount an effective resistance. The author of the *Chronicon* suggested that the local population had been hostile to the loyalist force since its first arrival and now threatened to rise in rebellion as the force from Bruges district approached.[40] Robert of Cassel quickly retreated to the more easily defended city of Veurne.

After accepting oaths of solidarity from the magistrates of Nieuwpoort, Janssone, Zannekin, and company set off for the nearby city of Veurne. The mere approach of the peasant force now began to inspire popular risings in both the city and countryside sufficient to put both urban and rural loyalists to flight without a fight. Robert of Cassel withdrew his force into Bergues district to regroup, as both the city and district of Veurne, represented by sympathetic magistrates and popularly chosen captains respectively, swore oaths of alliance with the rebels from Bruges district.[41] The presence of Zannekin, himself a peasant from the district of Veurne, appears to have been particularly effective in bringing the revolt to Veurne district. He was widely hailed as the liberator by his compatriots who had suffered much from the violence unleashed by Robert of Cassel.[42]

With the city and countryside of Veurne firmly on their side, the rebels moved on to Bergues district in pursuit of the loyalist force under Robert of Cassel's command. The author of the *Chronicon* described the rebel force at this time as consisting of three separate groups: one, commanded by Segher Janssone, contained a large number of well-armed men from the western part of Bruges district; a second, newly formed with recruits from the district of Veurne, was placed under Nikolaas Zannekin's command; a third, led by an unnamed captain, was drawn primarily from the town of Nieuwpoort, Veurne district. These forces of both peasants and townspeople proved to be too much for Robert of Cassel and his following, described by the author of the *Chronicon* as consisting of three hundred mounted nobles, armored in chain mail, accompanied by a "lazy and reluctant" infantry force[43]—the latter was reluctant perhaps because it had been recruited by force from the local, pro-rebel population.

Presumably leaving the force from the town of Nieuwpoort to guard against any loyalist counterattack in Veurne district, Janssone and Zannekin led their peasant forces into Bergues district. According to the author of the *Chronicon*, Robert of Cassel, learning that Janssone and Zannekin were proceeding toward the coastal city of Dunkirk, hurried there with a group of armed nobles prepared to stand firmly, but the forces under his command failed him. In an attempt to learn more about the movements of the advancing rebels, he had sent out a small party to make observations, but this party was discovered near the small coastal community of Zuidkote, seven kilometers east of Dunkirk, and in the struggle that ensued, six of the local population were killed by Robert's men. Almost immediately peasants from all the nearby communities mobilized and joined the rebellion while Robert's forces beat a hasty retreat. When in quick succession the peasants of the remainder of Bergues district and the districts of Bourbourg and

Cassel also mobilized and swore oaths of alliance to the rebels, Robert's retreat turned into a complete rout.[44] All he could do was seek refuge in the county of Artois as his houses in Dunkirk and Cassel went up in flames.

Segher Janssone and his force then turned eastward against the districts of Courtrai and Ypres, where they conquered the towns of Torhout (in Bruges district), Roeselare (in Ypres district), and began to close in on the cities of Ypres and Courtrai. The latter two cities remained in Count Louis' hands for the moment, but the presence of Janssone and his peasant army nearby prevented the count's forces from reinforcing the withering military force of Robert of Cassel in southwestern Flanders. With Janssone at his rear, Nikolaas Zannekin led his group into the districts of Cassel and Bailleul where he quickly gained control over city and countryside alike.[45] With the rebellion extended to all of southwestern Flanders, Zannekin and company took up a position at Poperinge, in the south of Veurne district, from which they could watch the city and district of Ypres, both of which still maintained at least the appearance of loyalty to Count Louis. All of this was accomplished presumably by some time in March 1325 (see the map in Figure 4).

The author of the *Chronicon* found himself at a complete loss for explaining how a primarily peasant army might prove so formidable against heavily armed and mounted nobles. All he could do was place the blame for rebel success on the city of Bruges, an explanation that he used repeatedly from then onward and that most historians looking at the revolt have adopted uncritically. He stated that Zannekin was not prepared to leave Poperinge and move against Ypres without the explicit command to do so from the city of Bruges,[46] suggesting erroneously that Bruges was now playing the coordinating and leadership role in the entire rebellion and that Zannekin, though a captain in the district of Veurne, received his instructions from Bruges.[47] There seems, however, to be no clear evidence of this. Rather, it was a matter of rural rebels coordinating efforts with the rebel city in an eventual assault on the cities of Ypres and Courtrai.

In fact, the rapid and overwhelming rebel successes in southwestern Flanders derived from forces actually on the scene. Most obviously, these included the rebel armies led by Nikolaas Zannekin and Segher Janssone. What was even more important, however, was the cooperation of local peasants themselves. Repeatedly, the mere approach of the rebel armies was paired with local collective action that was sufficient to drive lords and officials into exile. Indeed, the author of the *Chronicon* himself directly

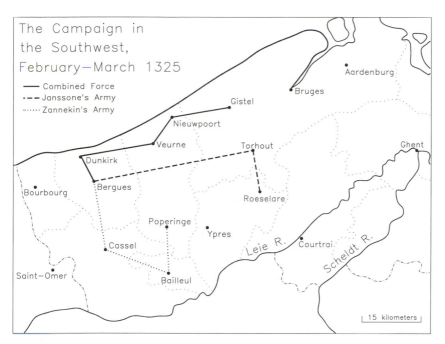

The Campaign in
the Southwest,
February—March 1325

——— Combined Force
- - - Janssone's Army
·····   Zannekin's Army

Aardenburg

Bruges

Gistel

Nieuwpoort

Veurne

Torhout

Ghent

Dunkirk

Bourbourg

Bergues

Roeselare

Poperinge

Ypres

Leie R.

Courtrai

Scheldt R.

Cassel

Saint—Omer

Bailleul

15 kilometers

Figure 4

confirmed this in his descriptions of the feeble loyalist efforts in the districts
of Veurne, Bergues, Bourbourg, Cassel, and Bailleul. Robert of Cassel and
his mounted warriors and reluctant foot soldiers had no chance of prevailing once the rural population rose en masse against them. The broad
support for the movement also was indicated by the fact that no occupying
armies remained behind—the real key to the phenomenal peasant successes
of February and March 1325. Newly liberated rural communities convened
assemblies to choose captains and other leaders to replace the exiled officials,[48] while the always modest peasant armies, fortified by a few additional
recruits, moved onward. Further, in southwestern Flanders as the rural
districts joined the rebellion, groups of artisans also acted by driving the
ruling oligarchies from power in a number of the smaller cities and towns
under the protective cover of the rebellion in the countryside. Nevertheless,
we can appreciate the position of the author of the *Chronicon*. Because he
was stationed near Saint-Omer, he was so close to the action that he might
have seen the smoke when Robert of Cassel's house in Cassel was burned.
The rapid and complete rebel successes doubtless shocked and confused

him. Such things simply were not supposed to happen. An army of peasants should not be able to defeat mounted, noble warriors.

While Janssone and Zannekin were liberating the southwestern end of Flanders from loyalist control, another rebel push was underway into the northeastern end of Flanders. Peasants from primarily the eastern part of the district of Bruges began an advance against the districts of Vier Ambachten and Land of Waas, to the north and northeast of Ghent respectively. They were led in this campaign by their captain Walter Ratgheer, a peasant from an unspecified rural community in Bruges district.[49] Under his command rebels were able to make significant inroads on Ghent's northeastern flank, for Ratgheer, with a force of about 500 armed men, occupied Assenede, district of Vier Ambachten, in early 1325. This gave the rebels a base for further operations in Vier Ambachten and Land of Waas as well as a vantage point from which to observe the loyalists in Ghent.

Primarily because of the close proximity to Ghent and stiff loyalist resistance, however, the initiative led by Ratgheer into northeastern Flanders was not as successful as those led by Janssone and Zannekin in southwestern Flanders. For example, some time in March, loyalist forces from Ghent temporarily were able to force Ratgheer and company back into the district of Bruges. But the rebels soon returned, for they were able to maintain control of the districts of Vier Ambachten and Land of Waas into and through the summer of 1325, despite the huge force of loyalists in nearby Ghent.[50] The author of the *Chronicon* believed that loyalists had missed an important opportunity to change the momentum by not pressing on more forcefully against the temporary rebel retreat from Assenede. He suggested that some among the loyalists were less than brave, perhaps even traitorous, in bringing their contingents back to the safety of Ghent and urging peace talks instead.[51]

Noble Intrigues and Lost Chances for Peace

It was within this context—the city of Bruges gradually allying itself with the rebellion, the continuing rout in southwestern Flanders, and rebel advances into the districts of Vier Ambachten and the Land of Waas—that Count Louis became convinced of the need to negotiate a settlement. A truce was arranged during late March 1325, bringing an end to the siege of Aardenburg and other hostile action, and on 7 April 1325, representatives from the cities of Ghent, Bruges, and Ypres began laying the groundwork for a settlement.[52] The magistrates of Ghent appear in particular to have urged this because some of their fellow citizens apparently had threatened to join the rebel side if their demands for a peaceful solution to the crisis were ignored,[53] suggesting that the people of this city were not unanimous in their support of the conservative patricians and the growing ranks of emigre nobles. A compromise was struck by which rebels would not be sentenced to death, mutilation, or banishment, and their possessions would remain safe if only they returned home. Subsequently, an investigation would be carried out by a special commission of arbitration consisting of Robert of Cassel and representatives from the cities of Ghent and Ypres.[54] An uneasy truce reigned as the commissioners began their inquiry.

No peaceful settlement resulted from the activities of the commission of arbitration, though in retrospect this is not particularly surprising. The rebels seem to have been divided on the prospects. On the one hand, there were those, including some captains, who were willing to commit themselves in advance to an eventual settlement. For example, Lambert Bonin, active as a captain in the eastern part of the district of Bruges, especially in the siege of Aardenburg, signed and sealed a document on 25 April 1325 in which he promised in the future to use all of his efforts to support rather than work against Count Louis.[55] But such submissions seem to have been both rare and of little lasting effect. Indeed, in the case of Bonin, we know that he quickly changed his mind and rejoined the rebellion, playing a leading role up to the Battle of Cassel in 1328.[56] On the other hand, there were many more rebels who were very suspicious of any findings that the commission might produce, since none of the commissioners seemed in the slightest way sympathetic to the rebellion. Especially suspicious were the rebels associated with Segher Janssone and Nikolaas Zannekin who had so recently liberated all of southwestern Flanders from the grasp of Robert of Cassel, the head of the commission. They were not eager to submit to the arbitration of their enemies after such a resounding victory.

By the beginning of June 1325, prospects for peace began to disappear entirely. The author of the *Chronicon* reported that many armed rebels from the district of Veurne had begun to follow the commissioners everywhere they went, complaining that so far only noble claims had been investigated and demanding in a threatening and abusive fashion that the punishment of those nobles allegedly responsible for murdering six peasants at Zuidkote be given the highest priority.[57] Hoping to placate a growing restlessness in the countryside, the commission agreed to begin investigating alleged noble atrocities at a meeting they scheduled for 11 June at Ter Duinen Abbey, in Veurne district. But the investigation never took place. A large, armed, and angry crowd, including Segher Janssone, Nikolaas Zannekin, and their followers, gathered at the monastery to express its dissatisfaction with the proceedings thus far.[58] Hearing of the welcome they were about to receive, the commissioners canceled their meeting. The author of the *Chronicon* defended the commissioners' timidity by explaining that the rebels had begun to rave at this time,[59] and it has been customary for historians following his lead to see the total breakdown of the peace process as due primarily to the menacing and irrational behavior of the rebels.[60] And within days peasant rebels not only reaffirmed their oaths of solidarity and reasserted control over the districts they had so recently liberated, but they also reestablished their alliance with the rebel city of Bruges.

To see the breakdown of the arbitration proceedings as due exclusively to the actions of peasants, however, is to miss a substantial portion of the political activity taking place at the time. Actions by others, apparently unknown to the author of the *Chronicon*, were as much to blame. In the weeks leading up to the Ter Duinen fiasco, Count Louis increasingly came under the influence of a group of nobles that was intent on preventing any settlement that might be even slightly prejudicial to them. When this group, apparently close to Louis' great uncle John of Namur, made a successful play for increased influence that was rewarded in the early days of June by appointment to Count Louis' *raad* or governing council, the fate of the peace initiative was sealed.[61]

Pressure to begin talks in 1325 had come primarily from townspeople, specifically citizens of Ghent who had threatened to join the rebellion unless serious negotiations began. The continuing rebellion, after all, was taking a substantial toll on the commerce and industry of Flanders. It was also representatives from the cities of Ghent and Ypres, not nobles, who made up the arbitration commission, while Robert of Cassel agreed to preside over the commission's activities. What the noble party feared most was a repeat of the previous year's arbitration verdict in the district of Veurne that had gone completely against them; that arbitration commission, too, had consisted of representatives from cities, not the nobility, and Robert of Cassel had presided over it. Nevertheless, such a repeat at least initially seemed highly unlikely, given the fact that peasants doubted the fairness of the proceedings and had begun harassing the commissioners about not attending to their complaints. But the noble party became alarmed and began to take more concerted action when, as the author of the

Chronicon described it, peasants were able to "twist back" or distort allegations of noble atrocities into a formal accusation which the commissioners then agreed to consider on 11 June 1325 at Ter Duinen Abbey.[62]

Robert of Cassel's participation in the arbitration proceedings deserves further examination in this connection because it may have convinced the nobles associated with John of Namur of the need to take some sort of action. Quite likely, Robert initially agreed to participate in the proceedings because he knew of no other way to forestall further destruction of his vast possessions in the part of Flanders now controlled by peasant captains. He had been powerless, after all, to stop the burning of his houses in Dunkirk and Cassel during the rebel advance through southwestern Flanders earlier in the year.[63] Since the beginning of the rebellion in 1323, however, the nobles close to John of Namur had not only seen Robert as their primary rival in providing advice and counsel to the count on the governance of Flanders, but also, after 1324, as far too willing to compromise with the rebels.[64] Indeed, it is highly unlikely that the commission could have agreed to look into peasant grievances without the consent of Robert, its presiding officer. In short, the real possibility of an arbitrated peace in mid-1325 frightened the noble party into taking direct action against Robert of Cassel designed to sabotage the arbitration process. The plan hatched by John of Namur and his associates was to remove Robert from the scene in the hope that this would destroy all chances for peace.

The first move was against Robert of Cassel as adviser to the count. On 9 June 1325, no doubt in response to increased pressure from the noble party and especially from John of Namur, Count Louis issued an act announcing changes in the membership of his *raad* or governing council for Flanders. The new council would consist of John of Flanders, lord of Nesles and Dendermonde, Robert, lord of Nevele and castellan of Courtrai, John of Verrières, castellan of Rupelmonde, and William of Auxonne. The first three were prominent nobles widely known to be against any arbitration or compromise and in favor of making the rebels pay dearly for the trouble they had caused; William of Auxonne was a cleric and lawyer who developed a reputation for seeking harsh repression in the years to come.[65] Conspicuously absent from the list was Robert of Cassel who had been one of count's principal advisers for the previous two years.

About the same time, John of Namur and his noble associates took steps to prevent Robert of Cassel from convening the meeting of the arbitration commission on 11 June. Apparently, they intended to seize him on his way to Ter Duinen Abbey, but Robert learned of the conspiracy against him and took refuge in his castle at Nieppe, north of the Leie River in the district of Cassel. Robert later maintained that the conspirators intended to kill him, though it is more likely they simply wanted to scare him enough to withdraw from the political scene.[66] The plan worked perfectly. The commissioners never arrived at the abbey on 11 June and headed for cover rather than face the angry crowd of rebels that had gathered there. Besides, there was little they could do by themselves without Robert of Cassel to preside over the meeting. The peace process had been subverted.

The Count's Capture

Count Louis was at Ypres when he heard of the events at Ter Duinen Abbey and of the renewed alliances between peasants associated with Segher Janssone and Nikolaas Zannekin and the city of Bruges. He began now to fear for his own safety. Apparently portions of both the city and rural population of Ypres were showing signs of increasing sympathy for the rebels.[67] He moved, therefore, to Courtrai with approximately 400 armed nobles where he was welcomed by the magistrates and many others of the city. Louis hoped to head off an expected attempt by rebels to take the city which would, if successful, drive a wedge between the two great cities still loyal to him, Ypres and Ghent.

Indeed, within days, hostile contingents began advancing on Courtrai. However, these were not the forces led by Janssone and Zannekin, but rather from the rebel city of Bruges. The author of the *Chronicon* said that the force from Bruges, about 5,000 strong, set out for Courtrai because some citizens of Bruges had been arrested and imprisoned there on the order of Count Louis, ostensibly for trying to subvert the city to the rebel side.[68] It is worth noting that the city of Bruges, though allied to the rural rebellion since February or March, had thus far taken no direct action in its support other than to accept prisoners captured by Segher Janssone and company at Gistel. And, when forces from the city first took to the road in mid June 1325, they did so for a typically urban reason—protection of the rights of free passage for its citizens—not explicitly in support of the ongoing peasant rebellion.

Though the magistrates and people of Courtrai initially gave Count Louis a warm and friendly welcome and swore loyalty to him,[69] their loyalty evaporated quickly in the wake of the count's subsequent blundering. Louis and his advisers were concerned that the Overleie quarter of Courtrai, the part that lay on the left bank or Bruges side of the Leie River, was badly exposed and thus very vulnerable to the approaching militia from the city of Bruges. In order to observe more clearly the approaching force and organize a more effective defense of Courtrai, Louis and his advisers, with the apparent consent of the magistrates of the city, decided to burn the Overleie suburbs. But a strong wind and excessive dryness caused the fire to rage out of control, jump the river, and spread to the main part of Courtrai. Furious at this turn of events, the ordinary people of the city who had not been warned or consulted about the planned fire renounced their loyalty to Louis, took to the streets in rebellion, and declared their solidarity with the approaching force from Bruges. A bloody battle took place within Courtrai on 20 and 21 June 1325 which proved to be disastrous to the count and his partisans.[70]

Count Louis and his force were caught between the raging fire and the angry people of Courtrai who, responding to the clamor and the ringing of church bells, turned out in great numbers to attack Louis' forces. As the mounted warriors attempted to flee, objects thrown from windows of houses hindered their escape, while men and women alike began literally to cut them to pieces with whatever weapons they had to hand. When the battle was over, the count's force had suffered heavy casualties. Among those killed, both during the hostilites and while being held prisoner, were some of the most prominent knights and nobles in Louis' retinue—Roger of Zaemslacht, the count's tutor, Baldwin of Zegerskapelle, a prominent knight, and three out of four new members of the count's revised *raad* or governing council: John of Verrières, John of Flanders, and Robert of Nevele.[71] Count Louis' great uncle, John of Namur, escaped during the melee with only light wounds and found temporary asylum in the monastery of St. Martin at Tournai, about 25 kilometers south of Courtrai along the Scheldt River. The count himself was captured and turned over to the militia of the city of Bruges, which transported him back to Bruges for more than five months of detention.[72]

As Count Louis was carted off to Bruges, his political situation deteriorated even further. Nikolaas Zannekin and his peasant army quickly moved into the district of Ypres which rallied to the rebel cause. About the same time, the artisans of the city of Ypres took to the streets, forcing the members of the conservative patrician oligarchy from their positions of power in the city and into exile. Artisan guild members themselves took over the reins of city government, seized the goods of patricians fleeing to France or Ghent, and began to fortify the suburbs of textile workers which, until then, had been without defense, a long-standing complaint of the ordinary people of the city.[73] An interesting illustration of a changed administration in the city of Ypres appeared in the form of a change of language for the city accounts, from French, the language of the ousted patricians, to Flemish, the language of the ordinary people of the city.[74]

Flanders Divided

With Louis a prisoner and the cities and districts of Ypres and Courtrai added to the rebellion, the rebels appeared to have gained the upper hand (the map in Figure 5 shows the extent of the revolt by the end of June 1325), and this prompted some interesting political realignments. Louis' uncle, Robert of Cassel, so recently a leader in the resistance to and himself a victim of rebel actions, now made common cause with the rebellion. Actually, the rebels were able to convince Count Louis to offer Robert the title of *ruwaart* or regent. On 30 June 1325, Robert accepted the administration of the County of Flanders on behalf of Count Louis and the magistrates of the city of Bruges until such time as the count should rescind the order. The officials of Bruges gave their consent to this arrangement not only for Bruges itself but also for the city of Ypres, the district of Bruges, and all the other confederates joined to them by oaths of solidarity.[75] While the act states that Count Louis approved of his uncle's regency, he probably had little choice in the matter.

About the same time that Bruges was arranging for Robert of Cassel to become regent of Flanders, Louis' great uncle, John of Namur, put himself at the head of the loyalist opposition at Ghent and claimed the regency for himself. It may well be that he sought to gain the support of the city of Ghent by forging a document attributed to Louis naming him regent, back-dated to 12 June 1325.[76] Forgery or not, by 20 September 1325 the king of France confirmed him as regent for the imprisoned count, and the political polarization of Flanders intensified once again. Alongside the original opposition between Flemish peasants and the politically and socially privileged of the countryside and the secondary opposition between the cities of Bruges and Ghent, there now appeared, by the beginning of

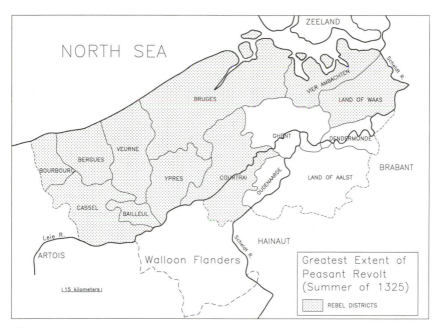

Figure 5

July 1325, an additional opposition between rival members of the ruling dynasty.

From the beginning of July 1325 onward, the revolt of Flanders came to include much more than strictly rural concerns, but for the next five months at least both rural and urban concerns were accommodated in a single movement. It had also acquired a form of traditional legitimacy with a member of the ruling dynasty at its head. The list of witnesses and the clerics who drew up the agreement of 30 June shows that some elites at least had accepted the count's imprisonment and Robert of Cassel's regency. The rebels now set about the task of adding the city of Ghent and its remaining allies to the cause, but the loyalists resisted this at every turn. The entire summer and fall of 1325 came to be dominated by this campaign, which was repeatedly accompanied by violence and ultimately cost hundreds of lives.

As regent of Flanders and suddenly the designated leader of the entire rebellion against the pro-French patricians and nobles ensconced at Ghent, Robert of Cassel did not neglect his own rivalry with John of Namur.

Indeed, much of what Robert did over the next five months was directed at least in part against his relative and rival. Initially at least, this personal vendetta did not interfere with his actions as regent for rebel Flanders because the rebels' enemies were the same as his. The act that made Robert regent contained a clause that stripped John of Namur of any authority in Flanders.[77] And almost immediately Robert began to use the military might at his disposal to move against John's primary base of support, the city of Ghent and the nearby districts of Ghent, Oudenaarde, Aalst, and Dendermonde. Apparently concluding that Ghent would be too difficult to take in a frontal assault, the rebels planned a complete encirclement of the city instead. Robert of Cassel at the head of the militia from the city of Bruges, presumably along with peasant contingents from western Bruges district and the districts of southwestern Flanders, would swing around the west and south side of Ghent, while Walter Ratgheer and the peasant forces from eastern Bruges districts and the districts of Vier Ambachten and Land of Waas would complete the circle around the north and east sides.

Robert of Cassel and his force set off, first of all, for Deinze, along the Leie River near the southwestern edge of the district of Ghent. In connection with a series of probes out of this base to gauge the kind of resistance they encountered, they managed to destroy a castle belonging to John of Namur at nearby Wijnendale. Their goal was the town of Oudenaarde along the Scheldt River, which protected the southern flank of Ghent, but the town was too well provisioned and defended to take with the force at hand. Not knowing exactly what to do next, Robert and his army attacked and occupied the nearby castle of Peteghem instead, which also happened to belong to John of Namur. Meanwhile, loyalist forces from Ghent had assembled in the village of Nevele, west of Ghent, presumably to begin a counter attack or to drive a wedge between the rebel forces and the bases of operation to the northwest of the Leie River. When the two sides clashed on 15 July 1325 at a bridge over the Leie River known as the Reckelings-brugge, near the town of Deinze, the rebels won a significant victory and control over the flow of supplies to Ghent via the Leie.[78] Despite this early success, however, Robert of Cassel and his portion of rebel forces were not able to capitalize on it. A later attempt to take Oudenaarde also ended in failure. In fact, by 22 September, John of Namur was able to refortify Oudenaarde and from then onward keep it firmly in the loyalist camp. About the same time he and the loyalists reasserted some military control over the city of Courtrai as well.[79]

While Robert of Cassel and his company were thus occupied in the areas to the south and west, Walter Ratgheer and peasant troops from the eastern part of Bruges district and from both Vier Ambachten and Land of Waas, supplemented by a contingent from the city of Bruges, attempted to consolidate and extend their control over the northern and eastern approaches to the city of Ghent. By late summer, the rebels finally gained control over Aardenburg and took up a position at Langerbrugge, in the northern part of Ghent district, from which they could launch raids and attempt to incite rebellion in the city and district of Ghent.[80] But every action they took was countered by the loyalists. John of Namur and the magistrates of Ghent maintained garrisons in the small towns of the district of Ghent and sent out agitators and agents to undermine rebel solidarity in Land of Waas.[81] With the onset of colder weather, however, Ratgheer and company withdrew from their exposed position at Langerbrugge to Eeklo in the district of Bruges.

The combined rebellion of peasants and the city of Bruges under the regency of Robert of Cassel never achieved the success that the primarily peasant rebellion did by itself during the first half of 1325. One of the essential reasons for peasant success was the fact that during the early months of 1325, throughout southwestern Flanders as well as in the districts of Vier Ambachten and Land of Waas, peasant armies spread the rebellion not so much by outright conquest as by breaking the grip of the landed elites, thereby allowing peasants to make their own rebellion. Protected by Ratgheer and company, peasants of these districts convened assemblies and replaced the count's officials by captains of their own choosing. There is no evidence at all that rebellion was forced on peasants in the districts of Vier Ambachten and Land of Waas. No occupying armies were left behind. The advancing peasant armies simply made rebellion possible in places where others had prevented it until then. Even the unsympathetic author of the *Chronicon* confirmed this in his descriptions of rebel risings in the districts of Veurne and Ypres, for example.[82]

After the count's capture, with a much heavier involvement of the city of Bruges and under the leadership of Robert of Cassel, the approach of the combined rebellion shifted away from the one that had worked so well for peasants up to that time. Neither Robert nor the city shared the desire for change in the countryside that motivated the peasant rebels. In fact, there was much less emphasis on creating conditions conducive to popular mobilization and rebellion during the second half of 1325 and much more emphasis on capturing cities and punishing rival cities or relatives. Even though the forces under Robert's direction presumably included peasant contingents from southwestern Flanders (though this is nowhere explicitly stated), they were directed primarily against John of Namur, which was in Robert's personal interest, and against the city of Ghent, which was in the interest of the rebel city of Bruges. Little or no attempt was made in this quarter to encourage and support peasant rebellion. Nor was the military might at Robert's disposal used to neutralize the strength of rural elites, except to the extent that attacks against the city of Ghent and its allies included action against exiled nobles who had fled to Ghent. In short, the part of the rebellion headed by Robert of Cassel and spearheaded by Bruges had abandoned its popular rural base, and, as a result, virtually all advances came to a halt by late in the year. In fact, the only places where additional progress was made after June 1325 were the districts of Vier Ambachten and Land of Waas where peasant armies supported local popular rebellions and then, presumably, turned the districts over to their own captains.[83]

To make matters worse, when Robert of Cassel decided that nothing further could be gained in continuing the squeeze on Ghent and withdrew his forces to Bruges, he left the peasant army north of the city of Ghent in a precarious position. Walter Ratgheer and his contingents from the districts of Bruges, Vier Ambachten, and Land of Waas, stationed very close to the city of Ghent at Langerbrugge, now faced the full force of the loyalists by themselves. At this point, the *Chronicon* mentioned dissension within rebel ranks.[84] At least part of the dissension should be attributed to Robert's withdrawal and a likely unwillingness by Ratgheer and company to do so.

Ratgheer and his peasant contingents were hesitant to withdraw because it would expose the rural districts of Vier Ambachten and Land of Waas to the violence of the noble loyalists who were expert at deploying mounted warriors against scattered rural populations. But with no aid coming from either the city of Bruges or Robert of Cassel they were forced, however reluctantly, to withdraw as far as Eeklo in the eastern part of the district of Bruges. What they feared the most began to happen almost immediately. Loyalist forces moved into the districts of Vier Ambachten and Land of Waas and began to crush the rebellion.[85] While rebels from the city of Bruges and Robert of Cassel apparently were willing to abandon a portion of the countryside to being despoiled and pillaged, the peasant captains definitely were not. Sometime during November 1325, therefore, a large peasant army drawn from the entire district of Bruges tried to counter the loyalists by advancing on Assenede.[86]

There is no evidence that either the city of Bruges or Robert of Cassel offered the slightest assistance in the move against Assenede. Facing the full force that loyalist Ghent and its allies could put in the field, they suffered a crushing defeat. The author of the *Chronicon* reported that more than 700 rebels were killed in the battle, including two captains, Walter Ratgheer and the previously unmentioned Blawrel Bockel.[87] Though captains Segher Janssone and Lambert Bonin managed to survive, the rebel advance had been halted, and a merciless repression began in northeastern Flanders.[88] The districts of Vier Ambachten and Land of Waas remained under the firm control of loyalist forces from then onward (see the map in Figure 6).

Though rebel forces were never able to obtain a solid foothold east of the Scheldt River, this does not mean that there was no sympathy for the rebellion in the towns and districts of southeastern Flanders. It means only that the loyalists were able to maintain military control there. Still, there were those who risked their lives and property by openly supporting the rebellion. First of all, around 23 September 1325, rebel supporters in the city of Geraardsbergen killed a number of loyalists as they entered the city. John of Namur escaped only because the rebels did not know exactly what he looked like and seized and killed the wrong man.[89] Though it had no lasting effect, the episode at Geraardsbergen shows that even in the most remote corners of the county there was some support for the rebellion.[90]

Secondly, there were some even within the loyalist city of Ghent who favored the rebel cause. Despite the firm grip of the conservative patriciate, reinforced by the continual influx of lords driven from rebel districts and patricians driven from rebel cities, the weavers of Ghent attempted to bring the city over to the rebel side sometime during August 1325. But their plans were discovered and they were charged by the conservative patriciate with treason. During September some weavers were executed and many more— at least 600; the author of the *Chronicon* said 3,000—were banished from the city for life.[91] From then onward, Ghent became a true stronghold of the conservative patricians and lords of Flanders. All dissent in Ghent was suppressed for years to come.[92]

Finally, the city magistrates of Dendermonde declared in late October that no enemies of the imprisoned count, of Robert of Cassel, or of the common people would be allowed to enter or pass through the city in the hope that this would keep the city in peace and quiet.[93] At the very least, this was an expression of willingness to cooperate with the rebels if the

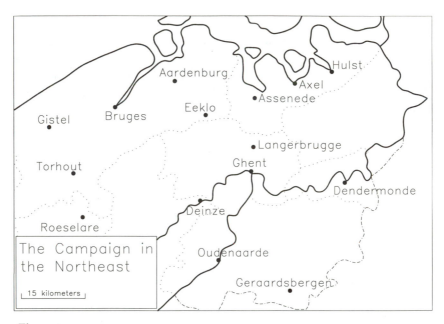

Figure 6

latter would refrain from attacking the city and district. However, since Dendermonde was punished the following year for aiding the rebellion, it must have done more than simply declare willingness to cooperate, but details regarding its support of the rebellion are lacking.[94] In any case, Dendermonde gave up all support of the rebellion around the end of 1325, most likely because it was completely isolated from the rest of rebel Flanders once the districts of Vier Ambachten and Land of Waas were forced back into the loyalist camp.

In summary, the actual military situation in November 1325 was as follows: the rebellion was general in the entire Flemish coastal portion and the rebels controlled the cities of Bruges, Ypres, and, at least for a while, Courtrai. The districts of Vier Ambachten and Land of Waas joined the rebellion in 1325, but under pressure from Ghent were lost to the rebellion. Though some temporary support or at least sympathy came from the towns of Geraardsbergen and Dendermonde, the Land of Aalst never showed much sympathy for the rebellion. Essentially, the Scheldt River formed the actual boundary between rebellious and loyal portions of the county, and this geographical alignment changed very little before 1328. Something resembling a stalemate had descended on Flanders.

The Beginnings of Royal and Papal Intervention

Though the geographical extent of the Flemish rebellion changed very little after late 1325, a significant change took place in the reaction of the outside world to Flemish affairs. Before the end of 1325, most rulers of northwestern Europe apparently viewed it as an essentially internal, local problem, best left to the count of Flanders to manage. Because the revolt persisted with no end in sight, and actually seemed to intensify over time, however, some rulers began to be concerned about the kind of precedent or encouragement it might provide for others to follow a similar course. Consequently, both secular and ecclesiastical lords outside of Flanders became increasingly critical of the Flemish revolt, ultimately condemning it and setting out to find ways of bringing it to an end. In particular, the French king could not remain totally indifferent to the situation in Flanders after the summer of 1325.

For the first two years of the revolt, the king of France seemed rather ambivalent about it. The peasant rebels of Flanders had directed their energies against the count's officers and administration and their allies the great lords, not against the count's overlord, the king. Besides, for centuries, the French monarchs had been seeking ways of gaining more direct control over the territory of Flanders. In the past, the greatest obstacles to such a policy had been the counts themselves as long as they had the support of the lords and patricians, the traditional power brokers of the Flemish countryside and cities. Thus, a challenge to the authority of the Flemish counts might well work to royal advantage over the long term. This helps to explain initial royal aloofness toward the rebellion in Flanders, or at least an apparent policy of allowing matters to play themselves out under close monitoring to see what might become of them. The immediate disadvantage of such a wait-and-see stance, however, was the fact that very little of the royal indemnity imposed by the 1305 treaty of Athis-sur-Orge and subsequent agreements had been paid since the beginning of the revolt.[95] There was always a need for cash, which could be alleviated at least partially by the regular and complete collection of the indemnity and its arrears. This required a count of Flanders who could exercise firm control over the cities and countryside of Flanders, but Count Louis had clearly lost all such control.

Royal ambivalence began to change to an active support for Count Louis during the summer and fall of 1325. In particular the increasing involvement of the city of Bruges in the rebellion changed matters considerably from the monarchy's point of view because of the decidedly anti-royal stance of that city. For example, Bruges attempted to prohibit the circulation of royal coin in Flanders, while its militia seized and garrisoned the castle of Helchin in the bishopric of Tournai, a stronghold supposedly under royal protection.[96]

But there was a larger principle involved in the Flemish revolt that the king of France could ignore no longer. As monarch he was supposed to be the guardian of the established order. Rebellions by ordinary people threatened such an order. First of all, a monarch owed protection to his vassals. When a particularly loyal vassal such as Count Louis of Flanders was driven from most of his principality by ordinary subjects who usurped his rights, appointed functionaries of their own, and ultimately captured and imprisoned him, it reflected very poorly on the image and reputation of the king. In addition, for many in French royal and aristocratic circles, the rebellion in Flanders was a continuing reminder that the humiliating defeat of the aristocratic French cavalry by ordinary Flemings in the Battle of Courtrai in 1302 had never been avenged. Knowing that many of those same Flemings were now directing their outrageous behavior against the count of Flanders, a peer of the French realm, only heightened the pain of that earlier defeat. A growing number of the king's advisers, therefore, were urging military action. Further, Flemish rebels had begun making diplomatic overtures toward England, something previous kings had tried to prevent even the counts of Flanders from undertaking. Finally, what was feared the most seemed to be coming true: ordinary people in other parts of northwestern Europe were beginning to take actions of their own in apparent imitation of Flemish rebels.[97] By 1328, in fact, the author of the *Chronicon* reported that civil unrest had visited parts of Picardy and Francia, the very heartland of the French kingdom.[98]

The worsening situation—the count imprisoned and no real possibility of anyone within Flanders being able to turn back the rebel tide, as well as the fear of rebellion spreading to his own lands—persuaded King Charles IV of France to take action. Shortly after Count Louis' capture, about the time Robert of Cassel began to act as regent, the king sent Alphonse of Spain as an emissary to Flanders to seek a resolution of the crisis. On several occasions during the summer and fall of 1325, Alphonse met with Robert and his rebel allies as well as with John of Namur and his loyalist allies to seek the count's release and the beginning of peace talks, but each time to no avail. The rebels refused to release the count until peace was concluded, while the loyalists refused to talk about peace until the count had been released.[99]

The next move by King Charles IV was to send a letter of instruction on 4 November 1325 to all bishops with jurisdiction over Flemish territory. After reviewing the infractions of the Flemish rebels against public order and accusing them of high treason, he ordered these churchmen to excommunicate the rebels and place the entire area controlled by the rebels under the interdict. Though it may seem odd today for the king rather than the pope to order this, at the time it was deemed appropriate. The papacy had endorsed the series of treaties concluded during the previous 20 years between the former king, Philip IV, and the former count, Robert of Béthune, and had declared that opposition to these treaties deserved punishment by excommunication and the interdict.[100] A letter of Pope John XXII, dated 1 February 1326, indicates that the Church had, in fact, granted Charles IV an extremely important lure that he could dangle in front of the Flemish rebels. The king had obtained permission selectively to lift the interdict whenever individuals or communities returned to obedience.[101] In addition, Charles placed loyalist Ghent under royal protection, loaned the city substantial sums of money, recognized John of Namur as rightful regent of Flanders, and prohibited all trade between rebel Flanders and France.[102] About the same time, he pressured Robert of Cassel by seizing some of the latter's property in northern France,[103] and began making preparations for a military campaign against the Flemish rebels by assembling troops and provisions at Lille and Saint-Omer.

These actions had an immediate effect on the rebel's situation. First of all, Robert of Cassel, acting since June 1325 as regent for the imprisoned Louis at the request of the rebels, though confirmed by Count Louis himself, now began to fear the consequences of continued association with the rebellion. Presumably to forestall further confiscations of his property, he began to look for ways of justifying his behavior to the king. As early as 30 November 1325, he appealed the censures and confiscations applied to him; on 20 March 1326, he attempted to explain his involvement in the Flemish troubles. As a result of these appeals and explanations, delegates of the king of France lifted the censures against Robert of Cassel on 20 March 1326, but from then onward the rebels had to manage without the support of Robert of Cassel and the symbolic legitimacy his regency was supposed to impart.[104]

Religious sanctions produced an interesting split among the clergy of rebel Flanders. Though excommunication and the interdict no doubt moved most priests to honor the sanctions by withholding their services, this was by no means a universal reaction. In April 1326, for example,

Bernard d'Albi, a young French cleric closely associated with the royal court and the Parlement of Paris,[105] was sent by the papacy into Flanders to investigate reports that members of the clergy in the city and district of Bruges had refused to carry out the provisions of the bans of excommunication and interdict. The commissioners who looked into these reports confirmed that at least two clerics were guilty. Nicholas, rector of the church at Klemskerke (15 kilometers west of Bruges) had told his associates to continue their duties because the letter announcing the bans was not authentic. William of Gravelgem, prior of the Augustinian friars in the city of Bruges, had publicly called on the clergy of the city to continue serving parishioners in defiance of the interdict.[106] Unfortunately, there is no way of knowing how many listened to them or whether they included rural priests, though the fact that the papacy authorized an investigation suggests that some must have done so. Presumably as a result of this investigation, Pope John XXII forgave a number of unnamed priests in early 1327 who had admitted to ignoring the Church's bans during late 1325 or early 1326.[107]

In an apparent attempt to break the stalemate that had developed, moderates, mostly from the city of Bruges, began to press for the release of the imprisoned count. Indeed, the author of the *Chronicon* maintained that the people of Bruges began to clamor for the count's release almost as soon as the French king moved against the rebellion.[108] But not everyone believed that releasing Count Louis would be such a good idea, for it would surrender the most effective leverage that the rebels possessed. On the other hand, until the count was in fact set free, there was no chance at all that the interdict or embargo would ever be raised or that anyone would talk with the rebels about peace.

All this suggests, however, that the dissension the author of the *Chronicon* had noticed within the rebel movement two months earlier had begun to develop into an actual split between those who wanted an agreement or compromise and those who believed that agreement or compromise was no longer possible. It was primarily an urban-rural split.

On the one hand, economic sanctions would have affected urban rebels more immediately than their rural allies. Urbanites depended on the reliable supply of agricultural surpluses on the urban market for their daily subsistence, while much of their work was dependent on a regular and plentiful supply of wool; much food and wool, in fact, came from outside of Flanders by the early fourteenth century. In contrast, peasants could always hold onto some basic level of subsistence as long as they had access to land and livestock. On the other hand, urban rebels—protected by city charters, cognizant of the power of their well-organized craft guilds in the past, and already possessing a recognized status in the Flemish political arena—would have been more willing than their rural compatriots to enter into agreements with their enemies. They knew they could survive long enough to take up arms another day if necessary to enforce any agreements entered into. For rural rebels, that possibility would have been much less certain. Peasants had no clearly recognized status as political players; almost any collective activity they undertook in defiance of those who dominated their lives could be condemned as illegal and thus subject to the harshest of punishments. Survival as a convincing movement, therefore, was much more problematic for rural rebels once they put down their arms than it was for urban rebels.

In the end, those seeking agreement or compromise prevailed. Indeed, since he was held by the city of Bruges, the decision to release Count Louis actually may have been taken without consulting rural rebels at all. In any case, on 30 November 1325, Count Louis swore an oath on the Holy Blood in the church of St. Basil at Bruges in which he promised a complete amnesty for all rebels, approval of all ruling measures taken in his name by Robert of Cassel as regent, and the establishment of a meaningful inquiry into the conduct of John of Namur as the self-appointed regent and rival of Robert of Cassel.[109] In exchange for these promises, Count Louis was released the following day, 1 December 1325, and moderates on the rebel side began urging new negotiations in the hope of forestalling a French invasion and removing the economic and religious sanctions placed on Flanders. Some, though, including even the otherwise unsympathetic author of the *Chronicon*, thought the city of Bruges had released the count without obtaining sufficient guarantees that something might actually come of this concession.[110]

Clearly, those who succeeded in gaining the count's release believed that such a gesture, as well as the conditions agreed to by Count Louis at that time, might well form the basis of an eventual agreement or compromise which they might find acceptable. But they soon had reason to question the wisdom of such assumptions. Almost immediately upon his release, Count Louis set out for Paris, determined to obtain the direct military intervention of the king of France that alone might bring the rebellion to an end in his favor. On 1 February 1326 Louis swore an oath to his feudal lord, King Charles IV, in which he promised to conclude no separate peace with his rebellious subjects; if he concluded such a peace, he would have to bear the entire cost of any future expedition that the kingdom of France might have to undertake to bail him out.[111]

Count Louis had thus sworn two oaths in the space of two months which, while not mutually exclusive, represented significantly different positions. In the first, he agreed to many rebel demands and held out the possibility of a peaceful resolution of the crisis; in the second, he entered an agreement with the king of France that was designed ultimately to crush the rebellion. It is perhaps safe to say that he never intended to honor his first oath, extracted, after all, under duress. In any case, it became ever more clear by February 1326 that the French king, at Count Louis' request, intended to invade Flanders with a force massive enough to overpower the rebels. That this was expected at the time in Flanders is suggested by the actions of the magistrates from the rebel town of Veurne, who entreated nearby Ter Duinen Abbey to accept their archives for safe keeping.[112] Increasingly, it seemed, a repeat of the Battle of Courtrai was the most that the Flemish rebels could hope for.[113]

The Peace of Arques

The expected French invasion proved more difficult to set in motion than was first expected. Though Charles IV began almost immediately to mass troops at Lille and Saint-Omer, the invasion was delayed. In fact, increasing English-French tensions, part of the prehistory to the Hundred Years' War, bought time for the Flemish rebels. If the English were to attack in south-western France, as many expected, an invasion of Flanders would represent a second front for French forces, perfect conditions for another resounding defeat of mounted French aristocratic forces at the hands of ordinary Flemish foot soldiers. Thus the king himself authorized negotiations with the Flemish rebels that resulted on 19 April 1326 in a peace, concluded at Arques, near Saint-Omer.[114] Claiming that the continuing rebellion in Flanders was a violation of the 1305 Peace of Athis-sur-Orge and subsequent agreements between France and Flanders, the king of France, not the count of Flanders, appeared as the aggrieved party. As a result, the Peace of Arques was negotiated by representatives of the king and representatives of the cities and districts of Flanders. The count of Flanders was only indirectly involved in the process.

Among other things, the Peace of Arques called for the removal of all new fortresses in the rebel districts, demanded the resumption of all payments owed the king from earlier treaties including all amounts in arrears, condemned all revolutionary innovations as well as the oaths of solidarity that underlay the political power of peasant captains, and restored the authority of Count Louis over Flanders. Many participants in the rebellion were assessed fines or forced to make pilgrimages, while the emigres from the countryside were to have their goods and property restored; the exiled weavers of Ghent, however, would not be allowed to return. The new peace also required the raising of additional sums of money in the rebel cities and districts sufficient to pay the count of Flanders 10,000 lbs. for his troubles and to make restitution for all damage done to churches and monasteries during the revolt. Further, the still unpaid fine of 66,000 lbs. levied by Count Louis against the city of Bruges in 1324 for the burning of Sluis was increased to 100,000 lbs. Finally, the cities of Bruges, Ypres, and Courtrai and the district of Bruges, were fined an additional 200,000 lbs., payable to the royal treasury. In return for all this, Charles IV promised to raise the bans of excommunication and interdict and to end the trade prohibition between France and Flanders.[115]

Notes

1. Arnold Fayen, ed., *Lettres de Jean XXII (1316–1334): textes et analyses*, Analecta Vaticano-Beligica publiés par l'Institut Historique Belge de Rome, II (Rome: M. Bretschneider, 1908), vol. 1, pp. 497–98, no. 1338.

2. Anonymous, *Chronicon comitum Flandrensium*, in *Corpus chronicorum Flandriae, sub auspiciis Leopoldi primi, serenissimi Belgarum regis: recueil des chroniques de Flandre*, vol. 1, J. J. DeSmet, ed., Académie Royale de Belgique, Commission Royale d'Histoire, Mémoires en quarto (Brussels: H. Hayez, 1837) (hearafter cited as *Chronicon*), p. 188: "in unum conceperunt intra se non esse bonum, nobiles inter ipsos mansiones habere fortes, et cum eis habitare, ne forte futuro tempore memores injuriarum sibi illatarum contra eos insurgerent ad vindictam."

3. On testing the limits of the possible, see James C. Scott, *Domination and the Arts of Resistance: Hidden Transcripts* (New Haven, CT: Yale University Press, 1990), pp. 192–97. Rebel opposition to the presence of nobles and others of privilege in the countryside is reminiscent of some categories of publically declared resistance to ideological domination compiled by Scott, p. 198: propagating notions of equality and negating the ruling ideology.

4. Henri Pirenne, ed., *Le soulèvement de la Flandre maritime, 1323–1328, documents inédites*, Académie Royale de Belgique, Commission Royale d'Histoire, Publications in-octavo (Brussels: P. Imbreghts, 1900), no. 4, p. 179, as well as the final sentence on p. 180: "Ende, ware dat sake dat eneghe verdonckerthede jof debaet worde in die vorseide points, die ghewijst ende ghezeid zijn bi mijn here Robracht van Vlaendre ende bi den drien ghoeden steden vorseid, daer verclaerzinghe toebehorde te doene van eneghen pointen, die voren ghewijst zijn, dat het staet ten verclarsene van mijnhere Robracht van Vlaendre ende van den drien ghoeden steden vorseid ende, daer zij 't verclaersen zouden, dat het daer ghehouden moeste bliven."

5. L. Gilliodts-van Severen, *Inventaire des archives de la ville de Bruges: section première, inventaire des chartes*, publié sous les auspices de l'administration comunale (Bruges: E. Gailliard, 1871), vol. 1, p. 348, no. 299; A. Schouteet, *Regesten op de oorkonden van het stadsarchief van Brugge*, vol. 2, *1301–1339*, Brugse geschiedbronnen uitgegeven door het Genootschap voor Geschiedenis "Société d'Émulation" te Brugge met steun van het Gemeentebestuur van Brugge, V (Bruges: Stadsarchief van Brugge, 1978), vol. 2, p. 155, no. 418; J. van Rompaey, "De opstand in het Vlaamse kustland van 1323 tot 1328 en de figuur van Nikolaas Zannekin," in *Nikolaas Zannekin en de Slag bij Kassel, 1328–1978: bijdrage tot de studie van de 14de eeuw en de landelijke geschiedenis van de Westhoek* (Diksmuide, Belgium: Kulturele Raad van Diksmuide, 1978), p. 109.

6. Gilliodts-van Severen, *Inventaire des archives de la ville de Bruges*, vol. 1, pp. 348–49, nos. 298, 301; Schouteet, *Regesten op de oorkonden van het stadsarchief van Brugge*, vol. 2, pp. 155–56, nos. 417, 420.

7. Published in part in Gilliodts-van Severen, *Inventaire des archives de la ville de Bruges*, vol. 1, p. 350, no. 304. See also Schouteet, *Regesten op de oorkonden van het stadsarchief van Brugge*, vol. 2, p.157, no. 423.

8. Gilliodts-van Severen, *Inventaire des archives de la ville de Bruges*, vol. 1, p. 351, no. 305, published a fragment of the act. See also Schouteet, *Regesten op de oorkonden van het stadsarchief van Brugge*, vol. 2, p. 157, no. 424; Sabbe, *Vlaanderen in opstand*, p. 33; van Rompaey, "De opstand in het Vlaamse kustland," p. 110.

9. Van Rompaey, "De opstand in het Vlaamse kustland," p. 111.

10. *Chronicon*, p. 188; Sabbe, *Vlaanderen in opstand*, p. 33. See also Scott, *Domination and the Arts of Resistance*, p. 198, where open descration of status symbols of the dominant is classified as a category of publically declared resistance to status domination.

11. The demands were aimed at the abbeys of St. Peter and St. Bavo at Ghent; see M. Vandermaesen, "Vlaanderen en Henegouwen onder het huis van Dampierre 1244–1384," in *Algemene geschiedenis der Nederlanden*, vol. 2 (Haarlem: Fibula-van Dishoeck, 1982), p. 422; Sabbe, *Vlaanderen in opstand*, p. 35; Pirenne, ed., *Le soulèvement*, p. xviii; Jacques Toussaert, *Le sentiment religieux en Flandre à la fin du moyen âge*, Civilisations d'Hier et d'Aujourd'hui (Paris: Plon, 1963), p. 318.

12. See Toussaert, *Le sentiment religieux en Flandre*, pp. 32, 452, 454.

13. Pirenne, ed., *Le soulèvement*, p. xviii.

14. See the the the text of the Treaty of Arques, of 19 April 1325, in T. De Limburg-Stirum, ed., *Codex diplomaticus Flandriae ab anno 1296 ad usque 1327, ou recueil de documents relatifs aux guerres et dissensions suscitées par Philippe-le-Bel, roi de France, contre Gui de Dampierre, comte de Flandre*, Société d'Émulation pour l'Étude de l'Histoire et des Antiquités de la Flandre (Bruges: De Plancke, 1889), vol. 2, pp. 385–403, no. 356, especially pp. 390–91.

15. Pirenne, ed., *Le soulèvement*, p. xxxv; David Nicholas, *Town and Countryside: Social, Economic, and Political Tensions in Fourteenth-Century Flanders*, Rijksuniversiteit te Gent, Werken uitgegeven door de faculteit van de letteren en wijsbegeerte, 152 (Bruges: De Tempel, 1971), p. 165, note 4.

16. Van Rompaey, "De opstand in het Vlaamse kustland," p. 111; Pirenne, ed., *Le soulèvement*, p. xix.

17. For additional information about these two, see Appendix B, below. On their status within their communities, J. Mertens, "De economische en sociale toestand van de opstandelingen uit het Brugse Vrije wier goederen na de slag bij Cassel (1328) verbeurd verklaard werden," *Revue Belge de Philologie et d'Histoire* 47 (1969), pp. 1131–53; and idem, "Het Brugse Vrije en de opstand van kust-Vlaanderen," *Spieghel historiael* 6 (1971), pp. 306–7.

18. *Chronicon*: p. 188, "primo illi de *Nort-Vrien*, quorum capitaneus erat Sigerus Johannis . . ."; p. 189, "Lambertus *Bonin*, capitaneus praedictus, cum suis et cum illis de *Oost-vrien*. . . ." For the role of assemblies and sworn delegates or proxies, see my discussion in the previous chapter.

19. Vandermaesen, "Vlaanderen en Henegouwen onder het huis van Dampierre," p. 423. Robert of Cassel mentioned the king's order a year later in a statement published in Henri Pirenne, "Un mémoire de Robert de Cassel sur sa participation à la révolte de la Flandre maritime en 1324–1325," *Revue du Nord* 1 (1910), p. 46.

20. *Chronicon*, p. 189; see also Sabbe, *Vlaanderen in opstand*, pp. 35, 37; van Rompaey, "De opstand in het Vlaamse kustland," p. 111.

21. Published in De Limburg-Stirum, ed., *Codex diplomaticus Flandriae*, vol. 2, p. 369, no. 348: "faites punir, grever et constraindre les devantdis chaus du Franc de Bruges, Colin Zannekin et les autres leur aidant et aliiet, en toutes les manières que vous sores et pores, soit par leur maison ardoir, soit par aus ochirre et tuer, soit par aus leur biens et leur terres faire noiier." Pirenne, ed., *Le soulèvement*, p. xx, demonstrates that De Limburg-Stirum dated it incorrectly to 1324. See also the facsimile of the document in van Rompaey, "De opstand in het Vlaamse kustland," p. 112.

22. See Robert of Cassel's statement of a year later in Pirenne, "Un mémoire de Robert de Cassel," pp. 46–47.

23. *Chronicon*, p. 188: ". . . domos popularium incendendo, et quotquot inveniebant ex illis vel perimendo, vel in captivitatem ducendo; et quos sic, vel in bello actuali, vel extra bellum, captivos abduxerant, vel decapitabant eos, vel absque redemptione aliqua supra rotas altas elevabant." See also H. van Werveke, "Vlaanderen en Brabant, 1305–1346: de sociaal-economische achtergrond," in *Algemene geschiedenis der Nederlanden*, vol. 3, *De late middeleeuwen, 1305–477* (Utrecht and Antwerp: De Haan and Standaard Boekhandel, 1951), p. 30; Sabbe, *Vlaanderen in opstand*, p. 36.

24. Vandermaesen, "Vlaanderen en Henegouwen onder het huis van Dampierre," p. 422; Sabbe, *Vlaanderen in opstand*, p. 34.

25. See, for example, Nicholas, *Town and Countryside*, chapters 2 and 3, where he discusses urban-rural relations with regard to textile production, staples markets, and waterways.

26. See, for example, Vandermaesen, "Vlaanderen en Henegouwen onder het huis van Dampierre," p. 422.

27. See the previous chapter for details.

28. Louis' letter to Robert of Cassel is published in De Limburg-Stirum, ed., *Codex diplomaticus Flandriae*, p. 369, no. 348, which fails to include the city of Bruges as among those aiding the rebellion. See also Pirenne, ed., *Le soulèvement*, p. xx, who provides the correct date; Sabbe, *Vlaanderen in opstand*, 36.

29. J. Bovesse, "Le comte de Namur Jean Ier et les événements du comté de Flandre en 1325–1326," *Bulletin de la Commission Royale d'Histoire* 131 (1965), p. 387; van Rompaey, "De opstand in het Vlaamse kustland," p. 111; Pirenne, ed., *Le soulèvement*, p. xix. Nicholas, *Town and Countryside*, p. 106, dates the beginning of involvement by the city of Bruges in the rebellion to 1324, one year too early.

30. *Chronicon*, p. 189: "Et tunc liquido patuit, quod illi de villa Brugensi favebant his popularibus, et eorum consilio dicti populares omnia faciebant."

31. *Chronicon*, pp. 189, 191. See Pirenne, ed., *Le soulèvement*, pp. xix, xxii, who, in turn, influenced others: for example, van Rompaey, "De opstand in het Vlaamse kustland," pp. 113–14; David Nicholas, *Medieval Flanders* (London and New York: Longmans, 1992), p. 214; Sabbe, *Vlaanderen in opstand*, p. 36.

32. F. W. N. Hugenholtz, *Drie boerenopstanden uit de veertiende eeuw: Vlaanderen 1323–1328, Frankrijk 1358, Engeland 1381; onderzoek naar het opstandig bewustzijn* (Haarlem: Tjeenk Willink, 1949), pp. 28–29, 105–8, as we shall see, rightly places the end of formal participation between the city of Bruges and the rural rebellion in April 1326, with the negotiation of the Peace of Arques.

33. David Nicholas, *The Van Arteveldes of Ghent: The Varieties of Vendetta and the Hero in History* (Ithaca, NY: Cornell University Press, 1988), pp. 6–7.

34. See the ordinance of 18 February 1325 published in De Limburg-Stirum, ed., *Codex diplomaticus Flandriae*, p. 370, no. 349.

35. Hugenholtz, *Drie boerenopstanden*, p. 29; and Nicholas, *The Van Arteveldes of Ghent*, p. 10.

36. *Chronicon*, p. 189; "et tunc cessit in vulgare proverbium: 'Non est securum, lupos cum lupis capere, et suorum adminiculo suos complices subjugare.' Ceciderunt ibidem XV viri fortes et animosi, et totidem vulnerati fugerunt ad munitionem, qui sequenti die reddiderunt se captos Sigero Johanni, et ducti sunt Brugas in custodia reservandi." Van Rompaey, "De opstand in het Vlaamse kustland," p. 111, places the battle in February 1325.

37. See Appendix B, below.

38. Published in De Limburg-Stirum, ed., *Codex diplomaticus Flandriae*, p. 369, no. 348: "chaus du Franc de Bruges, Colin Zannekin et autres leur aidant et aliiet." For more information concerning Zannekin, see Appendix B, below.

39. See Count Louis' instructions to Robert in De Limburg-Stirum, ed., *Codex diplomaticus Flandriae*, vol. 2, p. 369, no. 348.

40. *Chronicon*, p. 190.

41. *Chronicon*, p. 190: "Deinde venerunt ad villam Furnensem, quam sine resistentia possederunt, eamque sibi cum toto territorio astrinxerunt protinus per juramenta."

42. Bovesse, "Le comte de Namur Jean Ier et les événements du comté de Flandre en 1325–1326," p. 388.

43. *Chronicon*, pp. 190–91: "cum CCC loricatis stabat in servito comitis"; "cum armatorum nobilium parva multitudine, et peditum pigra et involuntaria."

44. *Chronicon*, p. 191: "et sic retrocedentes salvaverunt se equites universi: populares autem, qui cum ipsis venerant, haec videntes, gavisi sunt valde et protinus aliis popularibus firmiter se fide et juramento astrinxerunt. Hanc audiens victoriam popularium tota occidentalis vicinia, statim venerunt ad eos universi, se astringendo eis firmiter juramento. . . ."

45. Van Rompaey, "De opstand in het Vlaamse kustland," p. 113; Hugenholtz, *Drie boerenopstanden*, pp. 29–30.

46. *Chronicon*, p. 191: "Et mansit aliquibus diebus in villa de *Poperinghen*, non volens ulterius procedere, donec a Brugensibus aliud acciperet in mandatis: eorum etenim nutu omnia faciebat." The author of the *Chronicon* adopted a position that was not unusual during the middle ages. In his comparative study of fourteenth-century peasant revolts in Flanders, France, and England, Hugenholtz, *Drie boerenopstanden*, pp. 28–29, remarks that contemporary observers, convinced that peasants were incapable of making their own rebellions, claimed that urbanites instigated and led all three rebellions.

47. Van Rompaey, "De opstand in het Vlaamse kustland," pp. 113–14.

48. *Chronicon*, p. 191: "Et Nicolaus *Zannekin*, recepto fidelitatis juramento in Casleto ab illis de territorio Casletensi, et ab illis de Balliolo et ejusdem territorio, ordinatisque capitaneis et decurionibus inter eos, processit versus Ypram." See also Pirenne, ed., *Le soulèvement*, p. xxxv.

49. See Appendix B, below.

50. See, for example, *Chronicon*, pp. 192, 198; as well as Bovesse, "Le comte de Namur Jean Ier et les événements du comté de Flandre en 1325–326," p. 388; Sabbe, *Vlaanderen in opstand*, p. 37.

51. *Chronicon*, p. 192: "Nam, heu! quidam pusillanimes, ne dicamus pessimi proditores, fecerunt comitem et Gandenses retrocedere unde venerant in crastinum valde mane, et mox inceperunt de pace facienda tractare."

52. Gilliodts-van Severen, *Inventaire des archives de la ville de Bruges*, vol. 1, p. 355, no. 311; Schouteet, *Regesten op de oorkonden van het stadsarchief van Brugge*, vol. 2, p. 163, no. 440. See also Sabbe, *Vlaanderen in opstand*, p. 37.

53. See Robert of Cassel's statement published in Pirenne, "Un mémoire de Robert de Cassel," p. 47; and Bovesse, "Le comte de Namur Jean Ier et les événements du comté de Flandre en 1325–1326," p. 388.

54. *Chronicon*, p. 192. See also van Rompaey, "De opstand in het Vlaamse kustland," 114. Robert of Cassel referred to this peace effort in a statement published in Pirenne, "Un mémoire de Robert de Cassel," p. 47, but Pirenne, note 1, confused this attempt with the earlier arbitration of April 1324.

55. Published in Pirenne, ed., *Le soulèvement*, appendix 5, pp. 180–82.

56. Bonin was one of several peasant captains involved in a battle at Assenede, in the Vier Ambachten, sometime before the end of November 1325; see *Chronicon*, p. 199.

57. *Chronicon*, p. 193: "Sed populares semper insequebantur arbitros praedictos multitudine armata Furnis et alibi, et cum verbis contumeliosis quaerebant obtinere intentum, specialiter super correctione cujusdam homicidii super mare perpetrati per quosdam nobiles super inimicis suis." On the incident at Zuidkote, see *Chronicon*, p. 191; Sabbe, *Vlaanderen in opstand*, p. 38.

58. Mass demonstrations of this sort, as distinct from actual rebellion or revolt, is a common form of resistance to domination; see Scott, *Domination and the Arts of Resistance*, p. 198.

59. *Chronicon*, p. 193: "Ad quam diem populares in tanta venerunt multitudine . . . omnes armati, quod arbitri hoc audientes non fuerunt ausi comparere ad assignatum diem: nam videbatur, quod eis incipiebant iterum insanire populares."

60. See, for example, Pirenne, ed., *Le soulèvement*, pp. xxi–xxii; van Werveke, "Vlaanderen en Brabant," p. 31; and van Rompaey, "De opstand in het Vlaamse kustland," p. 114.

61. The information supplied by Bovesse, "Le comte de Namur Jean Ier et les événements du comté de Flandre en 1325–1326," pp. 387–99, is crucial for what follows.

62. *Chronicon*, p. 193: "Quod factum ipsi populares retorquebant in gravamen communitatis commissum, et volebant, quod simpliciter corrigeretur ad voluntatem eorum."

63. *Chronicon*, pp. 191–92.

64. Bovesse, "Le comte de Namur Jean Ier et les événements du comté de Flandre en 1325–1326," p. 395; Sabbe, *Vlaanderen in opstand*, pp. 38, 40.

65. Bovesse, "Le comte de Namur Jean Ier et les événements du comté de Flandre en 1325–1326," pp. 394–95; M. Vandermaesen, "Auxonne (Baudet, Baudot) Guillaume d' (Willem van)," *Nationaal biografisch woordenboek*, Koninklijke Academiën van België (Brussels: Paleis der Academiën, 1979), vol. 8, cols. 8–14.

66. Vandermaesen, "Cassel, Robrecht, heer van," cols. 86–87. See also Pirenne, ed., *Le soulèvement*, p. xxiii; Sabbe, *Vlaanderen in opstand*, p. 40. Bovesse, "Le comte de Namur Jean Ier et les événements du comté de Flandre en 1325–1326," pp. 389–99, provides a thorough discussion of the plot. Robert of Cassel, in a later statement published in Pirenne, "Un mémoire de Robert de Cassel," p. 47, claimed the plot was against his life.

67. For example, the city of Ypres increased the number of guards and crossbow shooters to protect the city by a factor of three between November 1324 and February 1325, and these numbers remained high into the summer; see G. Des Marez, and E. de Sagher, eds., *Comptes de la ville d'Ypres de 1297 à 1329*, Académie Royale de Belgique, Commission Royale d'Histoire (Brussels: P. Imbreghts, 1913), vol. 2, pp. 443–47.

68. *Chronicon*, 193.

69. *Chronicon*, p. 193. See also van Rompaey, "De opstand in het Vlaamse kustland," p. 114.

70. Bovesse, "Le comte de Namur Jean Ier et les événements du comté de Flandre en 1325–1326," p. 400. Sabbe, *Vlaanderen in opstand*, places the conflict a week earlier, on 13 and 14 June.

71. Though the account of this engagement in the *Chronicon*, p. 194, is very brief, some aspects of it resemble elements of another hastily organized battle at Ghent on 2 April 1302, during which ordinary people, in response to the banging of pots and pans, took to the streets in sufficient numbers to inflict a similiar, humiliating defeat on their mounted opponents; see W. P. Blockmans, *Een middeleeuwse vendetta: Gent 1300* (Houten, NL: Unieboek-De Haan, 1987), pp. 110–16.

72. Bovesse, "Le comte de Namur Jean Ier et les événements du comté de Flandre en 1325–1326," p. 400; Sabbe, *Vlaanderen in opstand*, p. 44.

73. H. Pirenne, "Documents relatifs à l'histoire de Flandre pendant la première moitié du XIVe siècle," *Bulletin de la Commission Royale d'Histoire* 5th ser., 7 (1897), p. 477–93; Nicholas, *Medieval Flanders*, p. 131; Sabbe, *Vlaanderen in opstand*, p. 45.

74. J. Merlevede, *De Ieperse stadsfinancien (1280–1330): bijdrage tot de studie van een Vlaamse stad*, Centrum voor Sociale Structuren en Economische Conjunctuur, Vrije Universiteit Brussel (Brussels: Uitgaven van de Vrije Universiteit, [1980]), p. 59; Nicholas, *Medieval Flanders*, p. 9.

75. De Limburg-Stirum, ed., *Codex diplomaticus Flandriae*, vol 2, p. 371, no. 350: "usque ad revocationem ipsius comitis;" "et predicti burgimagistri, scabini et consules, pro se et tota communitate ville Brugensis, etiam pro villa Yprensi, pro franco territorio Brugensi et pro omnibus aliis suis confederatis, et qui cum ipsis Brugensibus et eisdem prestiterunt juramenta." See also Robert of Cassel's statement, published in Pirenne, "Un mémoire de Robert de Cassel," p. 48.

76. Bovesse, "Le comte de Namur Jean Ier et les événements du comté de Flandre en 1325–1326," pp. 401–15, concludes it was a forged document.

77. De Limburg-Stirum, ed., *Codex diplomaticus Flandriae*, vol. 2, p. 372, no. 350: "revocavit et revocat expresse auctoritatem et potestatem quascunque, si quas retroactis temporibus concesserit comiti Namurcensi, super amministratione, gubernatione vel regimine predicti Flandrie comitatus."

78. *Chronicon*, pp. 195–96; Vandermaesen, "Cassel, Robrecht, heer van," col. 87; Bovesse, "Le comte de Namur Jean Ier et les événements du comté de Flandre en 1325–1326," pp. 409–10; Sabbe, *Vlaanderen in opstand*, p. 46.

79. Bovesse, "Le comte de Namur Jean Ier et les événements du comté de Flandre en 1325–1326," p. 416.

80. *Chronicon*, p. 198; Van Rompaey, "De opstand in het Vlaamse kustland," pp. 115–16; Sabbe, *Vlaanderen in opstand*, p. 46.

81. Pirenne, ed., *Le soulèvement*, p. xxii.

82. *Chronicon*, pp. 190, 195.

83. *Chronicon*, p. 198; Sabbe, *Vlaanderen in opstand*, p. 47.

84. *Chronicon*, p. 198.

85. Sabbe, *Vlaanderen in opstand*, p. 48.

86. *Chronicon*, p. 199: "congregata virorum magna multitudene de toto Franco armatorum electorum." For the date, see Bovesse, "Le comte de Namur Jean Ier et les événements du comté de Flandre en 1325–1326," p. 421.

87. See Appendix B, below.

88. *Chronicon*, p. 199; van Rompaey, "De opstand in het Vlaamse kustland," p. 116; Sabbe, *Vlaanderen in opstand*, pp. 48, 50. J. F. Verbruggen, *The Art of Warfare in Western Europe During the Middle Ages: From the Eighth Century to 1340*, Sumner Willard and S. C. M. Southern, trans., Europe in the Middle Ages: Selected Studies, 1 (Amsterdam and New York: North Holland Publishing, 1977), p. 162, says the rebels drew themselves up into the tightly packed crown formation that had been so successful at the Battle of Courtrai (1302), but the loyalist cavalry was able to break it up.

89. *Chronicon*, p. 197; Bovesse, "Le comte de Namur Jean Ier et les événements du comté de Flandre en 1325–1326," p. 416.

90. Erik Thoen, *Landbouwekonomie en bevolking in Vlaanderen gedurende de late middeleeuwen en het begin van de moderne tijden; testregio: de kasselrijen van Oudenaarde en Aalst (eind 13de–eerste helft 16de eeuw)*, Belgisch Centrum voor Landelijke Geschiedenis, no. 90 (Ghent: Belgisch Centrum voor Landelijke Geschiedenis, 1988), vol. 1, p. 43.

91. *Chronicon*, p. 197; Sabbe, *Vlaanderen in opstand*, p. 47; van Werveke, "Vlaanderen en Brabant," p. 32; van Rompaey, "De opstand in het Vlaamse kustland," p. 117; Bovesse, "Le comte de Namur Jean Ier et les événements du comté de Flandre en 1325–1326," p. 417.

92. Bovesse, "Le comte de Namur Jean Ier et les événements du comté de Flandre en 1325–1326," p. 417.

93. De Limburg-Stirum, ed., *Codex diplomaticus Flandriae*, vol. 2, p. 373, no. 351: "dat wy ne gheene viande myns heeren van Vlaendre, myns heer Robbrechts van Vlaenderen ende sghemeens lands houden, ghedoghen noch sousteneren ne zullen . . . zo begheren wy end verzouken, dat men hiermede zal laten de poert ende ons Joncheren land van Denremonde zitten in rusten ende in pais."

94. Van Rompaey, "De opstand in het Vlaamse kustland," p. 116.

95. Hugenholtz, *Drie boenenopstanden*, p. 30.

96. De Limburg-Stirum, ed., *Codex diplomaticus Flandriae*, vol. 2, p. 376, no. 352; Sabbe, *Vlaanderen in opstand*, p. 50.

97. De Limburg-Stirum, ed., *Codex diplomaticus Flandriae*, vol. 2, p. 375, no. 352: "turbato ordine regiminis universi."

98. *Chronicon*, 203: "ne, si terminos suos exirent, attrahere sibi possent communitates alias Picardiae et Franciae, et sic magnam confusionem facere nobilibus atque regno." See Pirenne, ed., *Le soulèvement*, pp. xxiii–xxiv.

99. See Robert of Cassel's statement, published in Pirenne, "Un mémoire de Robert de Cassel," pp. 48–49; Bovesse, "Le comte de Namur Jean Ier et les événements du comté de Flandre en 1325–326," p. 410; Sabbe, *Vlaanderen in opstand*, pp. 46–47; as well as *Chronicon*, pp. 196–97.

100. See, for example, Fayen, ed., *Lettres de Jean XXII*, vol. I, no. 411 (26 April 1317), pp. 145–46.

101. Fayen, ed., *Lettres de Jean XXII*, vol. 2, part 1, pp. 19–20, no. 1691.

102. Published in De Limburg-Stirum, ed., *Codex diplomaticus Flandriae*, vol. 2, pp. 374–78, no. 352. See also Sabbe, *Vlaanderen in opstand*, p. 48.

103. See Pirenne, ed., *Le soulèvement*, appendix 6, p. 183, in which Robert of Cassel authorized the payment of 800 lbs. (tournais) to the royal treasury to secure his property at Perche, in northern France, that had been seized because of his participation in the Flemish rebellion.

104. See the documents published in De Limburg-Stirum, ed., *Codex diplomaticus Flandriae*, vol. 2, pp. 378–84, nos. 353–55.

105. M. Vandermaesen, "Albi, Bernard d'," *Nationaal biografisch woordenboek*, Koninklijke Academiën van België, vol. 8 (Brussels: Paleis der Academiën, 1979), cols. 1–3.

106. The authorization for this investigation, dated 13 April 1326, is published in Fayen, ed., *Lettres de Jean XXII*, vol. 2, part 1, pp. 30–33, no. 1718. See also Sabbe, *Vlaanderen in opstand*, p. 103, note 224.

107. Fayen, ed., *Lettres de Jean XXII*, vol. 2, part 1, pp. 108–11, no. 1935 (31 March 1327). More serious, however, was the case of Peter de Senebeke, the priest of an unspecified place in rebel Flanders, who was later pursued by the Inquisition because he had openly opposed the Church's sanctions and showed no remorse for having done so. The authorization to pursue Senebeke, dated 28 November 1329, is

published in ibid, vol. 2, part 1, pp. 349–50, no. 2594. In addition, the count of Flanders confiscated property from a priest who lived at Schoondijke (about 28 kilometers northeast of Bruges, in The Netherlands today), presumably because of his association with the rebellion; see J. Mertens, ed., "Les confiscations dans la châtellenie du Franc de Bruges après la bataille de Cassel," *Bulletin de la Commission Royale d'Histoire* 134 (1968), p. 251: "Maes, f. Alard, prestres, 1 maison." See also Hugenholtz, *Drie boerenopstanden*, pp. 124–25.

108. *Chronicon*, p. 200: "Oportuit ergo consequenter, quod Brugenses ad clamorem populi comitem liberarent, et ipsum abire permitterent liberum et sine cautione quacumque, nisi quod eis indulsit injurias sibi factas in persona sua, et cum eis juravit, promittens se esse bonum dominum, dum tamen sibi essent populus subditus et fidelis."

109. The count carefully outlined the terms of his release in a letter he issued on 8 February 1327, on the occasion of his next visit to the city of Bruges, published in De Limburg-Stirum, ed., *Codex diplomaticus Flandriae*, vol. 2, pp. 405–8, no. 359.

110. *Chronicon*, p. 200: "sine cautione quacumque"; van Werveke, "Vlaanderen en Brabant," p. 32.

111. Van Rompaey, "De opstand in het Vlaamse kustland," pp. 120, 132.

112. Sabbe, *Vlaanderen in opstand*, p. 51; Pirenne, ed., *Le soulèvement*, pp. xxiv–xxv.

113. Van Rompaey, "De opstand in het Vlaamse kustland," p. 120; Pirenne, ed., *Le soulèvement*, p. xiv.

114. Van Rompaey, "De opstand in het Vlaamse kustland," p. 121; Sabbe, *Vlaanderen in opstand*, p. 52.

115. The text of the Treaty of Arques is published in De Limburg-Stirum, ed., *Codex diplomaticus Flandriae*, vol. 2, pp. 385–403, no. 356. See also Sabbe, *Vlaanderen in opstand*, pp. 52–53.

4. Stalemate, Invasion, and Victors' Vengeance

The Peace of Arques (April 1326), with its penalties more severe even than the Peace of Athis-sur-Orge (1305), seems more like a capitulation than an agreement. Yet a significant group of rebels, primarily city folk, were prepared to pay the price.[1] The list of those who subscribed to the Peace of Arques includes the names of forty-seven citizens of the city of Bruges as well as many others representing the cities and districts of Bruges, Ypres, and Courtrai.[2] Louis of Nevers, count of Flanders, immediately sent his bailiffs and other officials back into the principality to reoccupy the posts they had been forced to abandon in the rebel cities and districts and to set about reestablishing the central government's authority. Louis himself remained in France, seemingly in no hurry to return to the site of his recent humiliation and incarceration.[3]

Though many Flemings resigned themselves to the Peace of Arques, it brought no genuine peace to the county. Perhaps its most important achievement was ending the close cooperation that had existed between the rural rebels and the rebel cities of Bruges and Ypres during much of 1325. For example, there is no evidence that Bruges ever again played the important role in the rural rebellion that it did during the second half of 1325.[4] Though some individuals from Bruges and Ypres continued an informal or unofficial participation, official involvement of these cities in the peasant revolt was limited after November 1325 to maintaining relations with rural rebels but not supplying any direct aid or support.

The negotiations leading up to the Peace in April 1326 were conducted on the Flemish side by magistrates of the rebel cities and by the officials of the count who had been driven from the rural districts. Completely excluded from all deliberations were the true leaders of the rural revolt, the captains such as Lambert Bonin, Segher Janssone, and Nikolaas Zannekin, bound to their constituents by oaths of solidarity sworn at popular assemblies. As a result, while the rebel cities including Bruges and Ypres ended their hostilities, the rural rebellion was scarcely affected by the Peace of Arques.

Peasants in rebel districts of Flanders simply refused to accept a settlement that had been negotiated by their enemies without their participation. Their captains continued in their political functions, while groups of armed rebels systematically prevented bailiffs and other officials of the count as well as their supporters from returning. Within a few days of its imposition, therefore, the Peace of Arques was thwarted. Most of the cities and towns within the rebel districts, if they did not actively support the rebellion, at least learned to live with the situation and maintained some semblance of normal relations with rebel peasant regimes.[5]

Meanwhile, peace and tranquility were almost as elusive in the cities and towns that accepted the Peace of Arques as they were in the rebel countryside. There always had been considerable sympathy among ordinary urban people for the rural rebellion, especially among the rank and file of the craft guilds. But most cities and towns within the rebel districts, including Bruges and Ypres, now had new sets of magistrates which, at the very least, included coalitions of craft-guild leaders and patricians who had not been part of the former ruling oligarchies. Not surprisingly, those members of the old conservative oligarchies who tried to return to their former positions after the Peace of Arques received a cool reception at best, and in most cases they faced outright hostility. The primary reason for agreeing to the Peace of Arques had been to bring an end to religious and economic sanctions imposed by the king of France, not to restore the old guard to power. None of the new urban regimes was eager to begin paying the enormous fines that the new treaty called for, while the ordinary people of the cities and towns who bore the primary tax burden were adamantly opposed to additional levies for such purposes. In all likelihood, therefore, very few provisions of the Peace of Arques were actually being carried out.

Moreover, relations between the cities of Bruges and Ghent remained extremely contentious during the spring and summer of 1326 despite the cessation of most hostilities since the end of the previous year. Ghent had become the citadel of reaction, with its conservative oligarchy more firmly in control of the city's government than ever before. All internal dissent had been effectively stifled the year before with the mass execution or banishment of rebellious weavers, while the ever-increasing numbers of emigres from both the cities and districts of rebel Flanders only bolstered such reactionary tendencies.[6] Neither the ruling coalitions nor the ordinary people of the cities and towns of rebel Flanders were willing to cooperate with the city of Ghent to any significant degree.

Stalemate

When Count Louis finally returned to Flanders on 12 September 1326, five days before the fourth anniversary of his accession to the countship, there was very little for him to celebrate. Granted, he was not imprisoned as he had been on his third anniversary, and the armed truce between the cities of Ghent and Bruges seemed to be holding for the moment. But his rural subjects persisted in their refusal to allow county officials to return to their former posts in most of the districts. In fact, Louis' authority to rule thus far had been accepted by most Flemings for only fourteen out of forty-eight months in power, less than thirty percent of the time. He had also learned by this time that depending on the French monarch for assistance held little immediate promise, even when the monarch was his wife's uncle. After all, no sooner had he promised the king in early 1326 that he would not make a separate peace with the rebels than the king, without consulting him, made his own peace with the rebel cities and towns, if not the rebel districts. The promised military assistance, meanwhile, had been postponed indefinitely. A somewhat wiser Louis, therefore, decided to seek a resolution of the stalemate in Flanders by himself.

By this time, Count Louis had long abandoned any notion of negotiating or coming to terms with the peasant rebels. Ever since he had stacked his *raad* or governing council with nobles opposed to negotiating in early June 1325, his policy had been one designed to crush the peasant rebellion. But given such a goal, his practical options remained few in number. So far he could depend only on the support of aristocratic emigres and the city of Ghent, but this combination had already proved itself ill-suited to the task. His aristocratic warriors, while capable of remarkable brutality when numbers were in their favor, proved to be cowardly and ineffective when confronted with the possibility of real danger.[7] Furthermore, though the well-disciplined militia of Ghent would protect the city against most assaults, it could not be counted on to venture far outside the city's immediate hinterland to crush the rural rebellion. Louis' only chance of regaining control of his entire county was with a united front of the cities, especially the three great cities of Ghent, Bruges, and Ypres.

It is within this context that we must place the series of discussions that Count Louis undertook with the cities of Flanders from October to December 1326 and again in the early months of 1327.[8] Among other things, he attempted to court Bruges by not insisting on the strict observance of the Peace of Arques. During February 1327, he went so far as to renew the oath he had sworn just prior to his release by his captors in late 1325—a complete amnesty for all rebels, approval of all ruling measures taken in his name by Robert of Cassel as regent in 1325, and the establishment of a meaningful inquiry into the conduct of John of Namur, the self-appointed regent and rival of Robert of Cassel.[9]

The fact that Louis was willing to reaffirm this oath more than a year after he first swore it indicates the degree to which his options remained limited.[10] Probably about this same time, he concluded a curious and ultimately ineffective agreement with representatives from Ghent, Bruges and Ypres, as well as the craft guilds of the county, by which he promised to reside in Flanders, to appoint only Flemings to county offices, and to subject Flemings only to the judgments of local courts with actual jurisdiction over their places of residence. In return the cities and guilds forgave the count for following bad advice.[11] In the end, however, little came from these negotiations primarily because the magistrates of Bruges and Ypres feared that an agreement could serve only to expand the political influence of the conservative oligarchy of Ghent and the always dangerous John of Namur and his noble party. Some time after February 1327, therefore, Louis concluded that further talks were useless and once again sought assistance from the French monarchy.

When he returned to Paris in early 1327 in search of royal assistance, Count Louis left the task of resisting the revolt to the loyalist forces of Ghent. In fact, much of 1327 was spent in a bitter propaganda battle between the count and the conservative magistrates of loyal Ghent on the one side and the leaders of Bruges, Ypres, and their allied towns and cities on the other, with each party accusing the other of bad faith, breaking of agreements, and refusal to talk. Louis and the loyalists tried to use such charges to convince the king's council of the need for French military intervention in Flanders to restore his authority, while the leaders of the opposition used the same kinds of charges to counter that argument. All the while, Louis himself was coming increasingly under the influence of what can be described as the Ghent party with the appointment of members of the family of the castellan of Ghent to his *raad* or governing council, and this only made cooperation between the city of Ghent and the cities of Ypres and Bruges more remote than ever.[12]

A rapprochement between the great cities became even more unlikely in February 1328 when Bruges came under the direction of the radical party led by the Willem de Deken, a hotel keeper and broker who had long been a political figure in the city. His first involvement with the rebellion had been as a representative of Bruges on the arbitration commission in Veurne district in early 1324. By 1328, however, he and his party seemed intent on establishing a new regime in Flanders, essentially independent of the count's authority. During the summer of 1328 he even attempted to obtain English support for the project by suggesting to King Edward III of England that he declare himself the king of France and thus overlord of Flanders. Even though Willem de Deken involved himself primarily in urban matters, especially in ensuring that the small cities followed the leadership of Bruges, he also allied the city once again with rebels in the countryside.[13]

Meanwhile, the rural revolt continued without significant interruption. Peasant rebels quickly regained control of the districts of Bruges, Veurne, Bergues, Bourbourg, Cassel, Bailleul, Ypres, and Courtrai, driving loyalist magistrates and their supporters from the districts and seizing their properties. Once again the rebel administration pioneered during the first phase was reinstituted and continued to exercise public authority until the final, decisive battle at Cassel in August 1328. The general captains of the districts, who replaced the count's bailiffs, planned and coordinated rebel actions, while the local captains, replacing the count's *ammans*, served as the links between individual communities and the general captains. Peasants continued to collect taxes, convene courts, issue verdicts, make disbursements of public funds, and much more.[14] Ironically, we know much less about the general progress and far more about certain local details of the revolt after the Peace of Arques than before.

Some time after the suppression of the Flemish revolt, likely during 1329, a special commission looked into the losses and damages that certain individuals had suffered at the hands of rebels. This commission took testimony in the districts of Bourbourg and Bergues, presumably to determine which victims of the rebellion, if any, ought to receive compensation at public expense. All complainants appearing before the commission based their appeals for compensation at least partially on the assertion that they had suffered precisely because they had chosen to honor the Peace of Arques, though in some cases such a claim was challenged by others. In giving their testimony, however, the witnesses also revealed interesting details concerning the last phase of the revolt.

First of all, testimony given before the damages commission provides valuable information about two additional peasant captains, this time from the district of Bergues, who took their places alongside Lambert Bonin and Segher Janssone from the district of Bruges and Nikolaas Zannekin from the district of Veurne. Jacob Peyt served as a captain of the entire district of

Bergues at least from early 1326, around the time of the signing of the Peace of Arques, until his assassination at the end of 1327. Winnoc le Fiere succeeded Peyt and remained captain of Bergues district until the end of the revolt; he fell in the Battle of Cassel in August 1328.[15] Though Peyt must have been a native of the district of Bergues, it is difficult to attach him to a particular rural community; Coudekerque merely seems the most likely. Winnoc le Fiere, Peyt's successor, came from the parish of Hoymille (Bergues district).

Testimony before the same commission also provides some details of specific rebel activities. For example, in the district of Bergues, peasants took action once more against Ghis du Boos, a former magistrate for the district and the owner of considerable property near the town of Dunkirk. As we saw in chapter two, du Boos had been forced into the prison of the city of Bergues for twenty-one weeks during the initial phase of the revolt. While we do not know how he fared during the second phase, he was driven into exile in early 1326. According to his testimony, citizens of the rebel town of Dunkirk and peasants from the district of Bergues burned his manor house near Dunkirk and carried off his stored crops, his livestock, and his movable possessions while he was in exile, for which he now requested compensation. Jehan de Saint-Nicholay and Jehan Colin, both of Bourbourg district, asked compensation for burned houses and the confiscation of large quantities of crops and other possessions, though others challenged both of these requests. In particular, several witnesses claimed that de Saint-Nicholay had gone along with the rebellion for more than a year after the Peace of Arques and that those who had attacked his property were simply brigands and had not acted in the name of the rebellion.[16]

The remaining six complainants to testify before the damages commission were close associates of Pieron de le Dielf or Pieter van der Delft, the count's bailiff of Bergues district, and all were involved in what appear to have been confrontations concerning provisions of the Peace of Arques in the city of Bergues and in Hondschoote, on the eastern edge of the district. Benoit li Brol, according to allegations by his relatives, died when he was attacked by a large group of peasants in Bergues in February 1327. At one time or another in 1326 or 1327, Jehan li Vinc, Louwers Damman, Wautier le Scridere, Jehan Bankinoet, and Th. de Vinc were each driven from Hondschoote and sought sanctuary either in the *steen* or keep, which the bailiff continued to hold for some time, or in the church of the city of Bergues before heading off into exile.[17] According to the requests that they made for compensation, some of these exiles appear to have been extremely wealthy.

One of the most interesting features of the attacks on the property of exiles was the manner in which it was done—in a surprisingly orderly fashion, without looting. Anything of value was appropriated for the common good. For example, in the attack on the property of du Boos, the manor house was burned so that its bricks could be requisitioned for the fortifications of the city of Bergues, with the remainder going to citizens of Dunkirk and the rural district. Thousands of sheaves of wheat and oats, large quantities of vetch, livestock, equipment, and the contents of the house removed before the fire were seized by Jacob Peyt acting on the "order of the commons of the castellany [district] of Bergues" and sold or distributed in an orderly fashion. Damman, meanwhile, lost the contents of five houses, a stand of wood, stored crops, tools and equipment, and the production of some 66 hectares (about 165 acres) of land, all seized "on behalf of the district" by Jacob Peyt and his helpers. In these and other cases, the actions amounted to a redistribution of wealth confiscated not for individual enrichment but for purposes determined by common consent.[18]

Unfortunately, despite the existence of evidence concerning specific local peasant actions in Bergues and Bourbourg districts, it is very difficult to reconstruct what was happening in Flanders generally between April 1326 and August 1328. For example, the author of the *Chronicon* who had provided so much of the underlying narrative for the period leading up to the Peace of Arques, became extremely closemouthed thereafter. He dedicated less than one-tenth as much space to the 25 months of the revolt immediately following the Peace as he did for the preceding 24 months. In fact, he jumped over much of the period from 1326 to 1328 with the single remark that the "plague" of insurrection lasted for two more years, raging so violently that people became disgusted with life itself.[19] Nor were there any arbitration proceedings that might have brought some of the larger issues into sharper focus as they did for the earlier phases. All that we can be certain of is that little changed in geographical alignments.[20]

The quality of the information supplied by the author of the *Chronicon* declined seriously after the Peace of Arques as well. Until early 1326, he had always been well-informed about what was going on in Flanders, and his information was very reliable. Most of what he related could be corroborated by other, independent sources of information. For the last phase of the peasant revolt, however, he became ill-informed by comparison, and on a number of occasions other evidence suggests that he was simply wrong. For example, he made a series of errors with regard to the life and activities of the peasant captain, Jacob Peyt.[21] Not only did he render Peyt's name as

Jacobus Pric, but he also incorrectly identified him as a captain from the city of Bruges, while all other sources clearly make him a captain from the district of Bergues; he made the same mistake with Peyt's successor, Winnoc le Fiere. In addition, the passage in which he remarked that the revolt lasted an additional two years appeared right after his description of Peyt's death; independent sources clearly indicate, however, that Peyt was still alive in November 1327, while the author himself said later that the revolt ended by early 1329, about 15 months later.[22]

Because the author of the *Chronicon* was a monk, it is highly likely that he depended on clerical contacts within Flanders for much of his information, contacts that may have been broken after the Peace of Arques. On the other hand, a striking change of tone suggests another explanation. Though he had been opposed to the rebellion from the beginning, he had nevertheless discussed what happened, at least until the Peace of Arques (April 1326). Thereafter, he became totally dismissive, almost as though the revolt had become too evil or horrible for words. Whatever the reasons for the omissions, errors, and change of tone in the *Chronicon*, however, they have seriously affected how historians since then have viewed the last phase of the peasant revolt of Flanders.

Rebel Extremism or Elite Propaganda?

According to most historians who have given it serious consideration, the leaders of the peasant revolt of Flanders pursued goals and employed tactics during its last two years that were unacceptable to increasing numbers of people—in other words, the movement supposedly lost touch with its constituents. Specifically, they identify greater anti-clericalism and heightened violence, including horrible peasant atrocities, as the primary evidence of the movement's growing "extremism." There also is general agreement that the flight of significant numbers of "moderates" from the rebellion was somehow related to such presumed extremism, though whether as cause or as effect is not clearly established.[23]

While I agree that some in fact abandoned the revolt after the Peace of Arques, the evidence for the revolt taking on a more extreme character is not terribly convincing. Certainly, some of the issues became more sharply drawn over time leaving much less room for ambivalence, but the primary pressures behind the flight of the moderates must be found outside the movement. The Church's bans of excommunication and interdict and the

French king's massing of troops along the border forced people to choose sides in a way they had not really had to before. For the first time since the peasant revolt began, there were significant risks associated with defying traditional authorities, because both Church and king began construing anything less than full support for the Peace of Arques as highly suspect. As a result, all those not fully committed to the movement, those who would back only perceived winners as well as those lacking in personal courage, now began to do just as Robert of Cassel had done in late 1325. They began to put as much distance as they could between themselves and the ongoing rebellion so that they might save their property, their lives, and their souls once the rebellion was crushed.

We should keep in mind, however, that peasants and their captains had been systematically excluded from all deliberations leading up to the Peace of Arques and that the Peace itself called for nothing less than a complete capitulation. Not surprisingly, abandoning the rebellion now began to carry its own set of risks. If acceptance of the Peace of Arques became the symbol of submission and loyalty to the traditional authorities, it just as clearly marked off those who, by such submission, had declared themselves to be the enemies of the people and their captains. It is quite understandable, therefore, that rebels might now include them among those worthy of punishment. And indeed, the nine attacks referred to above in the districts of Bergues and Bourbourg, revealed by the testimony taken by a special damages commission, were planned and carried out by peasant rebels and their captains specifically because the victims had decided to honor the Peace of Arques.[24] Clearly, the time for fence-sitting had passed, but this does not by itself prove that the rebellion had lost touch with its constituents. In fact, any middle ground that might have existed until then had been removed not by the rebels but by those trying to impose the Peace of Arques.

Looking to outside pressures rather than supposed extremism within the rebellion as the primary reasons for the flight of the so-called moderates does not necessarily mean that the movement remained free of extremism during the last two years. After all, if the moderates abandoned the rebellion presumably only the more radical or determined elements remained. The entire case for rebel extremism depends primarily on an uncritical reading of two consecutive passages in the *Chronicon*.

First of all, the author of the *Chronicon* maintained that rebels condemned certain rich people to death because they held the lords in greater esteem than the communities from which they derived their living, and they forced close relatives of the condemned to carry out the death sentences.[25] Unfortunately, he provided no time or place for these actions, nor did he indicate how often this might have been done—all very uncharacteristic of the detailed and precise information found in most of his preceding descriptions of the rebellion. Indeed, the entire passage has the quality of unsubstantiated rumor about it. Though many have quoted this passage from the *Chronicon* as proof of heightened levels of violence and of peasant atrocities,[26] no independent sources corroborate it. I do not mean to suggest that the rebel peasants were nonviolent or that they never committed atrocities, only that this particular passage by itself alleges much but proves little. Indeed, most atrocities that can clearly linked to the last phase of the rebellion seem to have been committed by urban rebels.[27]

In the very next passage, the author of the *Chronicon* addressed the issue of anti-clericalism by describing the actions of Jacob Peyt (misspelled as Pric), captain of the district of Bergues (wrongly identified as a captain of Bruges).[28] He reported that Peyt claimed never to have set foot inside a church, that he would happily see the last priest in the world hanged, and that he would expel all priests from the land and confiscate their property. The author added that the judgment of God against Peyt was carried out when men from Veurne killed him, but frivolous people, seduced by the devil, began to revere him as a saint. For this reason, the bishop of Thérouanne later (most likely in December 1328 or January 1329) condemned Peyt as an arch-heretic, exhumed his bones, and burned them in a public ceremony.[29]

Certainly, there can be no doubt that anti-clericalism was an important part of the peasant revolt after the Peace of Arques, especially after 6 April 1327, the date on which Flanders was placed under the ecclesiastical sanctions of excommunication and interdict once again.[30] Other sources besides the *Chronicon* also indicate anti-clericalism, and they also link it largely to the person of Jacob Peyt. But the picture that such sources present differs drastically from the one offered by the author of the *Chronicon*.[31] It appears that Peyt's anti-clericalism was not only very popular but also highly calculated and tailored to counter certain specific actions by the Church. In a letter of 1329, Jean Lain, a priest of the town of Dunkirk and deacon of the city and countryside of Bergues, recounted an incident from November 1327 in which Peyt and a group of armed peasants disrupted a meeting of Church officials from all of southwestern Flanders. The purpose of the meeting was to remind all clergy of their requirement to honor the bans of excommunication and interdict, for some local priests apparently were reluctant to abandon their parishioners entirely.[32] However, the whole issue of clerical obedience became more urgent in late 1327 when peasants began pressuring priests to continue performing their duties. According to Lain, Peyt and his associates had organized a campaign to halt all payments and obligations to the churches and clergy honoring the bans in the district of Bergues and imposed fines on those "enemies of the community of the territory" who supported the anti-peasant clergy in any fashion.[33] In other words, Peyt and his peasant compatriots in Bergues district answered the Church's strictures with their own versions of excommunication and interdict.

It is difficult to understand how such actions qualified as the work of extremists, except perhaps in the minds of those clerics who equated any defiance of ecclesiastical authority with heresy. The monk of Clairmarais, it would appear, was one of the latter, for he set out to discredit Peyt and his associates during the last phase of the Flemish rebellion by labelling them heretics and dismissing them from further serious consideration. He clearly approved of the symbolic yet pathetic actions of the bishop of Thérouanne who exhumed Peyt's bones and burned them in an attempt to halt the martyr-like devotion that many peasants of Bergues district felt for their late captain.[34] Far from being an extremist out of touch with his fellow rebels, therefore, Peyt had become a popular hero because he dared to organize resistance to what, from the rebel perspective, were the unjust actions of the Church.

In short, there is no clear evidence that the rebellion lacked popular support during its last phase. The captains, deriving their authority from the popular assemblies that had chosen them, were able to maintain order without resorting to the harsh repression that the loyalists imposed on the districts of Vier Ambachten and Land of Waas from late 1325 onward. They collected taxes, convened courts, issued verdicts, made disbursements of public funds, and organized peasant militias which effectively contended with most forces sent against them. Though rebels practiced considerable violence at times, the surviving evidence indicates that it was clearly focused and never became all-pervasive. Indeed, once the count's officials and their aristocratic allies were driven out, the rebel countryside seemed to enjoy a measure of peace and tranquility, perhaps even a measure of prosperity—not only was the accumulated property of the exiles redistributed within the communities from which it had been extracted, but the pressure of very heavy taxation to pay royal indemnities or to line the pockets of former officials or their friends was probably lightened. Meanwhile, most ordinary peasants within the rebel districts continued to plant, harvest, and market their crops and tend to their livestock. What seemed like a series of peasant republics had replaced the count's authority in the rebel countryside, and the leaders of these republics cooperated closely with each other to provide solidarity within and even maintained what appear to have been normal contacts with cities and towns that had subscribed to the Peace of Arques.[35]

Invasion

By the end of 1327, few doubted any longer that a French invasion designed to restore the authority of the count of Flanders would occur eventually, but the sudden death of King Charles IV in early 1328 delayed all intervention for several months. In fact, Philip of Valois, while regent of France, tried one last time to reach a negotiated settlement by holding talks at Thérouanne (county of Artois) with representatives of Count Louis' court, the Flemish cities, and presumably exiled officials of the rebel rural districts (though not with peasant rebels), but he discontinued all such attempts when he became King Philip VI on 29 May 1328. Almost immediately, he began assembling troops for an invasion of Flanders. All knights in France owing service to him were ordered to assemble at Arras by 31 July 1328.[36] By the beginning of August, Philip had gathered 39 sub commands or banners of warriors in his own battle command or division, and they were soon joined by many more from the semi-autonomous principalities of France and even from several jurisdictions in the Empire. The invading force eventually came to consist of ten battle commands or divisions under 196 different banners, totalling around 4,000 knights.[37]

While Flemish peasant rebels knew as well as anyone that an invasion was imminent, they did not know which of several routes it would follow. For this reason, their captains drew up plans to watch and guard the three most likely ones. One group of 6,550 to 8,000 men, drawn primarily from the districts of Veurne, Bergues, Bourbourg, Cassel, and Bailleul under the command of Nikolaas Zannekin and Winnoc le Fiere, converged on the town of Cassel and established itself on the town's prominent hill—at 176 meters (around 575 feet), affording a clear view of the surrounding coastal plain. A similar force raised in the districts of Ypres and Courtrai stationed itself along the Leie River northwest of Lille. A third army of roughly equal size, drawn from district of Bruges and commanded by Segher Janssone

and Lambert Bonin, guarded the Scheldt route north of the city of Tournai.[38] At the same time the rebels prepared themselves for a possible attack
from the rear, along the Scheldt between Ghent and Oudenaarde, where
Count Louis had concentrated his forces since the middle of July, primarily
the strong militia of Ghent supplemented by contingents of emigre nobles
from the rebel districts.[39]

Though the three armies deployed in this fashion doubtless contained
city folk in their ranks, there is no clear evidence that any of the large cities
played an official role in trying to stop the invasion of the French king and
his allies. Always suspicious of the intentions of the conservatives in control
of Ghent, the magistrates of Bruges, headed by Willem de Deken, kept that
city's militia at home in a state of readiness, though they did send a
contigent of 100 archers to aid the rebels at Cassel.[40] Meanwhile the city of
Courtrai, which had joined the rebellion for a time during 1325, appears to
have made peace with Count Louis by accepting an amnesty offered on 24
June 1328 on the condition that it provide assistance in crushing the rebellion.[41] The stance of Ypres was more ambiguous. Though it sent a small
contingent to watch the Leie River approach and maintained contact with
the rebels at Cassel, it also sent representatives to Philip VI at various
junctures along his invasion route.[42] In the end, therefore, the vast majority
of those willing to risk their lives and property by physically opposing the
invasion were peasants.

The decision to divide the rebel forces in three to guard all possible
invasion routes worked to the serious disadvantage of the rebels. The
French-led force was far larger and better equipped than any one of the
three rebel armies, and because the latter were spread out over a distance of
sixty kilometers, they could not easily spring to each other's aid. From a
strictly military perspective, they might have fared far better had they kept
their forces concentrated somewhere around Bruges and waited for the
invading force to arrive. But such a strategy would have meant exposing all
of the western districts and part of the district of Bruges to the destruction
and plundering of the French and their allies, perhaps an acceptable choice
for non-peasants but totally unthinkable to the peasants constituting the
vast majority of the rebel forces. In addition, such a strategy would have
risked the possibility of the invading force linking up with the loyalists
under Louis' command, thus greatly strengthening the enemy.[43]

Philip VI wasted little time. Almost as soon as troops began assembling at Arras, he gave them orders to march. He and his advisers had

decided to concentrate their entire force against the rebels at Cassel, reasoning perhaps that the peasants from the most rural part of the county would be less formidable in battle than those drawn from the more highly urbanized districts stationed along the Leie and Scheldt Rivers. In any case, the invasion force was underway by 10 August, and a week later it was near the abbey of Ham, six kilometers south of the Leie River across from Cassel district. It crossed into Flemish territory on 20 August and encamped two days later below the town of Cassel (the invasion route and rebel positions are shown on the map in Figure 7). In an effort to create terror in the hearts of their opponents, the invaders burned, looted, and pillaged all around them as they proceeded.[44]

For a day and a night, the two sides observed each other closely. Though the rebels occupied an impregnable position atop Cassel's hill, their situation was far from ideal. The king and his allies not only possessed a force that was far greater than their own but also controlled access to their stronghold. The rebels knew that they probably could repel most attacks launched against them until reinforcements could arrive from elsewhere, but the extreme heat and limited supplies of fresh water made them restless. More serious, however, was the fact that the entire countryside of western Flanders where they and their families lived was totally unprotected. Almost immediately upon their arrival, the invaders had begun burning villages in the immediate vicinity of Cassel in the hope of luring some of the rebels out of their positions to put the fires out. No one broke ranks for the moment, but the lesson was clear. A long holdout in their secure position would only mean massive destruction in the countryside. According to the author of the *Chronicon*, when asked by Zannekin and the other peasant captains whether they wished to stay on the hill or descend and fight, the peasant troops overwhelmingly chose the latter.[45] On 23 August, therefore, they launched a surprise attack on the invaders encamped below.

Launching the attack was a very risky venture; peasants on foot could hope to achieve a victory against such a large force of primarily mounted warriors only as long as they kept themselves massed together, a difficult task when rushing against the enemy. Nevertheless, it almost worked. Because of the extremely hot weather, some of the king's warriors were out of armor, seeking relief from the heat in their tents. The rebels executed their attack in three groups with the purpose of converging on the royal contingents, and, indeed, they made considerable progress in the direction of the king's tent, sending some of his knights in flight to Saint-Omer. But

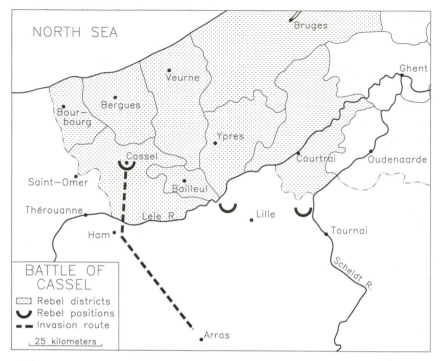

Figure 7

the peasant infantry lacked the speed and stamina to prevail against experienced mounted warriors who knew how to retreat and disperse themselves in front of the infantry and then regroup, charge, and envelop the infantry when the attackers ran out of breath and their ranks began to falter. After a short panic, the enemy regrouped and counterattacked. The Flemings drew themselves up into a compact circle or crown formation and vigorously repelled successive cavalry charges. At a given moment, however, some of the enemy feigned a retreat in the hope that the regimentation of the peasant infantry might weaken and that some might break ranks in pursuit. This is precisely what happened. Once they broke their ranks they were doomed, as the supposedly retreating knights wheeled around and pushed through the massed infantry formation. By the end of the day, the king of France and his allies had won, while 3,185 Flemish peasants lay dead on the battlefield, including captains Zannekin and le Fiere.[46] To all intents and purposes, the five-year peasant revolt of Flanders had been crushed.

Vengeance

Word of the outcome of the battle at Cassel traveled very quickly. As early as
5 September, Pope John XXII received the news at Avignon, and on the
following day he sent letters to the king and queen of France congratulating
them on their success. At the same time, he expressed the hope that the
remainder of the conquest might be concluded swiftly, and he urged the
king to show compassion to all Flemings who exhibited the slightest signs
of repentance.[47] And indeed, on the day after the battle, Philip VI began
receiving a long line of envoys from the rebel towns and districts of
Flanders sent to appeal for mercy, while submissions to Count Louis and
Robert of Cassel occurred in the weeks that followed. Anyone with money
or credit began making offers to Louis designed to obtain mercy. Even the
cities of Bruges and Ypres opened their gates to the king, the count, and the
returning loyalists with little resistence or hesitation.[48] In short, signs of
repentance were plentiful.

But compassion remained a truly scarce commodity among the victors
for some time to come, as a merciless repression unfolded. According to the
author of the *Chronicon*, the French cavalry immediately began subjecting
coastal Flanders to the flame and sword, massacring men, women, and
children alike. Doubtless for many of the aristocrats who constituted the
French cavalry, such actions finally brought the revenge they had long
sought for their humiliating defeat at the hands of ordinary Flemings in the
Battle of Courtrai in 1302. Returning Flemish nobles and patricians, however, were no better behaved as they sought revenge for their exile,[49]
though unlike their French counterparts, they tended to use the sword
without the flame—preferring to seize property rather than to destroy it.[50]
Official punishment while more disciplined was no less harsh. There were
countless executions over a period of more than a year, as peasant captains
and all those who had accepted posts from the rebels were decapitated or
broken on the wheel without any form of due process. At times, such
activities became grand spectacle; people came not only from Bruges and
Ghent but from as far away as Lille and Mechelen to observe executions of
rebels at Ypres, for example.[51]

Special attention was reserved, however, for Willem de Deken, a
former magistrate of the city of Bruges. At the express command of Philip
VI, he was brought to Paris for interrogation, torture, and finally a gruesome death on 23 December 1328. Even though he admitted under torture

to doing terrible things, including responsibility for burning a church in Aardenburg that contained a group of nobles who had sought sanctuary there in 1327, he was singled out because he apparently attempted to obtain English support for the rebellion. Specifically, he had urged Edward III, king of England, to declare himself the king of France, pledging that the Flemings would recognize him as such.[52] Edward declined for the moment, though a few years later he accepted the honor on the urging of a Fleming from Ghent, Jacob van Artevelde.

The pacification of Flanders proceeded quickly, as all significant opposition literally withered after the Battle of Cassel. Within a month, Philip VI transferred authority over the county of Flanders back to Count Louis along with the warning that the county would simply be incorporated into his royal domain if Louis ever needed to be rescued in this fashion again. By 26 September, Philip had returned to Paris.[53] On 4 October 1328, Pope John XXII wrote to Philip expressing pleasure that his venture in Flanders had proceeded so smoothly, and he was particularly pleased that a long-promised crusade headed by the king of France might soon become a reality.[54] By 19 October the pope gave his representatives in Flanders the authority to lift the bans of excommunication and interdict from Flanders.[55] However, only much later was forgiveness granted to those who had raised their hands against clerics or had directed other misdeeds against the Church.[56]

By all accounts, Count Louis took Philip's warning very seriously, and immediately set out to strengthen his authority over the cities and rural districts of Flanders. He ordered his bailiffs back to their posts in all cities and rural districts and his *ammans* or sheriffs in the rural communities with orders to deal harshly with all forms of dissent. As a result, openly-declared resistance to domination ceased. Even the attempt by Segher Janssone in February 1328 to raise the rebellion once again in the western part of the district of Bruges occasioned no massive response. The count's bailiff at Bruges easily neutralized the attempt and brought Janssone and his associates back to Bruges for particularly cruel forms of torture and a grisly public execution.[57] The same fate apparently awaited Rogier Monac when he and more than 200 associates attempted to raise the revolt in Ypres district in April 1331.[58] For a long time to come, resistance to domination within Flanders remained limited to the more common, concealed forms.[59]

Besides the direct physical punishment administered both officially and unofficially to large numbers of rebels, there were some indirect forms of punishment as well. Count Louis, for example, embarked on a significant project designed to centralize the government of Flanders more clearly. His primary means of doing so was to recall or rescind the charters of rights and privileges of many rebel cities and towns and to issue new ones that weakened their autonomy. He also gave the central administration the authority to oversee the selection of magistrates and to monitor the accounts that city and district officials kept. Finally, he attempted to restrict the ability of ordinary people in both city and countryside to chose their own leaders or proxies.[60] As a result of such actions, Louis emerged from the five-year peasant revolt much stronger than he had ever been before, largely because he now presided over the most highly centralized regime that Flanders had ever known.

Philip VI, meanwhile, refused to give in to the pressures of the victorious nobility to organize an expedition of wanton destruction.[61] While this decision seemed to accord with the pope's admonition to show mercy where appropriate, a more plausible motive was the principle that to the victor belong the spoils. He had decided to confiscate the property of all those who had fought against him in the Battle of Cassel by invoking the law of high treason. Almost as soon as it was safe to do so, therefore, royal agents began fanning out into the countryside of Flanders to make an inventory of the booty.[62] Count Louis had nothing to do with these confiscations, which served not only to punish the rebels but also to demonstrate conspicuously the sovereignty of the French crown within Flanders. After making this point, however, Philip consented in September 1328 to divide the income from the confiscations with Count Louis. Three months later, he showed the same favor to Robert of Cassel for the rural districts that constituted his appanage.[63] Count Louis undertook a more limited confiscation of rebel property in the city and district of Bruges.[64] I shall return to the confiscations of rebel property in Appendix A.

Notes

1. H. van Werveke, "Vlaanderen en Brabant, 1305–1346: de sociaal-economische achtergrond," in *Algemene geschiedenis der Nederlanden*, vol. 3, *De late middeleeuwen, 1305–1477* (Utrecht and Antwerp: De Haan and Standaard Boekhandel, 1951), p. 33.

2. The copy of the treaty published in T. De Limburg-Stirum, ed., *Codex diplomaticus Flandriae ab anno 1296 ad usque 1327, ou recueil de documents relatifs aux guerres et dissensions suscitées par Philippe-le-Bel, roi de France, contre Gui de Dampierre, comte de Flandre*, Société d'Émulation pour l'Étude de l'Histoire et des Antiquités

de la Flandre (Bruges: De Plancke, 1889), vol. 2, no. 356, pp. 385–403, came from the archives of the city of Bruges, and the signatories, pp. 385–86, represented the cities and rural districts of Bruges, Ypres, and Courtrai alone. However, the text of the treaty they were endorsing indicates, pp. 394–95, that representatives from the cities and rural districts of Veurne, Bergues, Bourbourg, Cassel, and Bailleul had been involved in its negotiations. Presumably another copy would have been subscribed to by officials from that part of Flanders—the apanage of Robert of Cassel—but no such copy seems to have survived.

3. M. Vandermaesen, "Vlaanderen en Henegouwen onder het huis van Dampierre 1244–1384," in *Algemene geschiedenis der Nederlanden*, vol. 2 (Haarlem: Fibula-van Dishoeck, 1982), p. 423; Jacques Sabbe, *Vlaanderen in opstand, 1323–1328: Nikolaas Zannekin, Zeger Janszone en Willem de Deken*, Genootschap voor Geschiedenis "Société d'Émulation" te Brugge, Vlaamse Historische Studies, VII (Bruges: Marc Van de Wiele, 1992), p. 53.

4. F. W. N. Hugenholtz, *Drie boerenopstanden uit de veertiende eeuw: Vlaanderen 1323–1328, Frankrijk 1358, Engeland 1381; onderzoek naar het opstandig bewustzijn* (Haarlem: Tjeenk Willink, 1949), pp. 106–7.

5. Van Werveke, "Vlaanderen en Brabant," p. 33; J. van Rompaey, "De opstand in het Vlaamse kustland van 1323 tot 1328 en de figuur van Nikolaas Zannekin," in *Nikolaas Zannekin en de Slag bij Kassel, 1328–1978: bijdrage tot de studie van de 14de eeuw en de landelijke geschiedenis van de Westhoek* (Diksmuide: Kulturele Raad van Diksmuide, 1978), p. 121.

6. J. Bovesse, "Le comte de Namur Jean Ier et les événements du comté de Flandre en 1325–1326," *Bulletin de la Commission Royale d'Histoire* 131 (1965), pp. 417–18, 431.

7. Anonymous, *Chronicon comitum Flandrensium*, in *Corpus chronicorum Flandriae, sub auspiciis Leopoldi primi, serenissimi Belgarum regis: recueil des chroniques de Flandre*, J. J. DeSmet, ed., vol 1, Académie Royale de Belgique, Commission Royale d'Histoire, Mémoires en quarto (Brussels: H. Hayez, 1837) (hereafter cited as *Chronicon*), pp. 189–92, said as much in recounting the events of early 1325.

8. *Chronicon*, p. 201; Vandermaesen, "Vlaanderen en Henegouwen onder het huis van Dampierre," p. 423. The accounts of the city of Ypres, G. Des Marez and E. de Sagher, eds., *Comptes de la ville d'Ypres de 1297 à 1329*, Académie Royale de Belgique, Commission Royale d'Histoire (Brussels: P. Imbreghts, 1913), vol. 2, contain frequent references to "parlemente" with representatives of Bruges, Ghent, and the count from early October 1326 to early February 1327 (pp. 656–67), as well as the following entry for 10 January 1327 (p. 664): "Item van te doen scrivene ende zeighelne 't compromis, dat was tusschen minen here van Vlaendren ende der stede van Ypre, ende van 2 leteren die de grave screef an den coninc, 44s. 4 d."

9. Contained in a letter Louis issued on 8 February 1327, published in T. De Limburg-Stirum, ed., *Codex diplomaticus Flandriae* (Bruges: De Plancke, 1889), vol. 2, pp. 405–8, no. 359. See also A. Schouteet, *Regesten op de oorkonden van het stadsarchief van Brugge (1089–1500)*, vol. 2, *1301–1339*, Brugse geschiedbronnen uitgegeven door het Genootschap voor Geschiedenis "Société d'Émulation" te Brugge met steun van het Gemeentebestuur van Brugge, V (Bruges: Stadsarchief van Brugge, 1978), pp. 169–70, no. 449.

10. Van Rompaey, "De opstand in het Vlaamse kustland," p. 120.

11. Summarized in Schouteet, *Regesten op de oorkonden van het stadsarchief van Brugge*, vol. 2, p. 164, no. 443, from an undated copy. Schouteet suggests a date of "ca. 1325," but, because it offers forgiveness to those who had been in revolt "over the past five years" and Louis took office in 1322, 1327 makes more sense.

12. Vandermaesen, "Vlaanderen en Henegouwen onder het huis van Dampierre," p. 423.

13. A. Vandewalle, "Willem de Deken (+1328) volksleider en makelaar," *Handelingen van het Genootschap voor Geschiedenis gesticht onder de benaming Société d'Émulation* 115 (1978), pp. 207–11; Sabbe, *Vlaanderen in opstand*, pp. 59–64.

14. Henri Pirenne, ed., *Le soulèvement de la Flandre maritime, 1323–1328, documents inédites*, Académie Royale de Belgique, Commission Royale d'Histoire, Publications in-octavo (Brussels: P. Imbreghts, 1900), p. xxxv; Sabbe, *Vlaanderen in opstand*, p. 62; David Nicholas, *Town and Countryside: Social, Economic, and Political Tensions in Fourteenth-Century Flanders*, Rijksuniversiteit te Gent, Werken uitgegeven door de faculteit van de letteren en wijsbegeerte, 152 (Bruges: De Tempel, 1971), p. 165, note 4.

15. The report of the damages commission, published in Pirenne, ed., *Le soulèvement*, appendix 16, pp. 206–18, contains multiple references to both. They were mentioned as well in *Chronicon*, pp. 202 and 204. For additional information on both Peyt and le Fiere, see Appendix B, below.

16. Pirenne, ed., *Le soulèvement*, appendix 16, pp. 207–11, 211–13.

17. Pirenne, ed., *Le soulèvement*, appendix 16, pp. 206–7, 213–18.

18. Pirenne, ed., *Le soulèvement*, appendix 16: p. 213: "et tous ces biens fi Jakeme Peit prendre par commandement du commun de le castelrie de Berghes"; and p. 214, "van slants halven." It seems to me that Madeleine Braekman, "Jacob Peyt, hérésie ou révolte social en Flandre au XIVe siècle?" *Bulletin de la Société du Protestantisme Belge* 7 (1979), p. 326, misinterprets these actions by suggesting that the rebels were seeking personal profit; the sources specifically refer to its being done for the common good, not for individual aggrandizement. The use of certain pieces of property might have been assigned to a captain by the commons in lieu of payment for services rendered or expenses incurred, for example.

19. *Chronicon*: for the period from April 1324 to April 1326, pp. 188–200 (13 pages) and for the period from April 1326 to May 1328, pp. 201–2 (just over one page); see especially p. 202: "Duravitque pestis ista postea per biennium, et in tantum ubique desaevit, quod taederet homines vitae suae."

20. Sabbe, *Vlaanderen in opstand*, pp. 58–59; van Rompaey, "De opstand in het Vlaamse kustland," p. 121.

21. For the examples that follow, see the evidence assembled in Appendix B, below.

22. *Chronicon*, pp. 202, 204, 208. Braekman, "Jacob Peyt, hérésie ou révolte social en Flandre," pp. 322–23.

23. Pirenne, ed., *Le soulèvement*, pp. xxv–xxvii; van Werveke, "Vlaanderen en Brabant," p. 33; David Nicholas, *Medieval Flanders* (London and New York: Longmans, 1992), p. 215; idem, *Town and Countryside*, pp. 162–63; van Rompaey, "De opstand in het Vlaamse kustland," p. 121; and Sabbe, *Vlaanderen in opstand*, pp. 55–

60, all see increasing extremism during the last phase. Hugenholtz, *Drie boerenop-standen*, pp. 30–32, suggests that the flight of the "moderates" made the movement more extreme.

24. The report of this damages commission, convened sometime after 1328, is published in Pirenne, ed., *Le soulèvement*, appendix 16, pp. 206–18.

25. *Chronicon*, p. 202: "Dicebant enim alicui diviti: 'Tu plus diligis dominos quam communitates de quibus vivis.' et nulla alia causa in eo reperta, talem expone-bant morti, et per unum de propinquioribus consanguineis (quod horrendum et inhumanum est audire) faciebant eum occidi, dicentes: 'Tu occides eum, vel tu incontinenti morieris.'"

26. On the basis of this passage, Pirenne, ed., *Le soulèvement*, pp. xxv–xxvii, concluded that the levels of violence and brutality visited upon Flanders by peasant rebels during the last phase of the revolt exceeded those of the French Jacquerie of 1358 and the English Rising of 1381, though the documents he published in this volume lend no support to such a conclusion. Other historians who have looked at the Flemish revolt have simply adopted Pirenne's conclusion uncritically; most recently, Nicholas, *Medieval Flanders*, p. 215.

27. The one truly infamous incident from the last phase of the revolt consisted of the murder of a number of nobles from Bruges district in early May 1328 by setting fire to the church in Aardenburg in which they had taken refuge. But it appears to have been the work of citizens from the city of Bruges, led by Willem de Deken, not of peasants or their captains. See Sabbe, *Vlaanderen in opstand*, pp. 60–61; van Rompaey, "De opstand in het Vlaamse kustland," p. 121; N. de Pauw, "L'Enquête de Bruges après la bataille de Cassel," *Bulletin de la Commission Royale d'Histoire* 68 (1899), pp. 667, 687.

28. For details concerning Peyt, see Appendix B, below.

29. *Chronicon*, p. 202: "Hoc horridum igitur mortis genus adinvenit cap-itaneus Brugensis, nominatus Jacobus *Pric*, proditor callidissimus et haereticus pessimus, qui optabat non esse nisi unum sacerdotem in mundo, et illum in aëre suspensum. Nam et ipse tanquam incredulus ecclesiam non intrabat, et modo inaudito atque tyrannico viros ecclesiasticos persequebatur; et ipsos omnes ex-pulisset a patria, bonis eorum primo confiscatis, nisi justo Dei judicio fuisset in Hontscota per Furnenses occisus, et postmodum, licet fatui populares eum tan-quam sanctum adorarent, diabolo ipsos seducente, per judicium praelatorum om-nium vicinorum et domini Morinensis, diocesani episcopi, tanquam pessimus haeresiarcha, igne concrematus." Braekman, "Jacob Peyt, hérésie ou révolte social en Flandre," p. 331, provides the time period for Peyt's exhumation.

30. Arnold Fayen, ed., *Lettres de Jean XXII (1316–1334): textes et analyses*, Analecta Vaticano-Beligica publiés par l'Institut Historique Belge de Rome (Rome: M. Bretschneider, 1909), vol. 2, part 1, no. 1942, pp. 113–18.

31. For further information regarding Peyt, see Appendix B, below.

32. Briefly discussed in the previous chapter.

33. See the letter of Jean Lain in Paul Fredericq, ed., *Corpus documentorum inquisitionis haereticae pravitatis Neerlandicae: verzameling van stukken betreffende de pauselijke en bisschoppelijke inquisitie in de Nederlanden*, vol. 3 (Ghent and The Hague: J. Vuylsteke and Martinus Nijhoff, 1909), p. 9: "sour paine d'estre anemy à la

communité dou pays." See also Sabbe, *Vlaanderen in opstand*, p. 56, who placed this episode in November 1325, however. On the dates, see Appendix B, below.

34. *Chronicon*, p. 202. It appears that the charges of heresy against Peyt were made official and acted upon only after the revolt, in late 1328 or 1329, but there was no real basis to them; see Braekman, "Jacob Peyt, hérésie ou révolte social en Flandre," pp. 331–32. Hugenholtz, *Drie boerenopstanden*, p. 88, arrived at the questionable conclusion that there must have been something to the charge of heresy simply because the bishop of Thérouanne charged Peyt with it.

35. The accounts of Ypres, published by Des Marez and de Sagher, eds., *Comptes de la ville d'Ypres de 1297 à 1329*, vol. 2, show that even though the city followed the requirements of the Peace of Arques (see, for example, an entry of 29 May 1327, p. 759: "Den grave van Cleirmont, ygheven in minderinghen van dat de steide sculdich was den coninc van Vrankerike van den pelerinen, die zi ysent zouden hebben in pelerinagen bi der vorme van den laetsten paise, 500 lb. tor. in vrancscher munte, die ygholden waren met vlaenderscher munte met 323 lb. 4 s. 2 d."), the rebels had numerous communications with the city from 1326 to 1328 (pp. 657–911), including the following explicit exchanges: p. 697 (2 May 1327), "Jan Taispile, isent te Roedsbrigghe ende te Cassele tote Jacob Peiten, van 2 daghen: 16 s."; p. 697 (9 May 1327), "Jan Famelse, ysendt in de castelrie van Ypre in veile prochien, van 2 daghen: 12 s."; p. 727 (30 May 1327), "Enen messagier, comende van Jacob Peiten: 4s."; p. 733 (11 July 1327), "Enen bode, comende van Jacob Peiten: 4 s."; and p. 823 (21 May 1328), "Van den costen die 3 hoofmannen van Berghen daden t'Ypre in Matheus herberghe van Warens, die t'Ypre camen van 's communs weghe dat te Cassele lach: 9 s. 6 d."

36. Pirenne, ed., *Le soulèvement*, p. xxvii; M. Vandermaesen, "Lodewijk II van Nevers," *Nationaal biografisch woordenboek*, Koninklijke Academiën van België, vol. 5 (Brussels: Paleis der Academiën, 1972), col. 528; idem, "Vlaanderen en Henegouwen onder het huis van Dampierre," pp. 423–24; Sabbe, *Vlaanderen in opstand*, p. 65; van Rompaey, "De opstand in het Vlaamse kustland," p. 122. For a chronological overview of the military operations of 1328, see J. Viard, "La guerre de Flandre (1328)," *Bibliothèque de l'École des Chartes* 83 (1922), pp. 362–82.

37. J. F. Verbruggen, *The Art of Warfare in Western Europe During the Middle Ages: From the Eighth Century to 1340*, Sumner Willard and S. C. M. Southern, trans., Europe in the Middle Ages: Selected Studies, 1 (Amsterdam and New York: North Holland Publishing, 1977), pp. 75, 79–80; Sabbe, *Vlaanderen in opstand*, pp. 67–68.

38. *Chronicon*, p. 204; Verbruggen, *The Art of Warfare*, pp. 144, 146; van Rompaey, "De opstand in het Vlaamse kustland," pp. 122–23. To help consolidate their position, Janssone and associates drove some loyalists from Bruges district out of the county; see Sabbe, *Vlaanderen in opstand*, p. 62.

39. *Chronicon*, p. 204; van Rompaey, "De opstand in het Vlaamse kustland," p. 122.

40. Pirenne, ed., *Le soulèvement*, p. xxviii; Sabbe, *Vlaanderen in opstand*, p. 67.

41. Van Rompaey, "De opstand in het Vlaamse kustland," pp. 118–19.

42. See Des Marez and de Sagher, eds., *Comptes de la ville d'Ypres*, vol. 2, pp. 853–59.

43. Van Rompaey, "De opstand in het Vlaamse kustland," p. 123.

44. Sabbe, *Vlaanderen in opstand*, p. 68; Viard, "La guerre de Flandre," pp. 366–67; Pirenne, ed., *Le soulèvement*, p.xxviii; *Chronicon*, p. 204: "Ignis ubique per terram ponitur, spolia diripiuntur, nulli parcitur."

45. Viard, "La guerre de Flandre," p. 370; *Chronicon*, p. 205.

46. *Chronicon*, pp. 205–6; Viard, "La guerre de Flandre," pp. 371–74; Verbruggen, *The Art of Warfare*, pp. 161–62; Pirenne, ed., *Le soulèvement*, pp. xxviii–xxx, 1–148; Sabbe, *Vlaanderen in opstand*, p. 72; van Werveke, "Vlaanderen en Brabant," p. 34; van Rompaey, "De opstand in het Vlaamse kustland," pp. 123–25; Robert Jennes, "De Slag bij Kassel, 23 augustus 1328," in *Nikolaas Zannekin en de Slag bij Kassel, 1328–1978: Bijdrage tot de studie van de 14de eeuw en de landelijke geschiedenis van de Westhoek* (Diksmuide, Belgium: Kulturele Raad van Diksmuide, 1978), pp. 142–49.

47. Fayen, ed., *Lettres de Jean XXII*, vol. 2, pp. 212–13, nos. 2221–23; Hugenholtz, *Drie boerenopstanden*, pp. 32–33.

48. *Chronicon*, p. 207; Pirenne, ed., *Le soulèvement*, pp. xxx, xxxiii. Willem de Deken's attempts to keep the rebellion alive collapsed almost immediately; see Sabbe, *Vlaanderen in opstand*, pp. 73, 75.

49. *Chronicon*, p. 206: "nam dum barones et majores natu sibi dicerent, ut illorum patriam, qui ipsum sic invaserant, daret incendio et uxores eorum cum filiis trucidaret."

50. See Pirenne, ed., *Le soulèvement*, pp. xxx–xxxi; F. Blockmans, "De bestraffing van den opstand van Brugge en Westelijk-Vlaanderen in 1328," *Beknopte Handelingen, XVe Vlaamsche Filologencongress* (1940), pp. 42–43.

51. Blockmans, "De bestraffing van den opstand van Brugge en Westelijk-Vlaanderen," pp. 42–43; Pirenne, ed., *Le soulèvement*, p. xxxi–xxxii; Sabbe, *Vlaanderen in opstand*, pp. 77–78.

52. See Vandewalle, "Willem de Deken (+1328) volksleider en makelaar," pp. 207–11; Sabbe, *Vlaanderen in opstand*, pp. 80, 82; van Rompaey, "De opstand in het Vlaamse kustland," pp. 121–22; H. Stein, "Les conséquences de la bataille de Cassel pour la ville de Bruges et la mort de Guillaume De Deken, son ancien bourgmestre," *Bulletin de la Commission Royale d'Histoire* 68 (1899), pp. 647–64; de Pauw, "L'Enquête de Bruges après la bataille de Cassel," pp. 665–704.

53. Viard, "La guerre de Flandre," p. 379.

54. Fayen, ed., *Lettres de Jean XXII*, vol. 2, pp. 217–18, no. 2238.

55. Fayen, ed., *Lettres de Jean XXII*, vol. 2, pp. 221–23, no. 2249.

56. See Hugenholtz, *Drie boerenopstanden*, p. 34, referring to acts of April 1330 and October 1333.

57. *Chronicon*, p. 207; Sabbe, *Vlaanderen in opstand*, pp. 82–83. See also the section on Janssone in Appendix B, below.

58. See Pirenne, ed., *Le soulèvement*, p. 222. He owned or leased 65 *mesures* (about 29 hectares or 71 acres) of land in Gistel, Bruges district; see J. Mertens, ed., "Les confiscations dans la châtellenie du Franc de Bruges après la bataille de Cassel," *Bulletin de la Commission Royale d'Histoire* 134 (1968), pp. 266–67.

59. See my discussion concerning resistance to domination in the introduction, above.

60. J. van Rompaey, "De Brugse keure van 1329 en de aanvullende privileges,"

Handelingen van het Koninklijke Commissie voor de Uitgave van de Oude Wetten en Verordeningen van België 21 (1965), pp. 35–40; idem, "De opstand in het Vlaamse kustland," pp. 117–19; M. Vandermaesen, "Lodewijk II van Nevers," in *Nationaal biografisch woordenboek*, Koninklijke Academiën van België, vol. 5 (Brussels: Paleis der Academiën, 1972), col. 529; Pirenne, ed., *Le soulèvement*, pp. xxxi–xxxii.

61. *Chronicon*, p. 206; Sabbe, *Vlaanderen in opstand*, p. 72.

62. Fortunately, much of the inventorization has survived and was published by Pirenne, ed., *Le soulèvement*, pp. 1–162, providing us with important information about the participants in the revolt.

63. See Pirenne, ed., *Le soulèvement*, appendices 7, 8, 11, pp. 184–88, 193–94.

64. The surviving documents were published in Mertens, ed., "Les confiscations dans la châtellenie du Franc de Bruges," pp. 239–84.

5. Ordinary People in a Changing World

Over the short term, the primary beneficiaries of the five-year peasant revolt were Philip VI, king of France, and Louis of Nevers, count of Flanders. In the wake of his victory at Cassel, Philip could legitimately claim to be the champion of right and privilege over the evils of popular pretension and disorder, while his treasury swelled from the rebel wealth that his agents began confiscating. Louis, meanwhile, was handed a principality much more docile than it had been at any time since the beginning of his reign, thanks to direct royal intervention, and he quickly built on this advantage by making his regime more centralized and authoritarian, using the French royal administration as his model. Ironically, however, neither ruler derived benefits from the defeated revolt that could help him over the long term. Philip spent much of the remainder of his life troubled by an English pretender to his throne, a point of vulnerability that Flemish rebels recognized as early as the 1320s, while Louis died in exile because a citizen of once loyal Ghent organized a new regime that rendered him superfluous. Nor was the long term particularly kind to Flemish aristocrats or particularly cruel to Flemish peasants. All that can be said with certainty is that Flanders never returned to being exactly what it had been before the revolt began.

The tragedy of the Flemish peasant revolt is that it actually was doomed by its own success. It came to an end not because of any internal weaknesses within the movement itself, for it was able to hold its own against all domestic opponents and even create a degree of normalcy within the rebel districts of Flanders. Rather, its fate was sealed when it provoked an international crusade replete with full ecclesiastical sanctions. Because it had significantly extended the realm of the possible for peasant political activity, it caught the attention of rulers throughout northwestern Europe who moved jointly to crush this challenge to traditional authority before it spread any further. Only massive force applied from the outside ended this bold and apparently unique experiment.

Count Louis wasted no time in establishing administrative control over his troublesome principality. As we saw in the previous chapter, not only did he order his officials to clamp down on all forms of dissent, but he also gave his chancery the task of rescinding the charters that defined the rights and privileges of many former rebel cities and districts and replacing them with more stringent ones. Simultaneously, the entire land was weighed down by an enormous tax pressure as all outstanding payments for indemnities, subsidies, and incomes called for in the French treaties became due immediately, with additional heavy fines levied on former rebel districts and cities. As an aid to extending his authority over all jurisdictions in Flanders, Louis also established new commissions controlled by his central administration to audit the accounts of local authorities and to oversee the annual appointment of rural and urban magistrates.[1] If nothing else, therefore, peasant insurrection indirectly aided the process of administrative centralization.

Obviously, peasants in the former rebel districts were the ones who suffered most immediately from the defeat of the revolt, and not only because thousands of their relatives and friends were killed in the battle at Cassel or because many others were brought to swift justice during the subsequent months and years. They suffered as well from the ruthless vengeance of aristocrats: from the French cavalrymen who dispensed destruction and mayhem with broad strokes and from returning *leliaart* Flemings who evened more personal scores.[2] Surprisingly, however, aristocrats derived no benefit beyond the fleeting pleasure of revenge. In contrast to peasants, who gradually recovered much of their former prosperity largely because the conditions of their original well-being remained in place, aristocrats lost out over the longer term. For example, nobles in the district of Bruges soon became indistinguishable from the wealthiest ranks of citizens in the city of Bruges.[3] To a certain extent, therefore, the peasant rebels saw one of their goals partially fulfilled—though aristocratic privilege in the countryside was not totally eliminated, it was nevertheless seriously undermined.

This does not mean that somehow the objective conditions affecting peasant life improved in Flanders after the revolt was crushed, only that they had changed irrevocably. As the influence of aristocracy and other relics of feudalism decayed in the Flemish countryside, their place was taken by the competing interests of the state with its ability to coerce and the cities with their control of markets and capital. The tax burden, meanwhile, weighed heavily upon them, though some may have preferred the more predictable nature of the state's demands to the often arbitrary demands of the old order. In the end, however, it was the cities that won out in Flanders and, while the influence of their markets tended to introduce greater risk by undermining peasant self-sufficiency, peasants could also prosper by selling their surpluses to townspeople, especially during the period of price rises over the next several decades.[4]

After August 1328, Flemish peasants were restricted to using concealed forms of resistance to domination, though their memories of the heroic time when they were public political actors doubtless lived on. After all, their revolt had been immensely successful by all accounts, at least until their defeat at Cassel. Not only had they rid the rebel countryside of corrupt officials and predatory aristocrats, they also succeeded in establishing a truly popular political regime that maintained order, contracted alliances with sympathetic cities and towns, and effectively defended itself against its domestic enemies. Contrary to the opinion of their detractors, Flemish peasants had showed themselves quite capable of managing their own affairs.

The key to their success throughout lay in their ability to overcome parochialism and engage in collective action that transcended individual rural communities, largely achieved by adapting existing institutions and traditions to new and subversive ends. But Flemish peasants were greatly aided in this enterprise by the unique opportunities offered by the complex political culture of Flanders. Because of the fractured and disputed nature of Flemish politics, no single individual or party possessed unified coercive force. Consequently, the official response to the peasants' initial public political activity was weak or at best ambiguous, which only encouraged them to assert themselves even more boldly, resulting eventually in their assumption of full political power in the rebel rural districts.

Peasant Revolt as Popular Politics

For the most part, historians have been reluctant to ascribe active political roles to pre-modern European peasants, preferring to assume that they simply followed the lead of non-peasants with greater political experience, especially during rebellions.[5] To a certain extent, they have been encouraged to do so by medieval chroniclers. Convinced that peasants were irrational beings and thus incapable of planning and implementing anything on their own, a number of chroniclers insisted, for example, that peasant revolts in Flanders, France, and England during the fourteenth century were instigated and led by non-peasants such as townspeople or renegade aristocrats. Indeed, in some cases, non-peasants may well have played leading roles in peasant rebellions. On the other hand, skepticism about peasant political activity and especially peasant leadership can be taken too far. We should not apply more rigorous tests to the assumption that peasants might have acted on their own behalf than we can apply to the assumption that non-peasants led them into revolt. In the Flemish case, there is absolutely no evidence of non-peasants playing a leadership role in the rural part of the rebellion. Peasants initiated and carried out their own rebellion.[6]

Skepticism about peasants playing active, political roles usually stems from the widely held assumption that peasant interests were exclusively parochial, limited to the rural communities in which they lived. As I have stressed throughout, Flemish peasants in fact lived and worked in rural communities. But the dramatic events of the 1320s clearly indicate that certain assumptions based on the central importance of rural communities in the lives of peasants are simply wrong. For example, peasant communities were not necessarily autonomous from each other, linked only through market towns or some other outside construct, as some have suggested, nor did peasants have to wait for the modern state to turn them into taxpayers and thus into a category that transcended local communities.[7] In the Flemish case, despite the parochial nature of their daily routines, peasants themselves developed horizontal linkages to form commons or coalitions that clearly transcended individual rural communities to encompass entire rural districts, and even multiple rural districts could be combined as in the unified peasant army under Nikolaas Zannekin's command at Cassel. We saw in chapter three that Norman peasants developed similar broad associations in their 996 revolt. The Flemish rebellion also shows clearly that peasants could make linkages to the non-peasant world in the form of alliances with numerous cities and towns.[8]

The Flemish revolt clearly illustrates the usefulness of placing revolts generally within the larger category of popular political practice, specifically as a rare extension of more common, concealed forms of resistance to domination. It also helps us to understand the roles played by individual leaders. For example, if revolt was but one of many possible types of peasant action and if it was used only on those occasions when other types of resistance to domination no longer seemed to work, then leadership of a particular confrontation or phase of a revolt becomes much less important. Leaders, in such a view, were not the creators of the revolt but rather those that peasants in revolt chose to follow.[9] In Flanders, even those who came the closest to playing preeminent leadership roles, Segher Janssone, Nikolaas Zannekin, and Jacob Peyt, were products of the insurrection, not its creators.

Though Europe in general saw numerous episodes of militant peasant action during the late Middle Ages, I know of none that even approached the success of the Flemish insurrection during the 1320s. This does not mean, however, that Flemish peasants were inherently superior to other peasants. Rather, the differences must be attributed to different types of political experience and different responses to initial acts of insurrection. Just as with the Flemish revolt, the key to understanding other late medieval revolts is to see them as extensions of popular political practice. What made the Flemish revolt so extraordinary was its great tenacity and resilience, its ability to survive for nearly five years compared to other medieval peasant revolts that lasted only a few weeks or months. In large part this was a result of the initially weak or ambiguous response of the count and his officials. There is little doubt that had the count of Flanders possessed the same authoritarian control over his subjects that the kings of France and England did in their lands, the outcome would have been quite different. Peasants were never likely to resort to openly declared forms of resistance to domination if it was likely to result in immediate, severe repression.

Because it persisted so long, however, the Flemish revolt ultimately exhibited features not always visible in others. For example, even though revolts lasting a short time experienced a certain amount of development or change in means and ends,[10] only in Flanders did such developments have a chance to develop fully. This is not to suggest that all revolts developed according to some common formula. On the contrary, they were always rooted in local conditions and responses. What the Flemish case does, however, is extend considerably the realm of what was possible for peasants to achieve, and it provides important points of comparison for other episodes of peasant insurrection.

Notes

1. J. van Rompaey, "De Brugse keure van 1329 en de aanvullende privileges," *Handelingen van het Koninklijke Commissie voor de Uitgave van de Oude Wetten en Verordeningen van België* 21 1965), pp. 35–40; idem, "De opstand in het Vlaamse kustland van 1323 tot 1328 en de figuur van Nikolaas Zannekin," *Nikolaas Zannekin en de Slag bij Kassel, 1328–1978: bijdrage tot de studie van de 14de eeuw en de landelijke geschiedenis van de Westhoek* (Diksmuide, Belgium: Kulturele Raad van Diksmuide,

1978), pp. 117–19; Ellen E. Kittell, *From* Ad Hoc *to Routine: A Case Study in Medieval Bureaucracy*, Middle Ages Series (Philadelphia: University of Pennsylvania Press, 1991), pp. 5, 139–41, 147–50.

2. It is possible to get an idea of the hatred that drove aristocrats in their revenge by reading the "Kerelslied," essentially the war chant of a fourteenth-century Flemish knight out to punish the peasants or *kerels* of Flanders for their incredible presumption in trying to force or constrain the knights—"si willen de ruters dwinghen." He comments on their size and appearance, their lack of manners, their eating and drinking habits, and much more, all in very demeaning terms. Raf Seys reprints the text from a 1966 reedition in "Zannekin en de Kerels van Vlaanderen in het volkslied: beknopte bloemlezing," in *Nikolaas Zannekin en de Slag bij Kassel, 1328–1978: Bijdrage tot de studie van de 14de eeuw en de landelijke geschiedenis van de Westhoek* (Diksmuide, Belgium: Kulturele Raad van Diksmuide, 1978), pp. 199–200, while David Nicholas, *Medieval Flanders* (London and New York: Longmans, 1992), pp. 253–54 translates part of it into English. Henri Pirenne, ed., *Le soulèvement de la Flandre maritime, 1323–1328, documents inédites*, Académie Royale de Belgique, Commission Royale d'Histoire, Publications in-octavo (Brussels: P. Imbreghts, 1900), p. xx, links the "Kerelslied" directly to the revolt of the 1320s.

3. David Nicholas, *Town and Countryside: Social, Economic, and Political Tensions in Fourteenth-Century Flanders*, Rijksuniversiteit te Gent, Werken uitgegeven door de faculteit van de letteren en wijsbegeerte, 152 (Bruges: De Tempel, 1971), p. 165.

4. See Rodney H. Hilton, "A Crisis of Feudalism," *Past and Present* 80 (1978), pp. 3–19; Charles Tilly, *Coercion, Capital, and European States, AD 990–1990*, Studies in Social Discontinuity (Cambridge, MA: Basil Blackwell, 1990), p. 19, and throughout.

5. See, for example, David Sabean, "The Communal Basis of Pre-1800 Peasant Uprisings in Western Europe," *Comparative Politics* 8 (1976), p. 359, who maintains that a common feature of pre-1800 peasant revolts was "the fact that leadership seldom, if ever, came from the peasants themselves." Pirenne, ed., *Le soulèvement*, p. xix, made this assumption for Flanders.

6. F. W. N. Hugenholtz, *Drie boerenopstanden uit de veertiende eeuw: Vlaanderen 1323–1328, Frankrijk 1358, Engeland 1381; onderzoek naar het opstandig bewustzijn* (Haarlem: Tjeenk Willink, 1949), pp. 28–29. See also Nicholas Brooks, "The Organization and Achievements of the Peasants of Kent and Essex in 1381," in *Studies in Medieval History Presented to R. H. C. Davies*, Henry Mayr-Harting and R. I. Moore, eds. (London and Ronceverte, WV: Hambledon Press, 1985), pp. 247–70; Richard Wunderli, *Peasant Fires: The Drummer of Niklashausen* (Bloomington: Indiana University Press, 1992), pp. 147–48.

7. See for example Sabean, "The Communal Basis of pre-1800 Peasant Uprisings in Western Europe," p. 355, who saw the communal focus of peasant life as so overwhelming that he "cannot think of a single case where peasants attempted to take power on a national scale, or even to insert themselves on a regular basis in the local or regional political apparatus." See as well Samuel Cohn, Jr., "Florentine Insurrections, 1342–1385, in Comparative Perspective," in *The English Rising of 1381*, Rodney H. Hilton and T. H. Aston, eds., Past and Present Publications (Cam-

bridge: Cambridge University Press, 1984), pp. 146–47, 161–62, who, in addressing the same issue in reference to the Ciompi Revolt in Florence in 1378, disagrees with Charles Tilly and George Rudé when they maintain that associational (as opposed to communal) movements were exclusively modern phenomena. See also Tilly, *Coercion, Capital, and European States*, pp. 99–103.

8. Besides Flemings and Normans, Florentines also developed associations that transcended neighborhood or community; see Cohn, "Florentine Insurrections, 1342–1385, in Comparative Perspective," pp. 143–64. See as well Susan Reynolds, *Kingdoms and Communities in Western Europe, 900–1300* (Oxford: Clarendon Press, 1984), pp. 110–11, 149–50, for associations of peasants in central Italy during the middle ages that clearly transcended local communities.

9. Sabean, "The Communal Basis of pre-1800 Peasant Uprisings," p. 359; Wunderli, *Peasant Fires*, p. 148.

10. Peter Bierbrauer, "Bäuerliche Revolten im Alten Reich: ein Forschungsbericht," in *Aufruhr und Empörung? Studien zum bäuerlichen Widerstand im Alten Reich* (Munich: H. Beck, 1980), pp. 44–45.

Appendix A: Economic and Social Conditions of the Rebels

From the historian's perspective, the inventories compiled as a prelude to the confiscation of rebel property by agents of the king of France and the count of Flanders are a gold mine. The two inventories that have survived, drawn up by different groups for quite different purposes, together provide important information concerning many participants in the revolt. Even though their use is not entirely free of difficulty—neither, for example, provides a cross section of the rebel population—they do permit us to make some tentative conclusions concerning the economic and social conditions of the Flemish rebels.

The largest of the two inventories, compiled by agents of the king of France, lists the names and property of 3,185 victims of the Battle of Cassel (23 August 1328), arranged according to the rural districts (Bailleul, Bergues, Cassel, and Veurne) and parishes in which they lived.[1] A majority, 2,294 or 72 percent, had property worth confiscating, while 891 or 28 percent were listed as owning none. Of the 2,294 listed as having property, some owned buildings but no land, others owned land but no buildings, but most owned both. On average, those listed in the inventory owned 0.6 buildings and 4.5 measures (French, *mesures*; Dutch, *gemeten*) or 2.0 hectares (4.9 acres) of land—one measure equaled 0.44 hectares (1.09 acres).[2] Table 1 shows the range of landholdings in measures per individual, arranged according to the four rural districts of southwestern Flanders for which information is available.

A somewhat different view is provided by the information contained in the second inventory, drawn up for the district of Bruges by agents of the count of Flanders. Unlike the royal inventory which contained a large sample, this one was very modest, listing the names and property of only 142 rebels from Bruges district and a handful of their allies in a number of towns and cities.[4] Because we know from other sources that much larger numbers participated in the revolt—for example, as many as 700 rebels from Bruges district died in a battle at Assenede in November 1325[5]—we

TABLE I. Range of Landholdings (in measures) per Rural District for South-western Flanders[3]

Size	Veurne	Bergues	Cassel	Bailleul	Total	% Total
0	513	655	21	0	1,189	37.3
1–5	629	490	61	3	1,183	37.1
5–10	248	164	35	2	449	14.1
10–15	93	56	16	0	165	5.2
15–20	56	32	12	0	100	3.1
20–25	17	17	5	0	39	1.2
25–30	9	7	4	0	20	0.6
30–35	8	3	0	0	11	0.3
35–40	6	9	2	0	17	0.5
40–45	2	1	0	0	3	0.1
45–50	4	1	1	0	6	0.2
50—	3	0	0	0	3	0.1
Totals	1,588	1,435	157	5	3,185	100.0

can only assume that this inventory refers to a small subset of all rebels from Bruges district. Unfortunately, the relationship of this sample to the total rebel population of the district is unknown. Whatever the criteria for inclusion, however, those listed owned an average of 0.95 buildings and had access to 14.7 measures of land. Table 2 summarizes the information concerning access to land embodied in the inventory of rebel property drawn up in Bruges district for the count of Flanders.

Clearly, there were differences between the two groups referred to in these inventories, perhaps most clearly indicated by the fact that the group from Bruges district had access to more than 3 times as much land per individual as did the group from southwestern Flanders—14.7 measures compared to 4.5 measures. This disparity can be attributed at least in part to the presence of 9 individuals in the inventory for Bruges district (representing 6 percent of the total) with access to more than 50 measures of land.[7] In contrast, only 3 out of 3,185 (less than 0.1 percent) in the inventory for southwestern Flanders had access to more than 50 measures of land. If we simply were to ignore these 9 individuals, the average would drop from 14.7 to 9.8 measures per individual, 2.2 times the amount for southwestern Flanders.

The disparity between the two groups can be explained further by the fact that no one included in the inventory for Bruges district was listed as totally lacking in land or buildings worth confiscating, a group that was

TABLE 2.   Range of Landholdings (in measures) for Bruges District[6]

Size	Owned	% Total	Leased	% Total	Combined	% Total
0	27	19.0	113	79.6	20	14.1
0.1–5	42	29.6	13	9.3	43	30.3
5.1–10	26	18.3	5	3.5	26	18.3
10.1–15	15	10.6	2	1.4	13	9.2
15.1–20	10	7.0	1	0.7	10	7.0
20.1–25	2	1.4	0	0.0	5	3.5
25.1–30	8	5.6	1	0.7	7	4.9
30.1–35	2	1.4	2	1.4	3	2.1
35.1–40	3	2.1	2	1.4	4	2.8
40.1–45	1	0.7	2	1.4	0	0.0
45.1–50	1	0.7	0	0.0	2	1.4
50.1—	5	3.5	1	0.7	9	6.3
Totals	142	100	142	100	142	100

represented by 891 individuals in the inventory for southwestern Flanders, 28 percent of all those listed. Why this was so may well be related to different procedures followed in compiling the inventories. In south-western Flanders, royal agents presumably began their work by listing the names of all rebels who fell in the Battle of Cassel—including an un-disclosed number of young men without property of their own living with parents or older siblings[8]—and subsequently attaching property to the list of names, a procedure apparently not followed in Bruges district where people without property worth confiscating were simply ignored. In any case, if 55 propertyless individuals were added to the Bruges group so that 28 percent of the total were without property worth confiscating, the amount of land at an individual's disposal would average out at 10.6 measures (or 6.9 measures if those having access to over 50 measures once again are eliminated).[9]

What the preceding hypothetical adjustments of the information pre-sented in the two inventories suggest is that neither represented a true cross-section of the rebel population of Flanders. While the list for south-western Flanders may have contained an inordinate number of propertyless individuals, the list for Bruges district may have placed an extra emphasis on those with more property to confiscate. The average rebel, if there really was such, most likely would have possessed land and buildings of a value somewhere between the two samples.

The question that still remains is whether or not the rebels were predominantly peasants, as I have maintained throughout this study. On the basis of my own examination of the confiscation lists, I see no reason to dissent from the prevailing opinion of all others who have given serious consideration to their social status. All agree that the rebels were primarily peasants.[10] The only real disagreement has been over their economic well-being, whether or not they should be considered impoverished or relatively well-off peasants.[11] However, this whole debate becomes moot if we abandon attempts to find a single average for all rebels and recognize as historians of peasants elsewhere have done that rich, poor, and middling peasants were customarily found side by side in the same rural communities. Clearly, the range of wealth stated in the confiscation lists corresponds closely to what we would expect to find (see the discussion in chapter 1, above). In southwestern Flanders, 74 percent of the rebels had access to 5 measures or less, 22 percent had access to between 5 and 20 measures of land, and 3 percent had access to more than 20 measures of land. The comparable figures for Bruges district are 44 percent, 34 percent, and 21 percent respectively.[12]

In the end, whether the rebels were peasants or not should be based not so much on purely quantitative considerations as on more qualitative concerns. Despite great differences in wealth between the poorest and richest peasants, they saw themselves as forming a group distinct from the great proprietors. Perhaps fairly typical of a peasant from the poorest group was Winnoc de le Brake, from Wormhout, Bergues district. The royal inventory merely tells us that he held 1.5 measures (0.7 hectares) of land.[13] In sharp contrast to him stood Coppijn van Roele, from the same parish, who owned a house, a grange, and 25 measures (11 hectares) of land.[14] Yet both most likely tilled the soil themselves and were joined together in a whole range of communal ties, such as sworn associations to combat fire and guard against cattle loss and an extensive system of mutual pledging and reciprocal obligations. In any case, they had much more in common with each other than either had with a great proprietor such as Simon de Rikelike, a prominent landowner in Bruges district during the 1320s and 1330s, who owned land and houses scattered over 11 parishes in the district. Much of what he owned was managed for him by agents who oversaw the collection of substantial rents, tithes, and payments in kind. Both Winnoc de la Brake and Coppijn van Roele viewed such people as the enemy because they lived primarily from the labor of others. Because Simon de Rikelike was so perceived by peasant rebels, explains the editor of his account book, collections of the rents, tithes, and payments owed him came to a virtual standstill during the revolt, causing him considerable financial embarrassment.[15]

Notes

1. Published in Henri Pirenne, ed., *Le soulèvement de la Flandre maritime, 1323–1328, documents inédites*, Académie Royale de Belgique, Commission Royale d'Histoire, Publications in-octavo (Brussels: P. Imbreghts, 1900), pp. 1–162. For Pirenne's description and analysis of the inventory and the circumstances under which it was drawn up, see pp. xxxvi–lxx.

2. Pirenne, ed., *Le soulèvement*, p. lxv. For the size of the measure, see J. Mertens, *De laat-middeleeuwse landbouweconomie in enkele gemeenten van het Brugse platteland*, Pro-Civitate, Historische Uitgaven, Reeks in 8to, nr. 27 (Brussels: Gemeentekrediet van België, 1970), p. 17.

3. Based on the summary information supplied by Pirenne, *Le soulèvement*, pp. lix–lxiv; by G. Des Marez, *Le problème de la colonisation franque et du régime agraire en Basse-Belgique*, Académie Royale de Belgique, Classe des Lettres, Mémoires, Collection en quarto, 2nd ser., vol. IX, fasc. 4 (Brussels: Maurice Lamertin, 1926), pp. 176–83; and by Louisa Hendrickx, "De sociale samenstelling van het Vlaamsche leger in den slag bij Cassel (1328)," *Nederlandsche historiebladen* 2 (1939), pp. 88–89.

4. Published in J. Mertens, ed., "Les confiscations dans la châtellenie du Franc de Bruges après la bataille de Cassel," *Bulletin de la Commission Royale d'Histoire* 134 (1968), pp. 245–75 (included in this inventory, pp. 275–78, were the confiscations of land and other property from four individuals who were treated separately because their vast holdings bore no relationship to the others in the list, while pp. 279–284 refer to the confiscation of 68 houses and other buildings from 55 individuals living in a number of towns and cities within Bruges district). Mertens provides a brief description of the inventory, pp. 239–44, with a more extensive analysis in a separate article: "De economische en sociale toestand van de opstandelingen uit het Brugse Vrije wier goederen na de slag bij Cassel (1328) verbeurd verklaard werden," *Belgisch tijdschrift voor filologie en geschiedenis* 47 (1969), pp. 1131–53.

5. See chapter three, above. We also know that Bruges district was able to form a sizeable force, perhaps several thousand strong, to guard the Scheldt route at Tournai against a French invasion in August 1328; see Chapter four above.

6. Compiled anew on the basis of Mertens, ed., "Les confiscations dans la châtellenie du Franc de Bruges," pp. 245–75, because there are a number of errors in Mertens, "De economische en sociale toestand van de opstandelingen uit het Brugse Vrije," pp. 1135–38, 1143–44 (Tables I and II).

7. Two of the nine (Jakemon le Garencopere and Rogier de Coudebrouc) were in fact citizens of the city of Bruges, while a third (Clais le Doiien) was the brother of a prominent Bruges citizen and magistrate, Willem de Deken; see Mertens, ed., "Les confiscations dans la châtellenie du Franc de Bruges," pp. 273–75.

Additional non-peasants were included among the smaller landholders: Jehans le Scotelare (citizen of Bruges), Pieters f. Pieter (citizen of Nieuwpoort, a city in Veurne district); and Rikewart de Strate (member of the prominent van Straten family); see ibid., pp. 253, 264, 254 respectively.

8. Hendrickx, "De sociale samenstelling van het Vlaamsche leger in den slag bij Cassel," p. 89. Hendrickx also points to several other reasons why the numbers of propertyless in this inventory may have been inflated, pp. 89–90, including the fact that very little account was taken of leased or rented land, a common phenomenon in the Flemish countryside by the beginning of the fourteenth century. For example, based on my own calculations, 20.9 percent of the land referred to in Table 2 was leased land compared to only 5.9 percent in Table 1; see Pirenne, ed. *Le soulèvement*, p. lviii.

9. Alternatively, if we were to strip out the 891 totally propertyless individuals from the group represented by the inventory for southwestern Flanders, the average amount of land available to those who remained would rise to 5.7 measures, up from the 4.5 measures when all are included.

10. Even though five in Bruges district and an unknown number for southwestern Flanders were citizens of cities and towns, with an additional handful of large proprietors who allied themselves with the rebels—see for example, the four treated separately in the Bruges list; Mertens, ed., "Les confiscations dans la châtellenie du Franc de Bruges," pp. 275–78.

11. Only Des Marez, *Le problème de la colonisation franque et du régime agraire en Basse-Belgique*, pp. 176–83, has argued that primarily the poorest peasants participated in the revolt. All others have concluded that the rebels were not an impoverished group: see Pirenne, ed., *Le soulèvement*, pp. lv–lxix; Hendrickx, "De sociale samenstelling van het Vlaamsche leger in den slag bij Cassel," pp. 88–90; and Mertens, "De economische en sociale toestand van de opstandelingen uit het Brugse Vrije," 1150–53.

12. Compare these figures to those provided by Adriaan Verhulst, *Précis d'histoire rurale de la Belgique* (Brussels: Éditions de l'Université de Bruxelles, 1990), pp.113–16; and Mertens, "De economische en sociale toestand van de opstandelingen uit het Brugse Vrije," pp. 1148–50.

13. Singled out only because his name, so similar to my own, caught my attention; Pirenne, ed., *Le soulèvement*, p. 113: "Winnoc de le Brake, 1-1/2 mesures de terre."

14. Pirenne, ed., *Le soulèvement*, p. 112: "Coppijn van Roele, 1 maison, 1 grange et 25 mesurez de terre."

15. Published by J. De Smet, ed., *Het memoriaal van Simon de Rikelike, vrijlaat te St. Pieters-op-den-dijk, 1323–1336*, Koninklijke Commissie voor Geschiedenis (Brussels: Maurice Lamertin, 1933); on the effects of the revolt, see pp. xxiii–xxv.

Appendix B: Peasant Captains, 1323–1328

The individuals examined here were special peasant captains or *hoofdmannen*. While many others were captains of single communities or localities, all of the following were captains of large portions of or even entire rural districts—they replaced the bailiffs of the count in the rebel rural districts. Even though they represented the top echelon of command and leadership for the entire revolt, all were peasants, chosen by the local captains of the districts within which they resided. Of those for whom we have information concerning ownership or leasing of property (Bockel, Bonin, le Fiere, Janssone, and Zannekin), all but one (le Fiere) belonged to the wealthiest ranks of the peasantry when we compare their landholdings to the information supplied in Appendix A above.

Blawrel Bockel

The only thing known for certain about Blawrel Bockel is that he was one of four captains who led peasant contingents from Bruges district in the November 1325 battle at Assenede, district of Vier Ambachten. The other three were Lambert Bonin, Segher Janssone, and Walter Ratgheer (see below). Bockel, along with Ratgheer, died in the battle.[1]

Bockel must have resided in the village of Nieuwerkerk, about 25 kilometers northeast of Bruges in the eastern part of Bruges district, since the lists drawn up for the purpose of confiscating the property of rebels at the end of the revolt mentioned a Hugh, son of Blauwel Beukels, a mother Blauwel, and a John, son of Blauwel Beukel. Together, they had access to nearly 25 hectares (over 60 acres) of land and owned several buildings.[2]

Lambert Bonin

Lambert Bonin was a captain for Bruges district during most of the rebellion. Even though Bonin was a very common name in both the city and rural district of Bruges,[3] identifying him with the village of Westkapelle, about twelve kilometers north of the city of Bruges, seems rather certain. According to the confiscation list compiled for that village at the end of the rebellion, Lambert Bonin owned and leased about 12 hectares (nearly 30 acres) of land.[4] That he was a wealthy peasant is shown by the fact that he possessed a seal for his own correspondence.[5]

Most of Bonin's activities as a captain were associated with the eastern part of the district of Bruges. In early 1325 he kept a contingent of loyalist forces occupied in Aardenburg while others, especially Segher Janssone and Nikolaas Zannekin (see below), liberated the southwestern rural districts of Flanders.[6] During a truce a short time later, he issued a statement on 25 April 1325 in which he promised in the future to use all of his efforts to support rather than work against Count Louis.[7] But his submission was of very short duration. He was one of four captains, along with Blawrel Bockel, Segher Janssone, and Walter Ratgheer (see above and below) who led peasant contingents from Bruges district in a battle at Assenede,[8] district of Vier Ambachten, shortly before the end of November 1325, and he continued to play a leading role up to the end of the rebellion.

Bonin did not participate in the decisive battle at Cassel, in August 1328. He and most of the other peasant rebels from Bruges district had assumed the task of guarding the easternmost of the possible routes the invading force might take and had thus stationed themselves along the Scheldt River near Tournai, some sixty kilometers east of Cassel.[9] In the general collapse of the rebellion that followed this battle, Bonin was captured and subsequently decapitated.[10]

Winnoc le Fiere

A native of the parish of Hoymille, in Bergues district, Winnoc le Fiere rose through the ranks to become captain for the district for the last year of the revolt, replacing Jacob Peyt (see below) after the latter's assassination. The earliest information we have about le Fiere actually predated his becoming the district captain. Testimony taken by a commission on damages after the Battle of Cassel implicated him along with fourteen others in the alleged murder on 9 February 1327 of a certain Benoit li Brol, of Hondschoote (Bergues district).[11] He is simply listed as a participant here, not as a district-wide captain; the group was led by the local captain of Hondschoote, Jehan le Valewe.[12]

It was only around the end of 1327 in the wake of Jacob Peyt's death,[13] that le Fiere was chosen captain of the entire district of Bergues. Additional testimony before the commission on damages claimed that le Fiere, as peasant captain of Bergues district in 1327, oversaw the seizure and sale of property belonging to Wautier le Scridere and Jehan Bankinoet, both of Hondschoote but imprisoned in the city of Bergues for opposing the rebellion.[14] The author of the *Chronicon* wrote that a Winnocus de Flere led the contingents from Bruges at the Battle of Cassel (August 1328),[15] which we should interpret to mean Winnoc le Fiere leading the contingents from Bergues.[16] Le Fiere died during the battle.

Compared to most of the other district captains that can be identified, le Fiere's landholdings were quite modest. After his death in the Battle of Cassel, his property, amounting only to a manor house with about a half hectare (nearly an acre and a half) of land, was confiscated by agents of the king of France.[17] Most of the other holdings in Hoymille were small as well. This village was very close to the city of Bergues, and many of its residents, including le Fiere, may have supplemented their agricultural activities with work in the city in one capacity of another.

Segher Janssone

Segher Janssone was one of several peasant captains for Bruges district. He was associated specifically with the northwest quadrant of the district, north and west of the city of Bruges.[18] Janssone was a resident of Bredene, 15 kilometers west of Bruges near the town of Oostende, where he owned and leased just over 11 hectares (about 27 acres) of land.[19]

Janssone first became visible in the sources around the end of 1324 as the leader of an armed, peasant force that besieged Gistel, a fortified town in the western part of Bruges district containing a contingent of Count Louis' forces. He was particularly active during 1325, however. With Niko-laas Zannekin (see below), he spearheaded the campaign that sent Robert of Cassel fleeing into Artois and brought all of southwestern Flanders into the rebel camp during the first months of that year. He was present in June 1325 when rebels confronted arbitration commissioners at Ter Duinen Abbey, and he participated in the ill-fated battle at Assenede during November 1325.[20] Though Janssone continued to play a leading role right up to the end of the rebellion, he did not participate in the decisive Battle of Cassel, in August 1328. He and most of the other peasant rebels from Bruges district assumed the task of guarding the easternmost of the possible routes the invading force might take; thus he most likely was stationed along the Scheldt River near Tournai, some sixty kilometers east of Cassel.[21]

In the general collapse of the rebellion that followed the Battle of Cassel, Janssone, unlike most of the other captains, evaded capture. He escaped to Zeeland, where he was joined by other rebels. During February 1329, he and his fellow exiles attempted to raise the rebellion once again by sailing from Zeeland to Oostende and swearing oaths of solidarity with many peasants from Oostende and Bredene. The rebels made their way as far as Oudenburg, where they eventually were defeated and Janssone was captured. Janssone was conveyed to Bruges were he was brutally tortured. The author of the *Chronicon* says his captors burned his entire body with red hot irons and broke his legs and arms before they decapitated him. His mutilated body was then suspended on a wheel for all to see. It was in connection with Janssone's gruesome death that the author of the *Chronicon* declared an end to the "plague of insurrection" that had raged for the previous six years.[22]

Jacob Peyt

Although Jacob Peyt (variants include Peit, Peiten) became one of the most important peasant captains during the last phase of the Flemish revolt, information about his career is fragmentary and in some cases controversial. It derives primarily from three independent sources: a passage by the anonymous author of the *Chronicon*; four episodes referred to in testimony before the previously-mentioned commission on damages convened after 1328; and a 1329 letter by Jean Lain, a priest of the town of Dunkirk and deacon of the city and countryside of Bergues.[23] Unfortunately these sources do not agree in all respects, and this ambiguity has been the cause not only of a certain amount of confusion but also of occasional error in the historical literature.

We know very little about Peyt's personal life. Because the peasants of Bergues district chose him as their captain, it is safe to assume that he was born in that district. All peasant captains that can be identified served in their native districts.[24] Perhaps his burial at Coudekerque, twelve kilometers west of the place where he was killed, indicates a tie to that particular community.[25] Historian Jacques Toussaert tried to identify Jacob Peyt with a monk named Pieter Peyt at Ter Duinen Abbey, at Koksijde in neighboring Veurne district, who presumably left Flanders around the time of the French invasion of 1300 because he objected to the pro-French (*leliaart*) sympathies of the abbey. According to Toussaert, this monk spent time at the abbey of Belfonds, in Hungary, before returning to Flanders during the 1320s.[26] In fact, Pieter Peyt most likely was Jacob's brother and apparently sympathized with his brother's cause.[27]

Peyt's entire career as peasant captain was played out in the years 1326 and 1327. The only historian to question the first date in any way is F. W. N. Hugenholtz who suggests on the basis of Peyt's well-known anticlericalism, expressed primarily as opposition to the imposition of excommunication and the interdict, that some of his activity might be placed as early as their first imposition on 4 November 1325 rather than their reimpostion of 6 April 1327. However, as Madeleine Braekman makes clear, there is no sufficient reason to accept the earlier date, nor does Hugenholtz really make a case for this date, only that it might have been a possibility. Hugenholtz quickly agrees, in fact, that most of his activities were after Peace of Arques (19 April 1326).[28] Indeed, all three primary sources clearly place his activities after the Peace of Arques.

All sources agree as well that Peyt remained active as a district captain until he was assassinated. It appears that he, like Nikolaas Zannekin (see below), had become a *buitenpoorter* of the city of Bruges—that is, he acquired citizenship in the city but maintained residence elsewhere, in his case in the rural district of Bergues.[29] The city of Bruges looked into the matter of Peyt's assassination for this reason, not because he was a resident of the city or because the city remained actively involved in the rebellion.[30] The results of the investigation are unknown.

Exactly when Peyt was assassinated is a somewhat contested matter. The anonymous author of the *Chronicon* mentioned Peyt's death: he was killed in Hondschoote, Bergues district, by people from Veurne, but whether by rivals within the movement or by agents of king, count, or church (or all three) is not indicated. The same author added, however, that the city of Bruges investigated the matter and that the revolt lasted another two years thereafter.[31] While to all intents and purposes the revolt ended shortly after the Battle of Cassel, in August 1328, the author of the *Chronicon* did not declare it concluded until after the torture and execution of Segher Janssone, the peasant captain from Bruges district who tried to reinstigate revolt in February 1329 (see above). This would place Peyt's death sometime around February 1327. But such a date clearly conflicts with other evidence. First of all, the city of Ypres sent a messenger to Peyt around the first of May 1327 and received messengers from him towards the end of May and as late as July 1327.[32] Further, a date of February 1327 for Peyt's death contradicts the testimony of Jean Lain who reported that Peyt was still active in November 1327.[33]

Braekman is the only historian who has attempted to build a case for placing Peyt's assassination before November 1327 as suggested by the author of the *Chronicon*, though she admits that this conflicts with the evidence supplied by Jean Lain.[34] She apparently was not aware of the fact that the city of Ypres received a messenger from Peyt as late as July 1327. She bases her argument primarily on an interpretation of testimony collected by the post-1328 damages commission referring to Peyt's successor, Winnoc le Fiere (see above) who she says had replaced Peyt by 9 February 1327—specifically, le Fiere was implicated in the death on that date of Benoit li Brol, of Hondschoote. However, as I argued above, there is no indication here that le Fiere was a district-wide captain at that time, only that he was a participant. The only captain mentioned in connection with this episode was a local one, Jehan le Valewe, *hoofman* or captain of Hondschoote. Thus, there is no need to assume from this passage that Peyt was already dead by February 1327 and that Winnoc le Fiere had taken his place.

The problem that remains is the statement in the *Chronicon*. Either the author was mistaken or he has been misread. But it would be difficult to interpret the statement differently; he clearly says that the revolt lasted two years after Peyt's death. However, as I have argued elsewhere (see chapter four), the author of the *Chronicon* seems to have been poorly informed about this part of the rebellion—after all, he rendered Jacob Peyt as Jacob Pric; he erroneously described him as a captain from Bruges district (instead of Bergues district);[35] and he wrongly saw the revolt as being directed by Bruges in this phase.[36] Because of the unreliability of the *Chronicon* for the third phase of the revolt and because two other sources clearly support the later date, it is safe to conclude that Peyt's assassination occurred sometime after 7 November 1327 and that the author of the *Chronicon* considered the fifteen-month interval between Peyt's death and the end of the revolt, which he placed in February 1329 (see the entry for Segher Janssone, above), to have been roughly two years.

Though Peyt was associated with several kinds of activities, including the driving of rural magistrates out of Bergues district shortly after the Peace of Arques in 1326 and overseeing the redistribution of their accumulated wealth, he gained his greatest notoriety for his actions against the clergy. There can be no doubt that Peyt took actions against the clergy after the Peace of Arques, especially after 6 April 1327, the date on which Flanders once again was placed under the ecclesiastical bans of excommunication and interdict.[37] In particular, he organized a series of actions against those members of the clergy in southwestern Flanders who had turned against the revolt, but such actions eventually earned for him the erroneous characterization of heretic.[38]

Walter Ratgheer

We know virtually nothing about Walter Ratgheer or where he came from. Because he led peasant contingents drawn primarily from the eastern part of Bruges district,[39] it is safe to assume that he resided in that part of the district. This conclusion is supported by the fact that all of his actions known to us consisted of three campaigns during 1325 from the eastern part of Bruges district into the northeastern rural districts, Vier Ambachten and Waas. Unfortunately, a review of the confiscation lists drawn up for Bruges district reveals no obviously similar names, so his place of origin remains uncertain.[40] Despite the fact that we know so little about him personally, we do know that he was a very important peasant captain. Ratgheer appears to have been in charge of the entire campaign to extend the revolt into the districts of Vier Ambachten and Land of Waas, a role he played right up to his death in the Battle of Assenede in November 1325.[41]

Nikolaas Zannekin

Nikolaas Zannekin, the best-known today of all the peasant captains of Flanders during the 1320s,[42] was a well-to-do peasant from Lampernisse, Veurne district, where he owned about 17 hectares (nearly 42 acres) of land.[43] His entire public career was associated with this district and the other districts of southwestern Flanders. Though it is perhaps safe to assume that most of the district captains began their rebel careers during the first phase of the revolt, there is evidence to that effect only for Zannekin. According to the author of the *Chronicon*, he was a captain for the entire district of Veurne as well as for all of southwestern Flanders during the disorders of 1323 to 1324.[44] For reasons not entirely clear today, he subsequently fled from Veurne district and like Jacob Peyt, became a *buitenpoorter*[45] of the city of Bruges, and he seemed to enjoy considerable popularity or notoriety there, depending on one's point of view.[46] In a letter of 21

January 1325 in which Count Louis asked his uncle, Robert of Cassel, for assistance in suppressing the rebellion, Zannekin was listed as an ally of the rebels of Bruges district.[47] He continued, however, to maintain very close ties to his home district of Veurne, apparently as a proxy or representative in temporary exile. His continuing leadership role in southwestern Flanders combined with his contacts in the city and district of Bruges made Zannekin one of the most important links in the organization of the Flemish peasant revolt.[48]

Little is known about Zannekin's actions for about three years after June 1325 except that he continued to act as a captain, not only for his native Veurne district but also for all of southwestern Flanders—essentially the lands that constituted the appanage of Robert of Cassel. Throughout this period the districts he oversaw remained loyal to the rebellion.

Zannekin reappeared in the written record during the summer of 1328 at the head of a large peasant army drawn from the districts of Veurne, Bergues, Bourbourg, Cassel, and Bailleul which was stationed in the town of Cassel to ward off the much expected invasion by the French and their allies. As we saw in chapter four, other rebel armies had been dispatched to cover other possible invasion routes: an army drawn from the districts of Ypres and Courtrai covered the Leie River and the city of Lille; the forces from Bruges district led by Janssone took up a position at Tournai to guard the Scheldt River.[49] Because the invaders chose the Cassel route, it was Zannekin (assisted by the captain from Bergues district, Winnoc le Fiere— see above) and the peasants of southwestern Flanders who received the full brunt of the massive invasion. According to the author of the *Chronicon*, after consulting with other captains as well as the rank and file of his army, on 23 August 1328 Zannekin decided to descend the impregnable but surrounded hill on which Cassel was founded to launch a surprise attack against the invaders on the plain below.[50] Most who have since examined the battle that ensued have concluded this was a mistake; the peasant infantry was stronger in defense against mounted warriors than on the offensive. In fact, by the end of the day, Zannekin and more than three thousand of his peasant warriors lay dead on the battlefield.[51]

Notes

    1. Anonymous, *Chronicon comitum Flandrensium*, in *Corpus chronicorum Flandriae, sub auspiciis Leopoldi primi, serenissimi Belgarum regis: recueil des chroniques*

de Flandre, vol. 1, J. J. DeSmet, ed., Académie Royale de Belgique, Commision Royale d'Histoire, Mémoires en quarto (Brussels: H. Hayez, 1837) (hereafter cited as *Chronicon*), p. 199. In my opinion, Jacques Sabbe, *Vlaanderen in opstand, 1323–1328: Nikolaas Zannekin, Zeger Janszone en Willem de Deken*, Genootschap voor Geschiedenis "Société d'Émulation" te Brugge, Vlaamse Historische Studies, VII (Bruges: Marc Van de Wiele, 1992), pp. 34–35, 46, 48, 78, 103. 112, confuses Blawrel Bockel with his son Hughe; the latter, seemingly a rebel as well, was executed for his activity after the Battle of Cassel—ibid., p. 103.

2. J. Mertens, ed., "Les confiscations dans la châtellenie du Franc de Bruges après la bataille de Cassel," *Bulletin de la Commission Royale d'Histoire* 134 (1968), pp. 247–48: "Huwes Blauwel f. Beukels," "la mer Blauwel," and "Jehan Blauwel, f. Beukel" together owned or leased more than 56 *mesures* of land and 3 buildings. One *mesure* (Dutch, *gemet*) was the equivalent of 0.44 hectares (or 1.09 acres) according to J. Mertens, *De laat-middeleeuwse landbouweconomie in enkele gemeenten van het Brugse platteland*, Pro-Civitate, Historische Uitgaven, Reeks in 8to, nr. 27 (Brussels: Gemeentekrediet van België, 1970), p. 17.

3. See David Nicholas, *Town and Countryside: Social, Economic, and Political Tensions in Fourteenth-Century Flanders*, Rijksuniversiteit te Gent, Werken uitgegeven door de faculteit van de letteren en wijsbegeerte, 152 (Bruges: De Tempel, 1971), pp. 312–14, note 150.

4. Mertens, ed., "Les confiscations dans la châtellenie du Franc de Bruges," p. 255: "Lambers Bonin, 1 manoir 4 mesures de fief que on tient de mons. de Flandres, desqueles une femme tient a se vie les 2 mesures. Item, 8 mesures de fief que on tient des enfans de Dudzele. Item, 13 mesures de terre qu'il achata dou sien propre."

5. Henri Pirenne, ed., *Le soulèvement de la Flandre maritime, 1323–1328, documents inédits*, Académie Royale de Belgique, Commission Royale d'Histoire, Publications in-octavo (Brussels: P. Imbreghts, 1900), appendix 5, p. 182.

6. *Chronicon*, p. 189: "Tunc Lambertus *Bonin*, capitaneus praedictus, cum suis et cum illis de *Oostvrien* obsedit villam de *Ardenborg*."

7. Published in Pirenne, ed., *Le soulèvement*, appendix 5, pp. 180–82.

8. *Chronicon*, p. 199.

9. J. van Rompaey, "De opstand in het Vlaamse kustland van 1323 tot 1328 en de figuur van Nikolaas Zannekin," in *Nikolaas Zannekin en de Slag bij Kassel, 1328–1978: bijdrage tot de studie van de 14de eeuw en de landelijke geschiedenis van de Westhoek* (Diksmuide, Belgium: Kulturele Raad van Diksmuide, 1978), p. 123.

10. *Chronicon*, p. 207: "Sic Lambertus *Bonin* capitaneus de Franco . . . decapitantur, rotantur cum multis aliis, qui per diversa supplicia in vindictam commissae nequitiae cogebantur extremum spiritum exhalare."

11. See Pirenne, ed., *Le soulèvement*, p. 216: "Jehan le Valewe ki a esté hoofman de Hondescote tout li muete durant et menoit de son maison lediit Benoit au Berghes pour lui mordrir, Winnoc le Fiere, Michiel le Varsche, Masin de Bieres, Michiel Boid, Jakemin Roze, David Loot, Clai Labaen, Jehan Brudoel, Willem Anbrois, Michiel Beier, Jehan Basin, Gill. Bode, Jehan le Mach, Danut Harbeen, et che furent cheaus ki faisoient chest orible fait de leur propre mains."

12. Madeleine Braekman, "Jacob Peyt, hérésie ou révolte social en Flandre au XIVe siècle?" *Bulletin de la Société du Protestantisme Belge* 7 (1979), p. 325, especially

note 105, misreads this passage by concluding that he was a district-wide captain by this time.

13. See the section on Jacob Peyt, below.

14. Pirenne, ed., *Le soulèvement*, pp. 215, 218: referred to as "Winnoc le Fiere adonc hoofman de Berghes . . ." and "Winnoc le Fiere, hoofman de le castelerie de Berghes et de tout le commun. . . ."

15. *Chronicon*, p. 204: "Fueruntque ibi congregati . . . Brugenses, quorum capitaneus erat Winnocus de *Flere*, pessimus homicida."

16. See Pirenne, *Le soulèvement*, p. 215, note. 1.

17. See Pirenne, ed., *Le soulèvement*, p. 116: "Winnoc le Fiere . . . le manoir là manoit avec 5 quartiers de terre."

18. *Chronicon*: p. 188, "illi de *Nort-Vrien*, quorum capitaneus erat Sigerus Johannis. . . ."

19. His holdings were described in the confiscation lists compiled after the Battle of Cassel, in 1328, published in Mertens, ed., "Les confiscations dans la châtellenie du Franc de Bruges après la bataille de Cassel," p. 272: "Sohiers, f. Jehan, 17 mesures et 2 lines de fief que on tient de le demisel de Rougebrucghe et 4 mesures et 50 verghes de terre et doivent par an les 4 mesures environ 10 s. 6 d."

20. For the events of 1325 and Jansonne's role in them, see chapter 3, above.

21. Van Rompaey, "De opstand in het Vlaamse kustland," p. 123.

22. *Chronicon*, pp. 208–9: "ibique cum ferro candenti membratim adustus, post tractus est ad patibulum, et fractis cruribus suis atque membris, decapitatus fuit et positus supra rotam, atque suspensus cum rota eadem in novum patibulum mirae altitudinis. . . . Sicque cessavit haec pestis popularium contra superiores suos rebellantium, quae de caetero, protegente Altissimo, non resurget, quae tamen sex annis continuis invaluit et duravit."

23. See respectively *Chronicon*, p. 202; Pirenne, ed., *Le soulèvement*, pp. 206–7, 211–13, 213–14, 216–17; and Paul Fredericq, ed., *Corpus documentorum inquisitionis haereticae pravitatis Neerlandicae: verzameling van stukken betreffende de pauselijke en bisschoppelijke inquisitie in de Nederlanden*, vol. 3 (Ghent and The Hague: J. Vuylsteke and Martinus Nijhoff, 1909), pp. 8–10.

24. As Braekman, "Jacob Peyt, hérésie ou révolte social en Flandre," pp. 322–23, notes, the author of the *Chronicon* (p. 202) wrongly identified Peyt as a captain of Bruges district instead of Bergues district. The two place names are similar in Latin; he should have written "capitaneus Bergensis" instead of "capitaneus Brugensis."

25. In the letter of Jean Lain, published in Fredericq, ed., *Corpus documentorum inquisitionis haereticae*, no. 11, p. 9, Peyt was identified as "Coppins Peyt li Renoyes" and "Coppin Peyt le Renoyet." One wonders whether Renoyes or Renoyet might be a form of Reynaerd. If so, perhaps Peyt was related to Jehan Reynaerd of Coudekerque; see Pirenne, ed., *Le soulèvement*, p. 117: "Jehan Reynaerd . . . le manoir et 14 mesures de terre." Another possibility might be to associate Peyt with Lauwer Paet of Quaedypre, 7 kilometers south of Coudekerque; see ibid., p. 111.

26. Jacques Toussaert, *Le sentiment religieux en Flandre à la fin du moyen-âge*, Civilisations d'Hier et d'Aujourd'hui (Paris: Plon, 1963), pp. 452, 454–55.

27. See Sabbe, *Vlaanderen in opstand*, pp. 56, 105, note 272.

28. F. W. H. Hugenholtz, *Drie boerenopstanden uit de veertiende eeuw: Vlaanderen 1323–1328, Frankrijk 1358, Engeland 1381; onderzoek naar het opstandig bewustzijn* (Haarlem: Tjeenk Willink, 1949), p. 96; Braekman, "Jacob Peyt, hérésie ou révolte social en Flandre," p. 325.

29. For the meaning and significance of *buitenpoorter*, see Nicholas, *Town and Countryside*, pp. 12, 221, 235–49.

30. N. de Pauw, "L'Enquête de Bruges après la bataille de Cassel," *Bulletin de la Commission Royale d'Histoire* 68 (1899), pp. 667, 686; Braekman, "Jacob Peyt, hérésie ou révolte social en Flandre," p. 323; Hugenholtz, *Drie boerenopstanden*, p. 33; and Nicholas, *Town and Countryside*, pp. 163–64.

31. *Chronicon*, p. 202: "fuisset in Hontscota per Furnenses occisus. . . . Duravitque pestis ista postea per biennium."

32. G. Des Marez and E. de Sagher, eds., *Comptes de la ville d'Ypres de 1297 à 1329*, vol. 2, Académie Royale de Belgique, Commission Royale d'Histoire (Brussels: P. Imbreghts, 1913): p. 697 (2 May 1327), "Jan Taispile, isent te Roedsbrigghe ende te Cassele tote Jacob Peiten van 2 daghen: 16. s."; p. 727 (30 May 1327): "Enen messagier, comende van Jacob Peiten: 4s."; p. 733 (11 July 1327), "Enen bode, comende van Jacob Peiten: 4 s."

33. His letter, published in Fredericq, ed., *Corpus documentorum inquisitionis haereticae*, vol. 3, pp. 8–10, is clearly dated to 16 February 1329 and refers to activity a year and fourteen weeks ("un an et XIIII semaines") earlier, around 9 November 1327.

34. Braekman, "Jacob Peyt, hérésie ou révolte social en Flandre," p. 325, especially note 105.

35. Braekman, "Jacob Peyt, hérésie ou révolte social en Flandre," pp. 322–24.

36. Hugenholtz, *Drie boerenopstanden*, p. 107.

37. Arnold Fayen, ed., *Lettres de Jean XXII (1316–334): textes et analyses*, Analecta Vaticano-Beligica publiés par l'Institut Historique Belge de Rome (Rome: M. Bretschneider, 1909), vol. 2, part 1, no. 1942, pp. 113–18.

38. Concerning the anti-clericalism of Peyt and his associates and the false charges of heresy, see Braekman, "Jacob Peyt, hérésie ou révolte social en Flandre," pp. 313–32, as well as Chapter four above.

39. *Chronicon*, pp. 192, 198: "capitaneus de *Vrien*, vocatus Walterus *Ratgheer*," "Walterus *Ratgheer* capitaneus de Franco," "Walterus *Ratgheer*, cum Ostvriensibus (Franconatus orientalis)," and "Walterus *Ratgheer* cum suis de *Ostvrien*."

40. The closest name I could come up with was Hanin, son of Clais Reinghier, who owned "1 maison 3 mesures et 41 verghe de terre" in the parish of Zevekote, about three kilometers west of Gistel; see Mertens, ed., "Les confiscations dans la châtellenie du Franc de Bruges," p. 266.

41. See, for example, *Chronicon*, pp. 198, 199: "Walterus *Ratgheer*, cum Ostviensibus (Franconatus orientalis) et cum Quatuor Officiis atque terra de *Waes*"; and "Walterus *Ratgheer*, congregata virorum magna multitudine de toto Franco armatorum electorum." For a review of Ratgheer's public career, see Chapter 3 above.

42. He remains today a popular Flemish folk hero, largely because he commanded the peasant forces in the 1328 Battle of Cassel. For a good idea of the breadth

and depth of his popularity, see J. Mertens, "Zannekin of de evolutie van het beeld van een volksheld," *De Franse Nederlanden—Le Pays-Bas français* (1978): 24–37.

43. See the list of confiscations compiled after the Battle of Cassel (1328), published by Pirenne, ed., *Le soulèvement*, p. 38: "Clais Zannekin . . . 38 mesures de terre."

44. *Chronicon*, p. 189: "Nicolaus *Zannekin*, qui in primo tumultu capitaneus fuerat territorii Furensis et totius terrae occidentalis. . . ."

45. See Nicholas, *Town and Countryside*, pp. 12, 221, 235–49. According to Sabbe, *Vlaanderen in opstand*, p. 24, Zannekin was implicated in disorders in Veurne revealed by an inquest of March 1323.

46. *Chronicon*, p. 189: "Fuit in diebus illis quidam magnae reputationis in villa Brugensi, nominatus Nicolaus *Zannekin*." See also Hugenholtz, *Drie boerenopstanden*, pp. 28, 106; and van Rompaey, "De opstand in het Vlaamse kustland," p. 113.

47. Published in T. De Limburg-Stirum, ed., *Codex diplomaticus Flandriae ab anno 1296 ad usque 1327, ou recueil de documents relatifs aux guerres et dissensions suscitées par Philippe-le-Bel, roi de France, contre Gui de Dampierre, comte de Flandre*, Société d'Émulation pour l'Étude de l'Histoire et des Antiquités de la Flandre (Bruges: De Plancke, 1889), vol. 2, p. 369, no. 348: "chil du Franc de Bruges, Colin Zannekin et autre leur aidant et aliiet."

48. Zannekin's activities during 1325 were reviewed in chapter 3, above.

49. J. van Rompaey, "De opstand in het Vlaamse kustland," p. 123.

50. *Chronicon*, 205.

51. Pirenne, ed., *Le soulèvement*, pp. xxviii–xxx, 1–162.

Bibliography

Alexandre, Pierre. *Le climat en Europe au moyen âge: contribution à l'histoire des variations climatiques de 1000 à 1425 d'après les sources narratives de l'Europe occidentale*. Recherches d'Histoire et de Sciences Sociales, number 24. Paris: École des Hautes Études en Sciences Sociales, 1987.

Anonymous. *Annales gandenses*. Edited and translated by Hilda Johnstone. Medieval Classics. London: Thomas Nelson and Sons, 1951.

———. *Chronicon comitum Flandrensium*. In *Corpus chronicorum Flandriae, sub auspiciis Leopoldi primi, serenissimi Belgarum regis: recueil des chroniques de Flandre*, edited by J. J. DeSmet, vol. 1, 34–57. Académie Royale de Belgique, Commission Royale d'Histoire, Mémoires en quarto. Brussels: H. Hayez, 1837.

Baerten, J. "Les mouvements paysans au moyen âge: reflexions sur deux ouvrages récents." *Le Moyen Age* 87 (1981): 455–64.

Bierbrauer, Peter. "Bäuerliche Revolten im Alten Reich: ein Forschungsbericht." In *Aufruhr und Empörung? Studien zum bäuerlichen Widerstand im Alten Reich*, 1–68. Munich: H. Beck, 1980.

Blickle, Peter. "Peasant Revolts in the German Empire in the Late Middle Ages." *Social History* 4 (1979): 223–39.

Bloch, Marc. *French Rural History: An Essay in Its Basic Characteristics*. Translated by Janet Sondheimer. Berkeley: University of California Press, 1966.

Blockmans, F. "De bestraffing van den opstand van Brugge en Westelijk-Vlaanderen in 1328." *Beknopte Handelingen, XVe Vlaamsche Filologencongress* (1940): 38–45.

Blockmans, W. P. "De ontwikkeling van een verstedelijkte samenleving (XIde–XVde eeuw)." In *Geschiedenis van Vlaanderen van de oorsprong tot heden*, edited by Els Witte, 43–103. Brussels: Historische Getuigen/La Renaissance du Livre, 1983.

———. *Een middeleeuwse vendetta: Gent 1300*. Houten, NL: Unieboek-De Haan, 1987.

Blockmans, W. P., J. Mertens, and Adriaan Verhulst. "Les communautés rurales d'ancien régime en Flandre: caractéristiques et essai d'interprétation comparative." In *Europe occidentale et Amerique—Western Europe and America*, vol. 5 of *Les communautés rurales—Rural Communities*, 223–48. Recueils de la Société Jean Bodin pour l'Histoire Comparative des Institutions, XLIV. Paris: Dessain et Tolra, 1987.

Blockmans, W. P., G. Pieters, Walter Prevenier, and R. W. M. van Schaik. "Tussen crisis en welvaart: sociale veranderingen 1300–1500." In *Algemene geschiedenis der Nederlanden*, vol. 4, 42–86. Haarlem: Fibula-van Dishoeck, 1980.

Bovesse, J. "Le comte de Namur Jean Ier et les événements du comté de Flandre en 1325–1326." *Bulletin de la Commission Royale d'Histoire* 131 (1965): 385–454.

———. "Notes sur l'Écluse et la maison comtale namuroise à la fin du XIIIe et au début du XIVe siècle." In *Hommage au professeur Paul Bonnenfant (1899–1965): études d'histoire médiévale dédiées à sa mémoire par les anciens élèves de son séminaire à l'Université Libre de Bruxelles*, edited by G. Despy, 231–53. Brussels: Universa, 1965.

Braekman, Madeleine. "Jacob Peyt, hérésie ou révolte social en Flandre au XIVe siècle?" *Bulletin de la Société du Protestantisme Belge* 7 (1979): 313–32.

Brinton, Crane. *The Anatomy of Revolution*. Revised edition. New York: Vintage, 1965.

Brooks, Nicholas. "The Organization and Achievements of the Peasants of Kent and Essex in 1381." In *Studies in Medieval History Presented to R. H. C. Davies*, edited by Henry Mayr-Harting and Robert I. Moore, 247–70. London and Ronceverte, WV: Hambledon Press, 1985.

Caenegem, R. C. van. "De Gentse februari-opstand van het jaar 1128." *Spiegel historiael* 13 (1978): 478–83.

Cohn, Samuel, Jr. "Florentine Insurrections, 1342–1385, in Comparative Perspective." In *The English Rising of 1381*, edited by R. H. Hilton and T. H. Aston, 143–64. Past and Present Publications. Cambridge: Cambridge University Press, 1984.

De Gryse, L. M. "Some Observations on the Origin of the Flemish Bailiff (bailli): The Reign of Philip of Alsace." *Viator: Medieval and Renaissance Studies* 7 (1976): 143–94.

De Limburg-Stirum, T., ed. *Codex diplomaticus Flandriae ab anno 1296 ad usque 1327, ou recueil de documents relatifs aux guerres et dissensions suscitées par Philippe-le-Bel, roi de France, contre Gui de Dampierre, comte de Flandre*. Vol. 2. Société d'Émulation pour l'Étude de l'Histoire et des Antiquités de la Flandre. Bruges: De Plancke, 1889.

De Pauw, N. "L'Enquête de Bruges après la bataille de Cassel, documents inédits publiés." *Bulletin de la Commission Royale d'Histoire* 68 (1899): 665–704.

De Smet, J., ed. *Het memoriaal van Simon de Rikelike, vrijlaat te St. Pieters-op-den-dijk, 1323–1336*. Koninklijke Commissie voor Geschiedenis. Brussels: Maurice Lamertin, 1933.

Derville, Alain. "Le nombre d'habitants des villes d'Artois et de la Flandre Wallonne (1300–1450)." *Revue du Nord* 65 (1983): 277–99.

Des Marez, G. *Le problème de la colonisation franque et du régime agraire en Basse-Belgique*. Académie Royale de Belgique, Classe des Lettres, Mémoires, Collection en quarto, 2nd ser., vol. IX, fasc. 4. Brussels: Maurice Lamertin, 1926.

Des Marez, G. and E. de Sagher, eds. *Comptes de la ville d'Ypres de 1297 à 1329*. 2 vols. Académie Royale de Belgique, Commission Royale d'Histoire. Brussels: P. Imbreghts, 1909, 1913.

Duby, Georges. *Rural Economy and Country Life in the Medieval West*. Translated by Cynthia Postan. History in Depth. Columbia: University of South Carolina Press, 1968.

———. *The Three Orders: Feudal Society Imagined*. Translated by Arthur Goldhammer. With a Foreword by Thomas N. Bisson. Chicago: University of Chicago Press, 1980.

Dunbabin, Jean. *France in the Making, 843–1180*. New York: Oxford University Press, 1985.

Fayen, Arnold, ed. *Lettres de Jean XXII (1316–1334): textes et analyses*. 2 vols. Analecta Vaticano-Beligica publiés par l'Institut Historique Belge de Rome, vols. II, III-1, III-2. Rome: M. Bretschneider, 1908, 1909, 1912.

Fourquin, Guy. *The Anatomy of Popular Rebellion in the Middle Ages*. Translated by Anne Chesters. Europe in the Middle Ages, Selected Studies. Amsterdam and New York: North Holland Publishing, 1978.

Fredericq, Paul, ed. *Corpus documentorum inquisitionis haereticae pravitatis Neerlandicae: verzameling van stukken betreffende de pauselijke en bisschoppelijke inquisitie in de Nederlanden*. Vols. 1, 3. Ghent and The Hague: J. Vuylsteke and Martinus Nijhoff, 1889, 1909.

Galbert of Bruges. *The Murder of Charles the Good, Count of Flanders*. Revised edition. Translated and edited by James Bruce Ross. Harper Torchbook. New York: Harper, 1967.

Genicot, Léopold. *Rural Communities in the Medieval West*. Johns Hopkins Symposia in Comparative History. Baltimore: Johns Hopkins University Press, 1990.

Gilliodts-van Severen, L. *Inventaire des archives de la ville de Bruges: section première, inventaire des chartes*. Vol. 1. Publié sous les auspices de l'administration comunale. Bruges: E. Gailliard, 1871.

Gosses, I. H. *De middeleeuwen*. Vol. 1 of *Handboek tot de staatkundige geschiedenis der Nederlanden*. Edited by R. R. Post. The Hague: Martinus Nijhoff, 1959.

Graus, Frantisek. *Pest-Geissler-Judenmorde: Das 14. Jahrhundert als Krisenzeit*. Veröffentlichungen des Max-Planck-Instituts für Geschichte, no. 86. Göttingen: Vandenhoeck und Ruprecht, 1987.

Hanawalt, Barbara A. *Crime and Conflict in English Communities, 1300–348*. Cambridge, MA: Harvard University Press, 1979.

———. "Peasant Resistance to Royal and Seignorial Impositions." In *Social Unrest in the Late Middle Ages: Papers of the Fifteenth Annual Conference of the Center for Medieval and Early Renaissance Studies*, edited by Francis X. Newman, 23–47. Medieval and Renaissance Texts and Studies, vol. 39. Binghamton, NY: Center for Medieval and Early Renaissance Studies, 1986.

———. *The Ties That Bound: Peasant Families in Medieval England*. New York and Oxford: Oxford University Press, 1986.

Hendrickx, Louisa. "De sociale samenstelling van het Vlaamsche leger in den slag bij Cassel (1328)." *Nederlandsche historiebladen* 2 (1939): 88–90.

Hilton, Rodney H. *Bond Men Made Free: Medieval Peasant Movements and the English Rising of 1381*. New York: Viking Press, 1973.

———. "A Crisis of Feudalism." *Past and Present* 80 (1978): 3–19.

———. *The English Peasantry in the Later Middle Ages: The Ford Lectures for 1973 and Related Studies*. Oxford: Clarendon Press, 1975.

———. "Introduction." In *The English Rising of 1381*, edited by Rodney H. Hilton and T. H. Aston, 1–8. Past and Present Publications. Cambridge: Cambridge University Press, 1984.

——. "Medieval Peasants: Any Lessons?" *Journal of Peasant Studies* 1 (1973–74): 207–19.

Hugenholtz, F. W. N. *Drie boerenopstanden uit de veertiende eeuw: Vlaanderen 1323–1328, Frankrijk 1358, Engeland 1381; onderzoek naar het opstandig bewustzijn.* Haarlem: Tjeenk Willink, 1949.

Jennes, Robert. "De Slag bij Kassel, 23 augustus 1328." In *Nikolaas Zannekin en de Slag bij Kassel, 1328–1978: Bijdrage tot de studie van de 14de eeuw en de landelijke geschiedenis van de Westhoek*, 142–49. Diksmuide, Belgium: Kulturele Raad van Diksmuide, 1978.

Kishlansky, Mark, Patrick Geary, and Patricia O'Brien. *Civilization in the West*. New York: HarperCollins, 1991.

Kittell, Ellen E. *From* Ad Hoc *to Routine: A Case Study in Medieval Bureaucracy*. Middle Ages Series. Philadelphia: University of Pennsylvania Press, 1991.

Ladurie, Emmanuel Le Roy. *Montaillou: The Promised Land of Error*. Translated by Barbara Bray. New York: Random House, Vintage, 1979.

Lambrecht, D., and J. van Rompaey. "De staatsinstellingen in het Zuiden van de 11de tot de 14de eeuw." In *Algemene geschiedenis der Nederlanden*, vol. 3, 77–134. Haarlem: Fibula-van Dishoeck, 1982.

Merlevede, J. *De Ieperse stadsfinancien (1280–1330): bijdrage tot de studie van een Vlaamse stad*. Centrum voor Sociale Structuren en Economische Conjunctuur, Vrije Universiteit Brussel. Brussels: Uitgaven Van de Vrije Universiteit, [1980].

Mertens, J. "Het Brugse Vrije en de opstand van kust-Vlaanderen." *Spieghel historiael* 6 (1971): 304–7.

——., ed. "Les confiscations dans la châtellenie du Franc de Bruges après la bataille de Cassel." *Bulletin de la Commission Royale d'Histoire* 134 (1968): 239–84.

——. "De economische en sociale toestand van de opstandelingen uit het Brugse Vrije wier goederen na de slag bij Cassel (1328) verbeurd verklaard werden." *Belgisch tijdschrift voor filologie en geschiedenis* 47 (1969): 1131–53.

——. *De laat-middeleeuwse landbouweconomie in enkele gemeenten van het Brugse platteland*. Pro-Civitate, Historische Uitgaven, Reeks in 8to, nr. 27. Brussels: Gemeentekrediet van België, 1970.

——. "Zannekin of de evolutie van het beeld van een volksheld." *De Franse Nederlanden—Le Pays-Bas français* (1978): 24–37.

Mieris, Frans van, ed. *Groot charterboek der graaven van Holland, van Zeeland en heeren van Friesland*. 4 vols. Leiden: Pieter van der Eyk, 1753–56.

Miller, David W. "Collective Violence in the Countryside." *Journal of Interdisciplinary History* 15, 3 (1985): 501–6.

Mollat, Michel, and Philippe Wolff. *The Popular Revolutions of the Late Middle Ages*. Translated by A. L. Lytton-Sells. London: Allen & Unwin, 1973.

Mullett, Michael. *Popular Culture and Popular Protest in Late Medieval and Early Modern Europe*. London: Croom Helm, 1987.

Nicholas, David. *Medieval Flanders*. London and New York: Longmans, 1992.

———. "Of Poverty and Primacy: Demand, Liquidity, and the Flemish Economic Miracle, 1050–1200." *American Historical Review* 96 (1991): 17–41.

———. *Town and Countryside: Social, Economic, and Political Tensions in Fourteenth-Century Flanders*. Rijksuniversiteit te Gent, Werken uitgegeven door de faculteit van de letteren en wijsbegeerte, 152. Bruges: De Tempel, 1971.

———. *The Van Arteveldes of Ghent: The Varieties of Vendetta and the Hero in History*. Ithaca, NY: Cornell University Press, 1988.

Nicholas, Karen S. "The Role of Feudal Relationships in the Consolidation of Power in the Principalities of the Low Countries, 1000–1300." In *Law, Custom, and the Social Fabric in Medieval Europe*, edited by Bernard S. Bachrach and David Nicholas, 113–30. Studies in Medieval Culture, XXVIII. Kalamazoo: Western Michigan University-Medieval Institute Publication, 1990.

Pirenne, Henri, ed. "Documents relatifs à l'histoire de Flandre pendant la première moitié du XIVe siècle." *Bulletin de la Commission Royale d'Histoire* 7 (1897): 477–93.

———, ed. *Le soulèvement de la Flandre maritime, 1323–1328, documents inédites*. Académie Royale de Belgique, Commission Royale d'Histoire, Publications in-octavo. Brussels: P. Imbreghts, 1900.

———. *Histoire de Belgique*. 3rd edition. Vol. 2. Brussels: Maurice Lamertin, 1922.

———. "Un mémoire de Robert de Cassel sur sa participation à la révolte de la Flandre maritime en 1324–1325." *Revue du Nord* 1 (1910): 45–50.

Pounds, Norman J. G. *An Historical Geography of Europe, 450 B.C.–A.D. 1330*. New York: Cambridge University Press, 1990.

Prevenier, Walter "La démographie des villes du comté de Flandre aux XIIIe et XIVe siècles: état de la question, essai d'interprétation." *Revue du Nord* 65 (1983): 255–75.

———. "Motieven voor leliaardsgezindheid in Vlaanderen." *De Leiegouw* 19 (1977): 273–88.

Prevenier, Walter and W. P. Blockmans, *The Burgundian Netherlands*. Translated by Peter King and Yvette Mead. Cambridge: Cambridge University Press, 1986.

Raftis, J. A. "The Concentration of Responsibility in Five Villages." *Mediaeval Studies* 28 (1966): 92–118.

———. "Social Change Versus Revolution: New Interpretations of the Peasants' Revolt of 1381." In *Social Unrest in the Late Middle Ages: Papers of the Fifteenth Annual Conference of the Center for Medieval and Early Renaissance Studies*, edited by Francis X. Newman, 3–22. Medieval and Renaissance Texts and Studies, vol. 39. Binghamton, NY: Center for Medieval and Early Renaissance Studies, 1986.

———. "Social Structures in Five East Midland Villages: A Study of Possibilities in the Use of Court Roll Data." *Economic History Review* 18 (1965): 83–100.

Reynolds, Susan. *Kingdoms and Communities in Western Europe, 900–1300*. Oxford: Clarendon Press, 1984.

Rompaey, J. van. "De Brugse keure van 1329 en de aanvullende privileges." *Handelingen van het Koninklijke Commissie voor de Uitgave van de Oude Wetten en Verordeningen van België* 21 (1965): 35–05.

———. "De opstand in het Vlaamse kustland van 1323 tot 1328 en de figuur van

Nikolaas Zannekin." In *Nikolaas Zannekin en de Slag bij Kassel, 1328–1978: bijdrage tot de studie van de 14de eeuw en de landelijke geschiedenis van de Westhoek*, 104–32. Diksmuide, Belgium: Kulturele Raad van Diksmuide, 1978.

Sabbe, Jacques. *Vlaanderen in opstand, 1323–1328: Nikolaas Zannekin, Zeger Janszone en Willem de Deken*. Genootschap voor Geschiedenis "Société d'Émulation" te Brugge, Vlaamse Historische Studies, VII. Bruges: Marc Van de Wiele, 1992.

Sabean, David. "The Communal Basis of Pre-1800 Peasant Uprisings in Western Europe." *Comparative Politics* 8 (April 1976): 355–64.

Schouteet, A. *1301–1339*. Vol. 2 of *Regesten op de oorkonden van het stadsarchief van Brugge (1089–1500)*. Brugse geschiedbronnen uitgegeven door het Genootschap voor Geschiedenis "Société d'Émulation" te Brugge met steun van het Gemeentebestuur van Brugge, V. Bruges: Stadsarchief Van Brugge, 1978.

Scott, James C. *Domination and the Arts of Resistance: Hidden Transcripts*. New Haven, CT: Yale University Press, 1990.

———. "Resistance Without Protest and Without Organization: Peasant Opposition to the Islamic *Zakat* and the Christian Tithe." *Comparative Studies in Society and History* 29 (1987): 417–52.

Seys, Raf. "Zannekin en de Kerels van Vlaanderen in het volkslied: beknopte bloemlezing." In *Nikolaas Zannekin en de Slag bij Kassel, 1328–1978: Bijdrage tot de studie van de 14de eeuw en de landelijke geschiedenis van de Westhoek*, 197–210. Diksmuide, Belgium: Kulturele Raad van Diksmuide, 1978.

Simons, W. *Stad en apostolaat: de vestiging van de bedelorden in het graafschap Vlaanderen (ca. 1225–ca. 1350)*. Verhandelingen van de Koninklijke Academie voor Wetenschappen, Letteren en Schone Kunsten van België, Klasse der Letteren, 49, no. 121. Brussels: Paleis der Academiën, 1987.

Sivéry, Gérard, *Terroirs et communautés rurales dans l'Europe occidentale au moyen âge*. Économies et Sociétés. Villeneuve-d'Ascq: Presses Universitaires de Lille, 1990.

Stein, H. "Les conséquences de la bataille de Cassel pour la ville de Bruges et la mort de Guillaume De Deken, son ancien bourgmestre (1328)." *Bulletin de la Commission Royale d'Histoire* 68 (1899): 647–64.

Strayer, Joseph R. *The Reign of Philip the Fair*. Princeton, NJ: Princeton University Press, 1980.

TeBrake, Wayne P. "Reconstructing the History of Popular Politics in Europe 1500–1850." Paper Presented at Netherlands Institute for Advanced Study. 1991.

TeBrake, William H. *Medieval Frontier: Culture and Ecology in Rijnland*. Environmental History Series, no. 7. College Station: Texas A & M University Press, 1985.

Thoen, Erik. *Landbouwekonomie en bevolking in Vlaanderen gedurende de late middeleeuwen en het begin van de moderne tijden; testregio: de kasselrijen van Oudenaarde en Aalst (eind 13de-eerste helft 16de eeuw)*. 2 vols. Belgisch Centrum voor Landelijke Geschiedenis, no. 90. Ghent: Belgisch Centrum Voor Landelijke Geschiedenis, 1988.

Tilly, Charles. *Big Structures, Large Processes, Huge Comparisons*. New York: Russell Sage Foundation, 1984.

————. *Coercion, Capital, and European States, AD 990–1990*. Studies in Social Discontinuity. Cambridge, MA: Basil Blackwell, 1990.

————. "Retrieving European Lives." In *Reliving the Past: The Worlds of Social History*, edited by Olivier Zunz, 11–52. Chapel Hill: University of North Carolina Press, 1985.

Toussaert, Jacques. *Le sentiment religieux en Flandre à la fin du moyen âge*. Civilisations d'Hier et d'Aujourd'hui. Paris: Plon, 1963.

Uytven, R. van. "Stadsgeschiedenis in het noorden en zuiden." In *Algemene geschiedenis der Nederlanden*, vol. 2, 188–253. Haarlem: Fibula-van Dishoeck, 1982.

Vandermaesen, M. "Albi, Bernard d'" In *Nationaal biografisch woordenboek*, vol. 8, 1–3. Koninklijke Academiën van België. Brussels: Paleis der Academiën, 1979.

————. "Auxonne (Baudet, Baudot), Guillaume d' (Willem van)." In *Nationaal biografisch woordenboek*, vol. 8, 8–14. Koninklijke Academiën van België. Brussels: Paleis der Academiën, 1979.

————. "Cassel, Robrecht, heer van." In *Nationaal biografisch woordenboek*, vol. 6, 79–89. Koninklijke Academiën van België. Brussels: Paleis der Academiën, 1974.

————. "Flote, Artaud." In *Nationaal biografisch woordenboek*, vol. 8, 317–21. Koninklijke Academiën van België. Brussels: Paleis der Academiën, 1979.

————. "Lodewijk II van Nevers." In *Nationaal biografisch woordenboek*, vol. 5, 523–34. Koninklijke Academiën van België. Brussels: Paleis der Academiën, 1972.

————. "Vlaanderen en Henegouwen onder het huis van Dampierre 1244–384." In *Algemene geschiedenis der Nederlanden*, vol. 2, 399–440. Haarlem: Fibula-van Dishoeck, 1982.

Vandewalle, A. "Willem de Deken (+1328) volksleider en makelaar." *Handelingen van het Genootschap voor Geschiedenis gesticht onder de benaming Société d'Émulation* 115 (1978): 207–211.

Verbruggen, J. F. *The Art of Warfare in Western Europe During the Middle Ages: From the Eighth Century to 1340*. Translated by Sumner Willard and S. C. M. Southern. Europe in the Middle Ages: Selected Studies, 1. Amsterdam and New York: North Holland Publishing, 1977.

Verhulst, Adriaan. "Occupatiegeschiedenis en landbouweconomie in het Zuiden circa 1000–1300." In *De middeleeuwen*, Vol. 2 of *Algemene geschiedenis der Nederlanden*, 83–104. Haarlem: Fibula-van Dishoeck, 1982.

————. "The 'Agricultural Revolution' of the Middle Ages Reconsidered." In *Law, Custom, and the Social Fabric in Medieval Europe*, edited by Bernard S. Bachrach and David Nicholas, 17–28. Studies in Medieval Culture, XXVIII. Kalamazoo: Western Michigan University-Medieval Institute Publication, 1990.

————. *Histoire du paysage rural en Flandre de l'époque romaine au XVIIIe siècle*. Collection "Notre Passé." Brussels: La Renaissance du Livre, 1966.

————. *Précis d'histoire rurale de la Belgique*. Brussels: Éditions de L'Université de Bruxelles, 1990.

Verhulst, Adriaan, and D. P. Blok. "Het natuurlandschap." In *Algemene geschiedenis der Nederlanden*, vol. 1, 116–64. Haarlem: Fibula-van Dishoeck, 1981.

Viard, Jules. "La guerre de Flandre." *Bibliothèque de l'École des Chartes* 83 (1922): 362–82.

Warlop, Ernest. "De vorming van de grote schepenbank van het Brugse Vrije (11de–13de eeuw)." *Anciens Pays et Assemblées d'États/Standen en landen* 44 (1968): 1–28.

Werveke, H. van. "Vlaanderen en Brabant, 1305–1346: de sociaal-economische achtergrond." In *De late middeleeuwen, 1305–1477*, Vol. 3 of *Algemene geschiedenis der Nederlanden*, 1–62. Utrecht and Antwerp: De Haan and Standaard Boekhandel, 1951.

———. "Les charges financières issues du traité d'Athis (1305)." *Revue du Nord* 32 (1950): 81–93.

Wunderli, Richard. *Peasant Fires: The Drummer of Niklashausen*. Bloomington: Indiana University Press, 1992.

Wyffels, C. "De oudste rekening der stad Aardenburg (1309–1310) en de opstand van 1311." *Archief: vroegere en latere mededelingen voornamelijk in betrekking tot Zeeland* (1949–50): 10–52.

Index

Aa River, 16

Aalst district, 88

Aardenburg, Bruges district, 73, 76, 81, 89, 146

rebel atrocities at, 124, 128 n.27

Aldermen, 23, 27, 30, 60

Alphonse of Spain, royal emissary, 94

Ambachten, 23

Ammans. See Sheriffs

Annales of Ghent, 32

Antwerp, 20

Aristocrats, 18–19, 26, 28

violence of, 123

See also Flanders, rural elites

Arques. *See* Peace of Arques

Arras, 16, 20, 120

population of, 38 n.15

Artaud Flote, councilor of Louis of Nevers, 54

Artois, 1–2, 16–17, 20, 78, 119

countess of, 50

Assenede, Vier Ambachten district, 80, 90–91

battle at, 91, 139, 145–47, 151

Athis-sur-Orge. *See* Peace of Athis-sur-Orge

Bailiffs, 22, 52, 55, 60, 112–13, 124

Bailleul, 78

Bailleul district, 73, 78–79, 112, 119, 139–40, 152

Baldwin II, count of Flanders, 16

Baldwin of Zegerskapelle, knight and loyalist, 85

Battle of Cassel. *See* Cassel, Battle of

Battle of Courtrai. *See* Courtrai, Battle of

Belfonds Abbey, Hungary, 149

Belgium, 15

Benoit li Brol, killed by rebels, Bergues district, 113, 146, 150

Bergues, 21, 53, 113–14, 147–48

bailiff of, 36

Bergues district, 25, 32, 36, 57, 60, 73, 77, 79, 112–19, 139–40, 142, 146–48, 150, 152

captains of, 53

Bernard d'Albi, royal agent, 96

Blawrel Bockel, peasant captain, 91, 145–46

presumed family of, 145

property of, 145

Bloch, Marc, 7

Bourbourg district, 25, 32, 53, 73, 77, 79, 112–14, 116, 119, 152

Brabant, 20

Braekman, Madeleine, 149–50

Bredene, Bruges district, 72, 147–48

British Isles, 18

Brittany, 2

Bruges, 15, 20–21, 26, 35, 46, 48–57, 67, 69–70, 72–74, 76, 78, 81, 84–86, 89–92, 96–97, 99, 108–9, 110–12, 115, 117, 120, 123–25, 133, 145–51

joins rebellion, 74–76, 80, 84–85, 89–90, 92–94

magistrates of, 50

Matins of. *See* Matins of Bruges

militia of, 50, 53, 84–85, 88–89, 120

population of, 20

St. Basil's Church at, 97

violence within, 33

Bruges district, 23, 25, 28, 46, 52–55, 67–78, 80–81, 86, 88–90, 99, 108, 112, 119, 124–25, 133, 139–42, 145–47, 149–52

Brugge. *See* Bruges

Burgundy, 2

Bylaws. *See* Rural communities, custom

Cambrai, 20

Canche River, 16

Captains, 35–36, 57–60, 68–69, 72, 77, 90, 108, 112, 117, 121. *See also* Blawrel Bockel; Lambert Bonin; Winnoc le Fiere; Segher Janssone; Jacob Peyt; Walter Ratgheer; Nikolaas Zannekin

Cassel, 1, 47, 78–79, 83, 120–21, 148, 152
    Battle of, 1–2, 10, 58, 81, 113, 121–25, 132–33,
        139, 141, 146–48, 152
Cassel district, 47, 73, 78–79, 84, 112, 119, 121,
        139–40, 152
Castelries. *See* Rural districts
Charles IV, king of France, 47–49, 72, 93–
        99, 109–10, 116, 119
Châtellenies. See Rural districts
Chronicon comitum Flandrensium, 1, 7, 32, 52,
        57, 67, 71, 74–84, 89–91, 94, 96–97, 114–
        17, 121–23, 147–52
    probable author of, 11 n.2
Church, 117–18
    excommunication and interdict by, 115,
        117–18, 124, 149
    See also Clergy; Jean Lain; John XXII;
        Monasteries
Clairmarais Abbey, Saint-Omer, 1, 68
Clergy, 58, 95–96, 106–7 n.107, 117–18, 150–51
Communities, definition of, 40. *See also*
    Rural communities
Coppijn van Roele, peasant of Bergues dis-
        trict, 142
Coudekerque, Bergues district, 148
Courtrai, 50, 72, 78, 84–86, 88, 92, 99, 108,
        120; Battle of, 33–34, 94, 98; peasant
        participation in, 33–34
    joins rebellion, 85
Courtrai district, 78, 86, 108, 112, 119, 152
Curatores. See Magistrates

Deinze, Ghent district, 88
Deken, Willem de. *See* Willem de Deken
Dender River, 16–17
Dendermonde, 17, 91–92
Dendermonde district, 88
Douai, 17, 20, 26, 35
    population of, 38 n.15
Douai district, 35
Drie steden, 21. *See also* Bruges; Ghent; Ypres
Dunkirk, 17, 21, 53, 77–78, 83, 113–14, 117,
        148

Échevins. See Aldermen
Edward III, king of England, 112, 124
Eeklo, 89–90
Elisabeth of Vermandois, wife of Count
        Philip, 16
Elites, 45, 68
    brutality of, 13 n.13

politics of, 46–52
violence of, 68, 123–25
England, 21, 25, 31, 74, 94, 98, 134
    trade with, 49
    See also Edward III
English Revolt of 1381, 3, 6

Flanders, 15–19, 25
    agriculture of, 17–18, 20–22, 29, 96
    cities of, 15, 19–22, 26–29, 34, 37, 50, 72, 96,
        123; magistrates, 49. *See also* Bruges;
        Cassel; Courtrai; Ghent; Lille; Ypres
    counts of, 15–16, 22–23, 26–27. *See also*
        Baldwin II; Guy of Dampierre; Robert
        of Béthune; Louis of Nevers; Philip
    economy of, 29
    French occupation of, 29
    industry of, 20, 22, 29, 36, 96
    northeastern, 80, 88–89, 91, 151
    population of, 15, 17–19, 22
    regents of. *See* Lords of Axel and Aspre-
        mont; Robert of Cassel
    rural communities. *See* Rural communities
    rural districts of, 22–23, 28, 34, 52, 57, 73,
        75, 123, 133. *See also* names of individual
        districts
    rural elites of, 23, 28; violence of, 68. *See
        also* Aristocrats; Great Proprietors;
        Lords; Nobles
    social composition of, 19, 26. *See also*
        Patricians
    southeastern, 91
    southwestern, 1, 16, 32, 52, 57, 68–69, 73,
        75–81, 88–90, 119, 139–42, 146, 151–52
    trade of, 20, 22, 29, 36, 96
    Transport of. *See* Transport of Flanders
    urban elites, 27–28, 30
    Walloon. *See* Walloon Flanders
    war with France, 29–30, 32–37, 48, 51, 72
France, 15, 45–47, 52–53, 86, 99, 119, 134
    kings, 16–17, 29, 31, 46, 110. *See also* Charles
        IV; Philip IV; Philip V; Philip VI
Francia, 94
French Jacquerie of 1358, 3, 5
French occupation of Flanders, 30

Gent. *See* Ghent
Geraardsbergen, 17, 91–92
German Empire, 16, 119
German Peasants' War of 1525, 3
Germany, 7

Ghent, 15–16, 19–21, 26–27, 30–31, 35, 46, 51–
    53, 56–57, 72–73, 76, 80–82, 84, 86–91,
    95, 109–11, 120, 124, 132
    aldermen of, 27, 31
    Council of Thirty-Nine, 21, 27, 30
    magistrates of, 37
    militia of, 53, 110, 120
    opposes rebellion, 75, 80, 86–92, 95, 108–
        11, 120
    population of, 19
    violence in, 33
    weavers of, 91, 109
Ghent district, 36, 88–89
Ghent party, 111
Ghis du Boos, magistrate of Bergues district,
    53, 60, 113–14
Gistel, Bruges district, 73, 75–76, 84, 147
Gravelines, Bourbourg district, 21
Great proprietors, 28, 33, 54. See also
    Flanders, rural elites; Simon de Rikelike
Guilds, 34, 36, 74, 96, 109, 111
    weavers, 73, 91, 109
Guy of Dampierre, count of Flanders, 30–
    32, 34

Hainaut, 2, 20, 48
Ham, Abbey of, in Artois, 121
Helchin, castle in bishopric of Tournai, 94
Holland, 48
Hondschoote, Bergues district, 113, 146–47,
    149–50
Hoofdmannen. See Captains
Hoymille, Bergues district, 113, 146–47
Hugenholtz, F. W. N., 149
Hundred Years' War, 98

Ieper. See Ypres
IJzer River, 76
Italy, 15, 45

Jacob Peyt, peasant captain, 112–15, 117, 136,
    146–51
    anticlericalism of, 117–18, 149
    charged with heresy, 118, 129 n.34
    murder of, 117–18, 149–50
Jacob van Artevelde, 124
Jacques de Châtillon, royal governor of
    Flanders, 32–33
Jean Lain, priest of Dunkirk, 117–18, 148, 150
Jehan Bankinoet, attacked by rebels, Bergues
    district, 113, 147

Jehan Colin, attacked by rebels, Bourbourg
    district, 113
Jehan de Saint-Nicholay, attacked by rebels,
    Bourbourg district, 113
Jehan le Valewe, peasant captain, 146, 150
Jehan li Vinc, attacked by rebels, Bergues
    district, 113
John of Flanders, count's councilor, 83, 85
John of Namur, great uncle of Louis of
    Nevers, 49–50, 62 n.10, 82–83, 85
    leader of loyalists, 86–91, 94, 97, 111
John of Verrières, count's councilor, 83, 85
John XXII, pope, 67, 95–96, 124

Kasselrijen. See Rural districts
Keuren. See Rural communities
Keurheren. See Magistrates
Keuriers. See Magistrates
Klauwaarts, 31–33, 35, 51
Kortrijk. See Courtrai

Lambert Bonin, peasant captain, 72–73, 76,
    81, 91, 108, 112, 120, 145–46
    death by decapitation, 146
    property of, 146
Lampernisse, Veurne district, 76, 151
Land of Aalst district, 92
Land of Waas district, 35, 80, 88–92, 118, 151
Langerbrugge, Ghent district, 89–90
Leie River, 17, 20, 84–85, 88, 119–21, 152
Leliaarts, 31–33, 35–36, 51, 56, 72, 133, 149
Lille, 17, 20, 26, 35, 37, 95, 98, 119, 152
    population of, 38 n.15
Lille district, 35
Lombardsijde, Veurne district, 59
London, 21
Lord of Aspremont, regent of Flanders, 52–
    53
Lord of Axel, regent of Flanders, 57, 67
Lords, 54, 71
Lorraine, 2
Louis I, count of Nevers and Rethel, 36, 47
Louis II, count of Nevers and Rethel
    Flanders. See Louis of Nevers
Louis of Nevers, count of Flanders, Nevers,
    and Rethel, 45–47, 67–70, 72–76, 78,
    80–87, 89–91, 93–99, 108–11, 119–20,
    124–25, 132, 146, 152
    allies of. See Loyalists
    confiscates rebel property, 139–42
    early life of, 46–47, 61 n.3

Louis of Nevers (*cont.*)
  governing council or *raad*, 49, 82, 83, 85,
    110–11
  imprisoned by rebels, 86–87, 89, 93–98
Louwers Damman, attacked by rebels,
  Bergues district, 113–14
Low Countries, 25–26
Loyalists, 73, 77, 79–80, 83–87, 89–90, 95, 120
  leadership of. *See* John of Namur
  repression imposed by, 118
  violence of, 76
  See also Noble party

Magistrates, 22
  abuse of office by, 54–57
  complaints against, 36, 51, 52
  punishment of, 55–57, 67, 70–71
  seized by rebels, 52–53
Margaret, daughter of Philip V, 47
Matins of Bruges, 33, 35
Mechelen, 20
Mediterranean Sea, 19–20
Monasteries, 71–72
  See also Belfonds Abbey; Clairmarais Ab-
    bey; St. Nicholas Abbey; Ter Duinen
    Abbey

Navarre, 2
Netherlands, 15
Nevele, Ghent district, 88
Nevers, 45–46, 50, 52, 57, 67
Nicholas, rector of Klemskerke, 96
Nieppe, Cassel district, 84
Nieuwerkerk, Bruges district, 145
Nieuwpoort, Veurne district, 21, 59, 76–77
Nikolaas Zannekin, peasant captain, 76–78,
    80–82, 84–85, 108, 112, 119, 121, 135–36,
    145–47, 149, 151–52
  death of, 122
  property of, 151
Noble party, 82, 83, 84, 111
Nobles, 32–35, 51, 55, 68, 120
  atrocities by, 81–82
  targeted by rebels, 71
  violence of, 123
  See also Flanders, rural elites
Normandy, revolt in (996), 60, 135
North Sea, 15–17, 49

Ongeld, 30
Oostburg, Bruges district, 71

Oostende, Bruges district, 21, 72, 147–48
Orchies, 35
Orchies district, 35
Oudenaarde, 88, 120
Oudenburg, Bruges district, 148

Papacy, 32. *See also* John XXII, pope
Paris, 16, 20–21, 37, 46, 48–49, 97, 111, 123–24
  Treaty of. *See* Treaty of Paris
  Parlement of. *See* Parlement of Paris
Parishes, 23–24, 58
Parlement of Paris, 47–48, 96
Patricians, 27, 30, 35, 51
  violence of, 123
Peace of Arques, 10, 98–99, 108–10, 112–17,
    119, 149–50
Peace of Athis-sur-Orge, 17, 23, 36, 51, 93, 98,
    108
  provisions of, 34–35
Peace of Sint-Andries, 55, 70
Peasant revolt, 7–10
  arbitration of, 54–57, 59, 68–69
  disease as metaphor for, 1, 7
  first phase of, 52–54
  leadership of, 135–36
  second phase of, 71–80, 84–86, 89–92
  third phase of, 112–14, 118–22
Peasants, 3–6, 8
  attack monasteries, 71–72
  attack rural elites, 53, 55, 67, 70, 71, 112, 113
  defy officials, 52–53, 70, 112
  redistribute or destroy property of elites,
    53, 55, 71, 112–14, 118
  grievances of, 54–57
  mobilization and organization of, 57–60,
    152
  politics. *See* Popular politics
  solidarity among, 26, 58–59, 67, 69, 78–79,
    82, 89, 108
  status groups, 25–26
  See also Captains; Rural communities
Peteghem, Oudenaarde district, 88
Philip, count of Flanders, 16
Philip IV (the Fair), king of France, 31–32,
    34–37, 95
Philip V, king of France, 37, 47
Philip VI, king of France, 119–25, 132
  confiscates rebel property, 139–42
Picardy, 20, 94
Pieron de le Dielf. *See* Pieter van der Delft
Pieter Peyt, monk, 148–49

Pieter van der Delft, bailiff of Bergues, 113

Poitou, 53

Political parties, 30–31
See also *Klauwaarts*; *Leliaarts*

Politics, 30, 34
general definition of, 14 n.37
See also Popular politics

Pontoise. *See* Treaty of Pontoise

Poperinge, Veurne district, 78

Popular assemblies. *See* Rural communities, assemblies

Popular politics, 45–46, 51–52, 68, 70–71, 134–36
notions of popular sovereignty, 45
peasant revolt as, 8–9
resistance to domination as, 8–9, 30, 33–34, 68, 134

Raad. *See* Louis of Nevers, governing council

Reckelingsbrugge, Ghent district, 88

Rethel, 45

Robert of Béthune, count of Flanders, 34–37, 47–48, 51, 95

Robert of Cassel, uncle of Louis of Nevers, 36, 47–48, 52, 55, 57, 64 n.43, 67–68, 72–73, 76–78, 81–84, 116, 125, 152
regent for Louis of Nevers, 86–91, 94–95, 97

Robert of Nevele, count's councilor, 83, 85

Roeselare, Ypres district, 78

Roger of Zaemslacht, count's tutor, councilor, 85

Rogier Monac, rebel leader, 124

Rural communities, 22–24, 26, 34
assemblies of, 24–25, 57–60, 67, 71, 89, 108; summoned by church bells, 57–58, 60, 70
custom within, 24, 58
leadership of, 25–26. *See also* Captains
mutual pledging in, 26, 58–60, 82, 89
proxies or agents within, 25, 58–60, 152
social composition of, 25–26
solidarity within, 26
solidarity between, 135
suppression of, 124, 133

Rural districts. *See* Flanders, rural districts

Saint-Omer, 1, 16, 20, 50, 68, 79, 95, 98, 121

Scandinavians, 18

Schelde River. *See* Scheldt River

Scheldt River, 15–17, 20, 85, 88, 912, 120–21, 146, 148, 152

Schepenen. *See* Aldermen

Schoondijke, Bruges district, 107 n.107

Second patriciate, 30–31

Segher Janssone, peasant captain, 72–73, 75–78, 80–82, 84, 91, 108, 112, 119, 135, 145–50, 152
property of, 147
torture and death of, 124, 148

Sheriffs, 23, 60, 72, 112, 124

Simon de Rikelike, great proprietor, 28, 142–43

Sint-Andries. *See* Peace of Sint-Andries

Sluis, 49–50, 54, 99

Sluis affair, 49–50, 54, 67, 70, 74, 99

Somme River, 16

St. Nicholas Abbey, Veurne, 56

Taxes, complaints regarding, 30, 52, 54, 56
opposition to collection of, 35–36, 51, 109

Ter Duinen Abbey, Koksijde, 70, 72, 82–84, 98, 147–49

Th. de Vinc, attacked by rebels, Bergues district, 113

Thérouanne, 119
bishop of, 117–18

Torhout, Bruges district, 78

Tournai, 85, 120, 146, 148, 152
bishopric of, 94
population of, 38 n.15

Toussaert, Jacques, 148–49

Transport of Flanders, 36, 49

Treaty of Paris, 37

Treaty of Pontoise, 35–36

Vermandois, 16

Veurne, 32, 59, 68, 72, 75–77, 98, 117, 149
aldermen of, 59
St. Nicholas Abbey, 56

Veurne district, 25, 36, 51, 53, 55–57, 59–60, 68–69, 72–73, 75–79, 81–82, 112, 119, 139–40, 149, 151–52
estimated population of, 59, 66 n.43

Vier Ambachten district, 80, 88–92, 118, 145–46, 151

Walloon Flanders, 17, 20, 23, 32, 35

Walter Ratgheer, 80, 88–91, 145–46, 151

War with France, 29–30, 32–37, 48, 51, 72

Wateringen, 23

Wautier le Scridere, attacked by rebels, Bergues district, 113, 147

Weavers, 73, 109

Westkapelle, Bruges district, 72, 146

Wijnendale, Ghent district, 88

Willem de Deken, citizen of Bruges, 11, n.7, 111–12, 120

    torture and death of, 123–24

William of Auxonne, count's councilor, 83

William of Gravelgem, Augustinian prior, Bruges, 96

Winnoc de le Brake, peasant of Bergues district, 142

Winnoc le Fiere, 113, 115, 119, 145–47, 150, 152

death of, 122

property of, 147

Wormhout, Bergues district, 142

Ypres, 20, 26, 36, 48, 51, 53, 56–57, 67, 72–73, 78, 81–82, 84–85, 92, 99, 108, 110–11, 120, 149–50

    aldermen of, 56, 69

    guilds of, 86

    joins rebellion, 85, 86, 92

    population of, 20

Ypres district, 36, 78, 84–86, 108, 112, 119, 124, 152

Yzendijke, Bruges district, 71

Zeeland, 48, 148

Zuidkote, Veurne district, 77, 81

Zwin waterway, Bruges, 49–50, 74

University of Pennsylvania Press
MIDDLE AGES SERIES
Edward Peters, General Editor

F. R. P. Akehurst, trans. *The* Coutumes de Beauvaisis *of Philippe de Beaumanoir.* 1992

Peter Allen. *The Art of Love: Amatory Fiction from Ovid to the* Romance of the Rose. 1992

David Anderson. *Before the Knight's Tale: Imitation of Classical Epic in Boccaccio's* Teseida. 1988

Benjamin Arnold. *Count and Bishop in Medieval Germany: A Study of Regional Power, 1100–1350.* 1991

Mark C. Bartusis. *The Late Byzantine Army: Arms and Society, 1204–1453.* 1992

J. M. W. Bean. *From Lord to Patron: Lordship in Late Medieval England.* 1990

Uta-Renate Blumenthal. *The Investiture Controversy: Church and Monarchy from the Ninth to the Twelfth Century.* 1988

Daniel Bornstein, trans. *Dino Compagni's* Chronicle *of Florence.* 1986

Maureen Barry McCann Boulton. *The Song in the Story: Lyric Insertions in French Narrative Fiction, 1200–1400.* 1993.

Betsy Bowden. *Chaucer Aloud: The Varieties of Textual Interpretation.* 1987

James William Brodman. *Ransoming Captives in Crusader Spain: The Order of Merced on the Christian-Islamic Frontier.* 1986

Kevin Brownlee and Sylvia Huot. *Rethinking the* Romance of the Rose: *Text, Image, Reception.* 1992

Matilda Tomaryn Bruckner. *Shaping Romance: Interpretation, Truth, and Closure in Twelfth-Century French Fictions.* 1993

Otto Brunner (Howard Kaminsky and James Van Horn Melton, eds. and trans.). Land *and Lordship: Structures of Governance in Medieval Austria.* 1992

Robert I. Burns, S.J., ed. *Emperor of Culture: Alfonso X the Learned of Castile and His Thirteenth-Century Renaissance.* 1990

David Burr. *Olivi and Franciscan Poverty: The Origins of the* Usus Pauper *Controversy.* 1989

David Burr. *Peaceable Kingdom: A Reading of Olivi's Apocalypse Commentary.* 1993

Thomas Cable. *The English Alliterative Tradition.* 1991

Anthony K. Cassell and Victoria Kirkham, eds. and trans. *Diana's Hunt/Caccia di Diana: Boccaccio's First Fiction.* 1991

John C. Cavadini. *The Last Christology of the West: Adoptionism in Spain and Gaul, 785–820.* 1993

Brigitte Cazelles. *The Lady as Saint: A Collection of French Hagiographic Romances of the Thirteenth Century.* 1991

Karen Cherewatuk and Ulrike Wiethaus, eds. *Dear Sister: Medieval Women and the Epistolary Genre.* 1993

Anne L. Clark. *Elisabeth of Schönau: A Twelfth-Century Visionary.* 1992

Willene B. Clark and Meradith T. McMunn, eds. *Beasts and Birds of the Middle Ages: The Bestiary and Its Legacy.* 1989

Richard C. Dales. *The Scientific Achievement of the Middle Ages.* 1973

Charles T. Davis. *Dante's Italy and Other Essays.* 1984

Katherine Fischer Drew, trans. *The Burgundian Code.* 1972

Katherine Fischer Drew, trans. *The Laws of the Salian Franks.* 1991

Katherine Fischer Drew, trans. *The Lombard Laws.* 1973

Nancy Edwards. *The Archaeology of Early Medieval Ireland.* 1990

Margaret J. Ehrhart. *The Judgment of the Trojan Prince Paris in Medieval Literature.* 1987

Richard K. Emmerson and Ronald B. Herzman. *The Apocalyptic Imagination in Medieval Literature.* 1992

Theodore Evergates. *Feudal Society in Medieval France: Documents from the County of Champagne.* 1993

Felipe Fernández-Armesto. *Before Columbus: Exploration and Colonization from the Mediterranean to the Atlantic, 1229–1492.* 1987

Robert D. Fulk. *A History of Old English Meter.* 1992

Patrick J. Geary. *Aristocracy in Provence: The Rhône Basin at the Dawn of the Carolingian Age.* 1985

Peter Heath. *Allegory and Philosophy in Avicenna (Ibn Sînâ), with a Translation of the Book of the Prophet Muḥammad's Ascent to Heaven.* 1992

J. N. Hillgarth, ed. *Christianity and Paganism, 350–750: The Conversion of Western Europe.* 1986

Richard C. Hoffmann. *Land, Liberties, and Lordship in a Late Medieval Countryside: Agrarian Structures and Change in the Duchy of Wrocław.* 1990

Robert Hollander. *Boccaccio's Last Fiction: Il Corbaccio.* 1988

Edward B. Irving, Jr. *Rereading* Beowulf. 1989

C. Stephen Jaeger. *The Origins of Courtliness: Civilizing Trends and the Formation of Courtly Ideals, 939–1210.* 1985

William Chester Jordan. *The French Monarchy and the Jews: From Philip Augustus to the Last Capetians.* 1989

William Chester Jordan. *From Servitude to Freedom: Manumission in the Sénonais in the Thirteenth Century.* 1986

Ellen E. Kittell. *From Ad Hoc to Routine: A Case Study in Medieval Bureaucracy.* 1991

Alan C. Kors and Edward Peters, eds. *Witchcraft in Europe, 1100–1700: A Documentary History.* 1972

Barbara M. Kreutz. *Before the Normans: Southern Italy in the Ninth and Tenth Centuries.* 1992

E. Ann Matter. *The Voice of My Beloved: The Song of Songs in Western Medieval Christianity.* 1990

María Rosa Menocal. *The Arabic Role in Medieval Literary History: A Forgotten Heritage.* 1987

Alastair J. Minnis. *Medieval Theory of Authorship.* 1988

Lawrence Nees. *A Tainted Mantle: Hercules and the Classical Tradition at the Carolingian Court.* 1991

Lynn H. Nelson, trans. *The Chronicle of San Juan de la Peña: A Fourteenth-Century Official History of the Crown of Aragon.* 1991

Charlotte A. Newman. *The Anglo-Norman Nobility in the Reign of Henry I: The Second Generation.* 1988

Joseph F. O'Callaghan. *The Cortes of Castile-León, 1188–1350.* 1989

Joseph F. O'Callaghan. *The Learned King: The Reign of Alfonso X of Castile.* 1993

William D. Paden, ed. *The Voice of the Trobairitz: Perspectives on the Women Troubadours.* 1989

Edward Peters. *The Magician, the Witch, and the Law.* 1982

Edward Peters, ed. *Christian Society and the Crusades, 1198–1229: Sources in Translation, including* The Capture of Damietta *by Oliver of Paderborn.* 1971

Edward Peters, ed. *The First Crusade:* The Chronicle of Fulcher of Chartres *and Other Source Materials.* 1971

Edward Peters, ed. *Heresy and Authority in Medieval Europe.* 1980

James M. Powell. *Albertanus of Brescia: The Pursuit of Happiness in the Early Thirteenth Century.* 1992

James M. Powell. *Anatomy of a Crusade, 1213–1221.* 1986

Jean Renart (Patricia Terry and Nancy Vine Durling, trans.). *The Romance of the Rose or Guillaume de Dole* 1993

Michael Resler, trans. Erec *by Hartmann von Aue.* 1987

Pierre Riché (Michael Idomir Allen, trans.). *The Carolingians: A Family Who Forged Europe.* 1993

Pierre Riché (Jo Ann McNamara, trans.). *Daily Life in the World of Charlemagne.* 1978

Jonathan Riley-Smith. *The First Crusade and the Idea of Crusading.* 1986

Joel T. Rosenthal. *Patriarchy and Families of Privilege in Fifteenth-Century England.* 1991

Teofilo F. Ruiz. *Crisis and Continuity: The Urban and Rural Structures of Late Medieval Castile.* 1993

Steven D. Sargent, ed. and trans. *On the Threshold of Exact Science: Selected Writings of Anneliese Maier on Late Medieval Natural Philosophy.* 1982

Sarah Stanbury. *Seeing the* Gawain-Poet: *Description and the Act of Perception.* 1992

Thomas C. Stillinger. *The Song of Troilus: Lyric Authority in the Medieval Book.* 1992

Susan Mosher Stuard. *A State of Deference: Ragusa/Dubrovnik in the Medieval Centuries.* 1992

Susan Mosher Stuard, ed. *Women in Medieval History and Historiography.* 1987

Susan Mosher Stuard, ed. *Women in Medieval Society.* 1976

Jonathan Sumption. *The Hundred Years War: Trial by Battle.* 1992

Ronald E. Surtz. *The Guitar of God: Gender, Power, and Authority in the Visionary World of Mother Juana de la Cruz (1481–1534).* 1990

William H. TeBrake. *A Plague of Insurrection: Popular Politics and Peasant Revolt in Flanders, 1323–1328.* 1993

Patricia Terry, trans. *Poems of the Elder Edda.* 1990

Hugh M. Thomas. *Vassals, Heiresses, Crusaders, and Thugs: The Gentry of Angevin Yorkshire, 1154–1216.* 1993

Frank Tobin. *Meister Eckhart: Thought and Language.* 1986

Ralph V. Turner. *Men Raised from the Dust: Administrative Service and Upward Mobility in Angevin England.* 1988

Harry Turtledove, trans. *The* Chronicle *of Theophanes: An English Translation of* Anni Mundi *6095–6305 (A.D. 602–813).* 1982

Mary F. Wack. Lovesickness in the Middle Ages: The Viaticum *and Its Commentaries.* 1990

Benedicta Ward. *Miracles and the Medieval Mind: Theory, Record, and Event, 1000–1215.* 1982

Suzanne Fonay Wemple. *Women in Frankish Society: Marriage and the Cloister, 500–900.* 1981

Jan M. Ziolkowski. *Talking Animals: Medieval Latin Beast Poetry, A.D. 750–1150.* 1993

This book has been set in Linotron Galliard. Galliard was designed for Mergenthaler in 1978 by Matthew Carter. Galliard retains many of the features of a sixteenth-century typeface cut by Robert Granjon but has some modifications that give it a more contemporary look.

Printed on acid-free paper.

3 5282 00497 8816